Fifth Edition Form A

Inside Writing

A Writer's Workbook

William Salomone
Palomar College

Stephen McDonald
Palomar College

THOMSON
™
WADSWORTH

Australia   Canada   Mexico   Singapore   Spain   United Kingdom   United States

THOMSON
™
WADSWORTH

Inside Writing, Form A, Fifth Edition
A Writer's Workbook
William Salomone
Stephen McDonald

Publisher: *Michael Rosenberg*
Acquisitions Editor: *Stephen Dalphin*
Production Editor: *Eunice Yeates-Fogle*
Executive Marketing Manager: *Ken Kasee*
Director of Higher Education Marketing:
   Lisa Kimball
Senior Print Buyer: *Mary Beth Hennebury*

Cover Designer: *Laek Designs*
Cover Art: *Lisa Houck*
Composition: *TBH Typecast, Inc.*
Production Management: *Hearthside Publishing
   Services*
Cover Printer: *Lehigh Press*
Text Printer/Binder: *Quebecor World*

Printed in the United States of America.
   3   4   5   6   06   05   04   03

For more information, contact: Wadsworth,
25 Thomson Place, Boston, MA 02210 USA,
or you can visit *http://www.wadsworth.com*

For permission to use material from this text
or product, contact us:

Tel 1-800-730-2214

Fax 1-800-730-2215

Web www.thomsonrights.com

ISBN: 0-15-50426-88

To Rosemary and Marlyle

Contents

Chapter Three Improving Sentence Patterns   **145**

Preface

Inside Writing was constructed on the premise that there is really only one reason for learning the essential rules of English grammar—to become better writers. In this text, we constantly stress that all college students are writers and that the aim of any college writing course—developmental or otherwise—is to improve writing. To this purpose, *Inside Writing* has been created with clear and simple organization, a friendly, non-threatening tone, thorough integration of grammar sections with writing sections, and unique thematic exercises.

The Reason for This Text

We are all aware of widespread disagreement about what should be presented in a first-semester developmental writing course. *Inside Writing* was written to address the resulting diversity of course content with a union of grammar and writing instruction. In it, we teach basic grammar and sentence structure, yet we also provide extensive practice in sentence combining and paragraph writing.

Moving Beyond a Traditional Approach. The traditional approach to developmental writing has been to review the rules of grammar, punctuation, and usage and then to test the students' understanding of those rules through a series of chapter tests. However, as research and experience have demonstrated, there is no necessary correlation between the study of grammar and the development of competent writers. As a result, many English departments have restructured their developmental courses to focus on the process of writing, developing courses that have very little in common with each other from one campus to the next. Today, some developmental writing instructors teach the traditional exercises in grammar, others focus on journal and expressive writing, others emphasize sentence combining, and still others teach the writing of paragraphs and short essays.

Using an Integrated Approach. *Inside Writing* responds to this spectrum of course content by integrating grammar instruction and writing practice. Certainly the practice of writing is important in a first-semester developmental class. Yet the study of traditional grammar, punctuation, and usage is also important because it provides a fundamental knowledge of sentence structure—knowledge that writers need not only to revise their own writing but also to discuss their writing with others. The writing practices in this text are specifically designed to support, not merely to supplement, the grammar instruction. As soon as students have mastered a particular grammatical principle, they are asked to put their knowledge into practice in the writing sections of each chapter. This immediate reinforcement makes it more likely that students will improve their writing as well as retain the rules of grammar, usage, and mechanics.

Text Organization and Features

Inside Writing is presented in six chapters. Each chapter consists of five sections that cover major principles of basic grammar, sentence construction, and paragraph writing. The text keeps this instruction as simple as possible, giving the students only the information that is absolutely essential.

- Each chapter's grammar instruction is broken into three sections so that the students are not presented with too much at once.

- Each of the three grammar sections includes various practices and ends with three exercises that give the students an opportunity to apply the concepts and rules they have learned.

- Each chapter is followed by a practice test covering the material presented in the first three sections of the chapter, and the text closes with a practice final examination.

- The fourth section of each chapter presents both instruction and exercises in sentence combining, based on the specific concepts and rules covered in the three grammar sections. For example, in the chapter covering participial phrases and adjective clauses, the sentence-combining section instructs the students to combine sentences by using participial phrases and adjective clauses.

- The fifth section of each chapter includes instruction in writing paragraphs and essays and a choice of several writing assignments, again designed to reinforce the grammar sections of the chapter by leading students to employ in their own writing the rules for sentence structure they have studied.

- At the end of the text, answers to the practices—but not to the exercises—are provided. These answers allow the students to check their understanding of the material as they read the text. The extensive exercises without answers permit the instructor to determine where more explanation or study is needed.

- Many of the practices and exercises develop thematic ideas or contain a variety of cultural, mythological, and historical allusions. Some exercises, for example, explain the origin of the names of our weekdays, tell the story of Cinque and the *Amistad*, or illustrate common urban legends. In addition, individual sentences within practices and exercises often provoke questions and discussion when they refer to characters and events from history, mythology, or contemporary culture. This feature of *Inside Writing* encourages developmental writing students to look beyond grammar, mechanics, and punctuation. It reminds them—or it allows us as instructors to remind them—that the educated writer has command of much more than the correct use of the comma.

Connecting Concepts and Writing Practice. To emphasize further the connection between the writing assignments and the grammar exercises, the writing assignment in each chapter is modeled by three thematic exercises within the grammar sections of the chapter. For instance, in Chapter 3, Exercises 1C, 2C, and 3C are paragraphs that use examples to support a statement made in a topic sentence. The writing practice section then extends this groundwork by presenting instruction in the writing of a similar expository paragraph or essay.

In each writing assignment, the students are introduced gradually to the writing process and encouraged to improve their writing through prewriting and careful revision. They are also introduced to the basic concepts of academic writing—thesis statements, topic sentences, unity, specificity, completeness, order, and coherence. However, the main purpose of the writing instruction is to give the students an opportunity to use their new knowledge of grammar and sentence structure to communicate their own thoughts and ideas.

Changes to This Edition

We have improved this Fifth Edition of *Inside Writing* in several areas:

- The writing section of each chapter (Section 5) has been expanded and revised to include a more thorough explanation and illustration of the writing process. New exercises to assist the student writer appear in several of the writing sections.

- At the request of many instructors, we have moved the instruction in essay writing from the Appendix to Chapter 3, and we have revised the writing sections of Chapters 3, 4, 5, and 6 so that they now include both paragraph and essay assignments. Each of these chapters also includes a sample student paragraph and essay.

- We have added new thematically related practices and exercises. In addition to exercises that focus on the American cowboy, Alcatraz Prison, Indiana Jones, Betsy Ross, the *Amistad,* and Native American folklore, we have included material ranging from a comparison of King Lear and Willy Loman to a lament of the problems caused by a chocolate addiction.

- As with all previous editions, we have continued to include single-sentence allusions that are designed to interest both the instructor and the student. For example, in Section 1 of Chapter 2 alone are references to all of the following: Circe, Iago, Ophelia, Ishmael, the Battle of Bull Run, Snow White, Beowulf, Puck, Mount Vesuvius, Billie Holiday, Thelonious Monk, Miles Davis, John Coltrane, Bill Gates, Steve Jobs, Prometheus, Dr. Jekyll and Mr. Hyde, the Ides of March, and San Francisco's Pier 39.

Many instructors use these allusions as part of their classes, asking students if they know what they refer to, or, if a joke is involved, whether or not they get the joke. Here's an example from page three: "Pandora stared curiously at the box in her hand." Instructors can use this sentence as they would any other sentence in the practice (underlining nouns), or they can stop for a moment and ask if anyone knows whether Pandora opened that box—or if she should open the box. A few students at this level will have heard of Pandora, but not many. Those who can answer the question teach the other students a little about mythology. Not all the allusions are serious. Some are just fun: "Dr. Frankenstein proudly told his neighbors about the success of his latest experiment" or "Neptune was looking forward to a hefty fillet-of-fish sandwich." The point is that such allusions provide a depth of content and a light-hearted tone that go beyond the rote recitation of practices and exercises.

■ We have rewritten nearly 50 percent of all practices, exercises, and practice tests.

An Exceptional Support Package

The Instructor's Manual provides suggestions for how to use the text, answers to the exercises, diagnostic and achievement tests, a series of six chapter tests and six alternate chapter tests, a final examination, answers to the tests and final examination, additional writing assignments, and model paragraphs. With this material, the instructor can use a traditional lecture approach, working through each chapter and then testing the students together, or the instructor can allow the students to work through the book at their own pace, dealing with the students' questions individually and giving students tests as they complete each chapter.

This text will be available in an alternate version, "Form B," for added teaching flexibility in the second semester.

Acknowledgments

We thank our friends and colleagues in the English Department at Palomar College, particularly Jack Quintero, who has consistently and generously given his encouragement and advice, as well as Brent Gowen and Bruce Orton, whose valuable comments and suggestions have contributed to this text.

We extend our thanks to Stephen Dalphin at Heinle, who has encouraged us from the start, to Eunice Yeates-Fogle, also at Heinle, and to Laura Horowitz of Hearthside Publishing Services, who has effortlessly stepped us through the production process of this revision. We also gratefully acknowledge the following students, who graciously allowed us to use their paragraphs as models: Michael Heading, Kelli Newell, Lana Futch, Brian Yeskis, Cathy Martin, Laurence Suiaunoa, Patricia Muller, and Dora Cerda.

We are very grateful to the following professors who provided valuable input for this book: Tammis Bennett, San Joaquin Valley College; Dianne E. Rutherford, Middle Georgia College; Paula Ingram, Pensacola Junior College; Cari Kenner, Texas State Technical College—Harlingen; Brenda Rawson, College of Eastern Utah.

In addition, we thank spouses, children, and friends who gave us room and time to work.

William Salomone
Stephen McDonald

Naming the Parts

Let's face it. Few people find grammar a fascinating subject, and few study it of their own free will. Most people study grammar only when they are absolutely required to do so. Many seem to feel that grammar is either endlessly complicated or not important to their daily lives.

The problem is not that people fail to appreciate the importance of writing. The ability to express oneself clearly on paper is generally recognized as an important advantage. Those who can communicate their ideas and feelings effectively have a much greater chance to develop themselves, not only professionally but personally as well.

Perhaps the negative attitude toward grammar is due in part to the suspicion that studying grammar has little to do with learning how to write. This suspicion is not at all unreasonable—a knowledge of grammar by itself will not make anyone a better writer. To become a better writer, a person should study *writing* and practice it frequently.

However, the study of writing is much easier if one understands grammar. Certainly a person can learn to write well without knowing exactly how sentences are put together or what the various parts are called. But most competent writers do know these things because such knowledge enables them not only to develop their skills more easily but also to analyze their writing and discuss it with others.

Doctors, for example, don't necessarily have to know the names of the tools they use (stethoscope, scalpel, sutures), nor do mechanics have to know the names of their tools (wrench, screwdriver, ratchet). But it would be hard to find competent doctors or mechanics who were not thoroughly familiar with the tools of their trades, for it is much more difficult to master any important skill and also more difficult to discuss that skill without such knowledge.

The terms and concepts you encounter in this chapter are familiar to most of you but probably not familiar enough. It is not good enough to have a vague idea of what a linking verb is or a general notion of what a prepositional phrase is. You should know *precisely* what these terms mean. This chapter and subsequent chapters present only what is basic and necessary to the study of grammar, but it is essential that you learn *all* of what is presented.

A sound understanding of grammar, like a brick wall, must be built one level at a time. You cannot miss a level and go on to the next. If you master each level as it is presented, you will find that grammar is neither as difficult nor as complicated as you may have thought. You will also find, as you work through the writing sections of the text, that by applying your knowledge of grammar you can greatly improve your writing skills.

Subjects and Verbs

Of all the terms presented in this chapter, perhaps the most important are **SUBJECT** and **VERB**, for subjects and verbs are the foundation of every sentence. Sentences come in many forms, and the structures may become quite complex, but they all have one thing in common: <u>Every sentence must contain a SUBJECT and a VERB.</u> Like most grammatical rules, this one is based on simple logic. After all, without a subject you have nothing to write about, and without a verb you have nothing to say about your subject.

Subjects: Nouns and Pronouns

> **noun**
>
> A noun names a person, place, thing, or idea.

Before you can find the subject of a sentence, you need to be able to identify nouns and pronouns because the subjects of sentences will always be nouns or pronouns (or, occasionally, other words or groups of words that function as subjects). You probably know the definition of a noun: **A noun names a person, place, thing, or idea**.

This definition works perfectly well for most nouns, especially for those that name concrete things we can *see, hear, smell, taste,* or *touch.* Using this definition, most people can identify words such as *door, road,* or *tulip* as nouns.

 EXAMPLES

    N   N   N

Paula reads her favorite **book** whenever she goes to the **beach.**

    N   N   N

My **brother** likes to watch **football** on **television.**

Unfortunately, when it comes to identifying <u>ideas</u> as nouns, many people have trouble. Part of this problem is that nouns name even more than ideas. They name **emotions, qualities, conditions,** and many other **abstractions.** Abstract nouns such as *fear, courage, happiness,* and *trouble* do not name persons, places, or things, but they <u>are</u> nouns.

Following are a few examples of nouns, arranged by category. Add nouns of your own to each category.

Persons	*Places*	*Things*	*Ideas*
Paula	New York	spaghetti	sincerity
engineer	beach	book	anger
woman	India	sun	democracy
artist	town	bicycle	intelligence
_____	_____	_____	_____
_____	_____	_____	_____
_____	_____	_____	_____

PRACTICE   Place an "N" above all the nouns in the following sentences.

           N   *N*   *N*   *N*
1. Brad asked Jennifer to look in the mirror at her hair.

2. Huck and Jim had accidentally passed Cairo in the fog.

3. Pandora stared curiously at the box in her hand.

4. Humpty hoped the men near the wall would solve his problem.

5. Frazier thought his sophistication would win the love of Lydia.

To help you identify <u>all</u> nouns, remember these points:

1. Nouns can be classified as **proper nouns** and **common nouns**. **Proper nouns** name specific persons, places, things, and ideas. The first letter in each of these nouns is capitalized (Manuelita, Missouri, Mazda, Marxism). **Common nouns** name more general categories. The first letter of a common noun is not capitalized (man, mansion, moss, marriage).

2. **A, an,** and **the** are noun markers. A noun will always follow one of these words.

EXAMPLES

                   N   N
The young **policeman** was given **a** new **car**.

           N   N   N   N
The final **point** of the **lecture** concerned **an inconsistency** in the last **report**.

3. If you are unsure whether or not a word is a noun, ask yourself if it **could be introduced with a, an,** or **the.**

EXAMPLE

           N   N   N
My **granddaughter** asked for my **opinion** of her new **outfit**.

4. Words that end in **ment, ism, ness, ence, ance,** and **tion** are usually nouns.

EXAMPLE

                 N   N

Her **criticism** of my **performance** made me very unhappy.

PRACTICE   Place an "N" above all the nouns in the following sentences.

                            N   N   N

1. Her new Chevrolet with all of its accessories pleased Valerie.

2. Persephone reached for the pomegranate at the top of the bush.

3. Homer stared at the huge plate of Spam sitting on the table.

4. The huge ship hit an iceberg and sank as the band played a cheerful tune.

5. Lewis told Clark that the woman would guide them across the mountains.

6. Alice stared in amazement at the cat with the enormous grin.

7. Love and tolerance are not usually characteristics of racism and prejudice.

8. Dr. Frankenstein proudly told his neighbors about the success of his newest experiment.

9. Carol Burnett combines wit, humor, intelligence, and empathy for her fellow humans.

10. The poet treated simple situations in the city or in nature with a quirky insight.

---

pronoun
A pronoun takes the place of a noun.

A pronoun takes the place of a noun. The "pro" in *pronoun* comes from the Latin word meaning "for." Thus, a pronoun is a word that in some way stands "for a noun." Pronouns perform this task in a variety of ways. Often, a pronoun will allow you to refer to a noun without having to repeat the noun. For instance, notice how the word *John* is awkwardly repeated in the following sentence:

John put on John's coat before John left for John's job.

Pronouns allow you to avoid the repetition:

John put on his coat before he left for his job.

In later chapters we will discuss the use of pronouns and the differences among the various types. For now, you simply need to be able to recognize pronouns in a sentence. The following list includes the most common pronouns. Read over this list several times until you are familiar with these words.

Personal Pronouns

I	we	you	he	she	they	it
me	us	your	him	her	them	its
my	our	yours	his	hers	their	
mine	ours				theirs	

Indefinite Pronouns

some	everyone	anyone	someone	no one
all	everything	anything	something	nothing
many	everybody	anybody	somebody	nobody
each				
one				
none				

Reflexive/Intensive Pronouns

myself	ourselves
yourself	yourselves
himself	themselves
herself	
itself	

Relative Pronouns

who, whom, whose
which
that

Demonstrative Pronouns

that	this
those	these

Interrogative Pronouns

who, whom, whose
which
what

PRACTICE   Place an "N" above all nouns and a "Pro" above all pronouns in the following sentences.

1. Erik noticed their boat was drifting toward the falls, so he dropped its anchor.

2. The guard at the border argued with her officer about whether to let us pass.

3. The investigator hurt himself while he was inspecting the scene of the crime.

4. Some of the players on our team celebrated the victory by giving their jerseys to their opponents.

5. Do you know what P.T. Barnum said about suckers?

6. The dancer picked up the rattlesnake and draped it over his shoulders.

7. Who knows anything about quarks and quasars?

8. Each of us should know which little piggy went to market.

9. My collection of rare books does not include anything by Herman Melville or Nathaniel Hawthorne.

10. Everyone for whom the bell tolls will receive a free tour of the home of John Donne and a copy of his poems.

PRACTICE

In the following sentences, write nouns and pronouns of your own choice as indicated.

1. The _*sailor*_ (N) on the _*pier*_ (N) stared at _*his*_ (Pro) _*pipe*_ (N).

2. _____ (N) will share _____ (Pro) _____ (N) with _____ (Pro) _____ (N).

3. _____ (Pro) told _____ (Pro) about _____ (Pro) _____ (N) at the _____ (N).

4. _____ (N) liked the _____ (N) that _____ (Pro) bought at the _____ (N).

5. After _____ (N) washed _____ (Pro) _____ (N), _____ (Pro) asked _____ (Pro) _____ (N) to go to the _____ (N) with _____ (Pro).

Verbs

verb
A verb either shows action or links the subject to another word.

Once you can identify nouns and pronouns, the next step is to learn to identify verbs. Although some people have trouble recognizing these words, you should be able to identify them if you learn the following definition and the few points after it: **A verb either shows action or links the subject to another word.**

As you can see, this definition identifies two types of verbs. Some are "action" verbs (they tell what the subject is <u>doing</u>), and others are "linking" verbs (they tell what the subject is <u>being</u>). This distinction leads to the first point that will help you recognize verbs.

Action Verbs and Linking Verbs

<u>One way to recognize verbs is to know that some verbs can do more than simply express an action.</u> Some verbs are action verbs; others are linking verbs.

ACTION VERBS

Action verbs are usually easy to identify. Consider the following sentence:

The deer leaped gracefully over the stone wall.

If you ask yourself what the **action** of the sentence is, the answer is obviously *leaped*. Therefore, *leaped* is the verb.

 EXAMPLES OF ACTION VERBS *run, read, go, write, think, forgive, wait, laugh*

 PRACTICE   Underline the action verbs in the following sentences.

   1. Madonna <u>leaned</u> on the drummer.

   2. The *Titanic* sank in the North Atlantic in 1912.

   3. Hortense dyed her hair magenta yesterday.

   4. Sam eats green eggs and ham for breakfast, lunch, and dinner.

   5. Mr. Lincoln talked to General Grant on his cell phone.

LINKING VERBS

Linking verbs are sometimes more difficult to recognize than action verbs. Look for the verb in the following sentence:

Helen **is** a woman of integrity.

Notice that the sentence expresses no real action. The verb *is* simply links the word *woman* to the word *Helen*.

EXAMPLES OF LINKING VERBS   forms of *be*: am, is, are, was, were, be, being, been

forms of *become, seem, look, appear, smell, taste, feel, sound, grow, remain*

Linking verbs can link three types of words to a subject.

1. They can link nouns to the subject:

   Hank <u>became</u> a hero to his team. (*Hero* is linked to *Hank*.)

2. They can link pronouns to the subject:

   Cheryl <u>was</u> someone from another planet. (*Someone* is linked to *Cheryl*.)

3. They can link adjectives (descriptive words) to the subject:

   The sky <u>was</u> cloudy all day. (*Cloudy* is linked to *sky*.)

PRACTICE   Underline the linking verbs in the following sentences.

1. The author <u>was</u> sad about the lack of success of his novel.

2. Mr. Gates is successful in business.

3. *Apocalypse Now* seemed longer this time.

4. Rip Van Winkle felt dizzy after his long nap.

5. I am wild for okra.

Verb Tense

<u>Another way to identify verbs is to know that they appear in different forms to show the time when the action or linking takes place.</u> These forms are called *tenses*. The simplest tenses are present, past, and future.

Present		*Past*	
I walk	we walk	I walked	we walked
you walk	you walk	you walked	you walked
he, she, it walks	they walk	he, she, it walked	they walked

Future	
I will walk	we will walk
you will walk	you will walk
he, she, it will walk	they will walk

Note that the verb *walk* can be written as *walked* to show past tense and as *will walk* to show future tense. When a verb adds "d" or "ed" to form the past tense, it is called a **regular verb**.

Other verbs change their forms more drastically to show past tense. For example, the verb *eat* becomes *ate*, and *fly* becomes *flew*. Verbs like these, which do not add "d" or "ed" to form the past tense, are called **irregular verbs**. Irregular verbs will be discussed in Chapter Six. For now, to help you identify verbs, remember this point: Verbs change their forms to show tense.

PRACTICE

In the following sentences, first underline the verb and then write the tense (present, past, or future) in the space provided.

present **1.** Aeneas <u>praises</u> Dido once a week.

_____ **2.** Odysseus wanted to go home.

_____ **3.** Homer and Hortense will visit Gatorland, Louisiana, on their anniversary.

_____ **4.** A strong earthquake destroyed much of San Francisco in 1906.

_____ **5.** Yo-Yo Ma practices almost every day.

Helping Verbs and Main Verbs

A third way to identify verbs is to know that the verb of a sentence is often more than one word. The **MAIN VERB** of a sentence may be preceded by one or more **HELPING VERBS** to show time, condition, or circumstances. The helping verbs allow us the flexibility to communicate a wide variety of ideas and attitudes. For example, note how adding a helping verb changes the following sentences:

I run indicates that an action is happening or happens repeatedly.

I will run indicates that an action is not now occurring but will occur in the future.

I should run indicates an attitude toward the action.

The **COMPLETE VERB** of a sentence, then, includes a **MAIN VERB** and any **HELPING VERBS**. The complete verb can contain as many as three helping verbs.

      MV
He *writes.*

    HV   MV
He *has written.*

    HV HV   MV
He *has been writing.*

    HV   HV   HV   MV
He *might have been writing.*

You can be sure that you have identified all of the helping verbs in a complete verb simply by learning the helping verbs. There are not very many of them.

These words are **always** helping verbs:

can	may	could
will	must	would
shall	might	should

These words are sometimes helping verbs and sometimes main verbs:

Forms of have	*Forms of* do	*Forms of* be		
have	do	am	was	be
has	does	is	were	being
had	did	are		been

In the following examples, note that the same word can be a helping verb in one sentence and a main verb in another:

      MV

Anna **had** thirty pairs of shoes.

      HV   MV

Thomas **had** thought about the problem for years.

      MV

She **did** well on her chemistry quiz.

      HV MV

Bob **did** go to the game after all.

      MV

The bus **was** never on time.

      HV   MV

He **was** planning to leave in the morning.

When you are trying to identify the complete verb of a sentence, remember that any helping verbs will always come before the main verb; however, other words may occur between the helping verb(s) and the main verb. For instance, you will often find words like *not, never, ever, already,* or *just* between the helping verb and the main verb. Also, in questions you will often find the subject between the helping verb and the main verb.

 EXAMPLES

      HV   S   MV

Will the telephone company raise its prices?

      S   HV   MV

Nobody has **ever** proved the existence of the Loch Ness Monster.

PRACTICE   In the spaces provided, identify the underlined words as main verbs (MV) or helping verbs (HV).

_MV_   **1.** The cowboy <u>is</u> a popular figure in American folklore.

_____   **2.** Early cowboys in the Southwest <u>had</u> the Spanish title of *vaquero*.

_____   **3.** Soon American pronunciation <u>had</u> changed *vaquero* to *buckeroo*.

_____   **4.** Buckeroos <u>were</u> not called cowboys until the 1820s.

_____   **5.** Cowboys <u>were</u> mostly simple ranch hands.

_____   **6.** They <u>did</u> many physically demanding jobs on the ranch.

_____   **7.** However, they <u>did</u> not drive cattle across country until the late 1860s.

_____   **8.** Texans had <u>been</u> raising cattle for many years before that.

_____   **9.** But their problem had always <u>been</u> the distance between Texas and the markets to the north and east.

_____   **10.** In response, the cowboys <u>would</u> move hundreds of thousands of cattle across the country from Texas to the railheads in Kansas and Nebraska.

PRACTICE   **A.** In the following sentences, place "HV" over all helping verbs and "MV" over all main verbs.

             HV MV

1. Tony Gwynn has set many baseball records.

2. The Sirens have caused many shipwrecks.

3. Venus was selling herbal remedies to some of the older gods.

4. Has General Washington crossed the river yet?

5. Ishmael could have stayed safely at home.

B. In the following sentences, write helping verbs and main verbs of your own choice as indicated.

             MV

6. John Lee Hooker _played_ some blues for his friends.

                              MV   MV

7. The chef _____ the snails and _____ them to his mother.

                 HV   MV

8. Janus _____ _____ both ways at the same time.

          HV   MV   MV

9. _____ Shakespeare _____ the tragedy that I _____ him for?

                       HV   HV   MV

10. Lady Godiva _____ not _____ _____ her horse when

              HV   MV

she _____ not _____ any clothes.

Verbals

<u>A fourth way to identify verbs is to recognize what they are not.</u> Some verb forms do not actually function as verbs. These are called **VERBALS.** One of the most important verbals is the **INFINITIVE,** which usually begins with the word *to* (*to write, to be, to see*). The infinitive cannot serve as the verb of a sentence because it cannot express the time of the action or linking. *I wrote* communicates a clear idea, but *I to write* does not.

    Another common verbal is the "-ing" form of the verb when it occurs without a helping verb (*running, flying, being*). When an "-ing" form without a helping verb is used as an adjective, it is called a **PRESENT PARTICIPLE.** When it is used as a noun, it is called a **GERUND.**

 EXAMPLES

    MV   Verbal

I **hope to pass** this test.

    HV   MV

I **should pass** this test.

            Verbal   MV

The birds **flying** from tree to tree **chased** the cat from their nest.

          HV   MV

The birds **were flying** from tree to tree.

   Verbal MV

Jogging is good cardiovascular exercise.

   MV

I **jog** for the cardiovascular benefits of the exercise.

PRACTICE   In the following sentences, write "HV" above all helping verbs, "MV" above all main verbs, and "Verbal" above all verbals.

               HV MV   *Verbal*

1. Paradise should be a good place to sleep late.

2. Standing on third base, Barry could not believe his luck.

3. To please Hortense, Homer had prepared a Spam and celery omelette.

4. The class was looking at a picture of Mother Teresa giving a sick man a

   drink of water.

5. The people picking potatoes ignored Vincent.

 PRACTICE   Place "HV" above all helping verbs and "MV" above all main verbs in the following sentences. Draw a line through any verbals.

               HV   MV

1. Paul had intended ~~to reach~~ Damascus before dark.

2. People have been talking about Mr. Gates's attempt to monopolize the

   market.

3. Does Oedipus really want to marry Jocasta?

4. The Sphinx has a rather simple riddle for you.

5. The lost campers were yelling and waving at the helicopter circling above

   them.

6. Picking up his guitar, Woody Guthrie was wondering what to play next.

7. Andres Segovia should not have been so critical of today's guitarists.

8. As a boy, George Reeves was always jumping higher than anyone else.

9. The prospectors have been trying to find the Lost Dutchman's mine.

10. Have you asked Queequeg to bring his harpoon?

Identifying Subjects and Verbs

Finding the Subject

Most sentences contain several nouns and pronouns used in a variety of ways. One of the most important ways is as the subject of a verb. In order to identify which of the nouns or pronouns in a sentence is the subject, you need to identify the complete verb first. After identifying the verb, it is easy to find the subject by asking yourself "Who or what ___(verb)___ ?"

EXAMPLE

S   HV MV
The **man** in the green hat **was following** a suspicious-looking stranger.

The complete verb in this sentence is *was following,* and when you ask yourself "Who or what was following?" the answer is "the man." Therefore, *man* is the subject.

 Remember, most sentences contain several nouns and pronouns, but not all nouns and pronouns are subjects.

EXAMPLE

S   MV
The **people** from the **house** down the **street** often borrow our **tools**.

This sentence contains four nouns, but only *people* is the subject. The other nouns in this sentence are different types of **objects**. The noun *tools* is called a **direct object** because it receives the action of the verb *borrow*. The nouns *house* and *street* are called **objects of prepositions**. Direct objects will be discussed in Chapter Four. Objects of prepositions will be discussed later in this chapter. For now, just remember that not all nouns and pronouns are subjects.

PRACTICE

In the following sentences, place an "HV" above any helping verbs, an "MV" above the main verbs, and an "S" above the subjects.

S HV MV
1. Al Capone was sent to Alcatraz Federal Penitentiary in 1932.

2. The famous prison sits in the middle of San Francisco Bay.

3. Escaping prisoners would drown in the cold waters of the bay.

4. Over the years, several men were shot while trying to escape.

5. After only twenty-nine years as a prison, Alcatraz was closed in 1963.

Subject Modifiers

Words that modify or describe nouns or pronouns should not be included when you identify the subject.

 EXAMPLE

                 S   MV

The red **wheelbarrow is** in the yard.

The subject is *wheelbarrow*, not *the red wheelbarrow*.

     Remember that the possessive forms of nouns and pronouns are also used to describe or modify nouns, so do not include them in the subject either.

 EXAMPLES

                 S   MV

My brother's **suitcase is** very worn.

         S   MV

His **textbook was** expensive.

The subjects are simply *suitcase* and *textbook*, not *my brother's suitcase* or *his textbook*.

Verb Modifiers

Just as words that describe or modify the subject are not considered part of the subject, words that describe or modify the verb are not considered part of the verb. Watch for such modifiers because they will often occur between helping verbs and main verbs and may be easily mistaken for helping verbs. Notice that in the following sentence the words *not* and *unfairly* are modifiers and, therefore, not part of the complete verb.

 EXAMPLE

  S   HV   MV

Parents should **not unfairly** criticize their children.

Some common verb modifiers are *not, never, almost, just, completely, sometimes, always, often,* and *certainly*.

 PRACTICE

Place "HV" over helping verbs, "MV" over main verbs, and "S" over the subjects of the following sentences.

            S   *HV*   *MV*

1. The fight for Little Roundtop has not yet begun.

2. Fried okra was served with the hushpuppies.

3. Pearl could sometimes be seen at Starbucks on Saturdays.

4. Norman's reward was a kiss from Patty.

5. Charging up the hill, Pickett's men bravely faced the rifles and cannons.

Multiple Subjects and Verbs

Sentences may contain more than one subject and more than one verb.

 EXAMPLES

    S   MV
Fred petted the dog.

    S   S   MV
Fred and **Mary petted** the dog.

    S   S   MV   MV
Fred and **Mary petted** the dog and **scratched** its ears.

    S   MV   S   MV
Fred petted the dog, and **Mary scratched** its ears.

    S   S   MV   S   MV
Fred and **Mary petted** the dog before **they fed** it.

 PRACTICE

Place "HV" over helping verbs, "MV" over main verbs, and "S" over subjects in the following sentences.

                     S   *MV*

1. For twenty years, Telemachus helped his mother.

2. The owl and the pussycat were enemies.

3. Superman and Batman grabbed the gold and headed for the hills.

4. Wolverine wanted to go with them, but they had not invited him.

5. Before the whale-watching boat departed, Ishmael and Starbuck

came aboard.

Special Situations

SUBJECT UNDERSTOOD

When a sentence is a command (or a request worded as a polite command), the pronoun *you* is understood as the subject. *You* is the only understood subject.

 EXAMPLES

    MV
Shut the door. (Subject is *you* understood.)

        MV

Please **give** this book to your sister. (Subject is *you* understood.)

VERB BEFORE SUBJECT

In some sentences, such as in questions, the verb comes before the subject.

EXAMPLE

MV   S

Is your **mother** home?

The verb also comes before the subject in sentences beginning with *there* or *here*, as well as in some other constructions.

EXAMPLES

    MV S

There **is** a **bug** in my soup.

  MV   S

Here **is** another **bowl** of soup.

         MV   S

Over the hill **rode** the **cavalry**.

             MV   S

On the front porch **was** a **basket** with a baby in it.

PRACTICE

Place "HV" over helping verbs, "MV" over main verbs, and "S" over subjects in the following sentences. Verbals and verb modifiers should not be included in the complete verb.

1. Give the nose spray to Cyrano.

2. Near the piano was Thelonious.

3. Could Lee have won at Gettysburg?

4. There are two extraterrestrial beings in my living room.

5. Raise the flag at dawn.

PRACTICE

Underline all subjects once and complete verbs twice in the following sentences. Remember that the complete verb contains the main verb and all helping verbs and that verbals and verb modifiers should not be included in the complete verb.

1. <u>You</u> certainly <u>wear</u> those baggy shorts with style.

2. Sonny could have treated the injured dog better.

3. Neil Armstrong might have hesitated before taking that first step.

4. Beethoven's hearing had begun to diminish.

5. Does the Israeli delegate want to address the UN?

6. Godzilla was looking forward to his vacation in Jurassic Park.

7. Tell those Munchkins to stop their obnoxious singing.

8. Gregor had become an insect, so he refused a latte.

9. There were election problems in Florida.

10. The Little Mermaid looked at Aladdin and winked.

 PRACTICE   Write sentences of your own that follow the suggested patterns. Identify each subject (S), helping verb (HV), and main verb (MV).

1. A statement with one subject and two main verbs (S-MV-MV):

   S   MV
   A large black cat hopped off the fence

   *   MV*
   and crept into our yard.

2. A statement with a subject and two main verbs (S-MV-MV):

   _____

   _____

3. A statement with one subject, one helping verb, and one main verb (S-HV-MV):

   _____

   _____

4. A question with one helping verb, one subject, and one main verb (HV-S-MV):

   _____

   _____

5. A command that begins with a main verb (MV):

_____

_____

6. A statement that starts with "There" and is followed by a main verb and a subject ("There" MV-S):

_____

_____

7. A statement with two subjects and one main verb (S-S-MV):

_____

_____

8. A statement with one subject, one helping verb, and one main verb followed by "after" and another subject and another main verb (S-HV-MV "after" S-MV):

_____

_____

9. A statement with a subject, a helping verb, and a main verb followed by ", and" and another subject, helping verb, and main verb (S-HV-MV ", and" S-HV-MV):

_____

_____

10. A statement with a subject and main verb followed by "because" and another subject and main verb (S-MV "because" S-MV):

_____

_____

Section One Review

1. A **noun** names a person, place, thing, or idea.

   a. **Proper nouns** name specific persons, places, things, or ideas. They begin with a capital letter. **Common nouns** name more general categories and are not capitalized.

   b. **A, an,** and **the** are noun markers. A noun always follows one of these words.

   c. If you are unsure whether or not a word is a noun, ask yourself if it **could** be introduced with **a, an,** or **the.**

   d. Words that end in **ment, ism, ness, ence, ance,** and **tion** are usually nouns.

2. A **pronoun** takes the place of a noun.

3. A **verb** either shows **action** or **links** the subject to another word.

4. Verbs appear in different **tenses** to show the time when the action or linking takes place.

5. The **complete verb** includes a **main verb** and any **helping verbs.**

6. **Verbals** are verb forms that do not function as verbs.

   a. The **infinitive** is a verbal that begins with the word *to.*

   b. The "-ing" form of the verb without a helping verb is called a **present participle** if it is used as an adjective.

   c. The "-ing" form of the verb without a helping verb is called a **gerund** if it is used as a noun.

7. To identify the **subject** of any sentence, first find the verb. Then ask "Who or what <u>(verb)</u>?"

8. **Subject modifiers** describe or modify the subject. They should not be included when you identify the subject.

9. **Verb modifiers** describe or modify verbs. They are not considered part of the verb.

10. Sentences may contain **multiple subjects** and **multiple verbs.**

11. When a sentence is a command (or a request worded as a polite command), the pronoun *you* is understood as the subject. *You* is the only understood subject.

12. In some sentences the verb comes before the subject.

Exercise 1A

In the spaces provided, indicate whether the underlined word is a subject (write "S"), a helping verb (write "HV"), or a main verb (write "MV"). If it is none of these, leave the space blank.

__*MV*__ **1.** Homer <u>scorched</u> his armadillo-and-beet soup.

_____ **2.** Tony Soprano looked at his <u>wife</u> and smiled.

_____ **3.** <u>Ulysses</u> knew that it would be ten more years before he saw his wife, Penelope.

_____ **4.** The last great redwood <u>crashed</u> heavily to the ground.

_____ **5.** The New York <u>firemen</u> gathered for a memorial at the church.

_____ **6.** Narcissus <u>could</u> see his reflection in the water.

_____ **7.** In the <u>pan</u> my mother was frying okra.

_____ **8.** The game <u>was</u> almost over when we decided to leave.

_____ **9.** Alicia <u>had</u> just finished when her cell phone rang.

_____ **10.** The rain was coming down hard, so Alcee <u>decided</u> to stay.

_____ **11.** Frustrated by the bad weather, <u>Icarus</u> canceled his flight.

_____ **12.** Michael Jordan could <u>do</u> things with a basketball that no one else could do.

_____ **13.** <u>Somebody</u> noticed that Santa had forgotten his suspenders.

_____ **14.** The Chernobyl nuclear power plant <u>suffered</u> a major meltdown in 1986.

_____ **15.** Amanda <u>was</u> not expecting the American gladiator to return her call.

Exercise 1B

A. Underline all subjects once and complete verbs twice in the following sentences. Remember that a sentence may have more than one subject and more than one verb.

1. Indiana Jones was not entirely a fictional character.

2. In fact, *Raiders of the Lost Ark* was written in part about a real person.

3. Vendyl Jones is the head of the Institute for Judaic-Christian studies.

4. The writer of the story had met Jones on an archeological dig.

5. Do you remember the gigantic rolling boulder in the movie?

6. The real-life Vendyl Jones and his assistants escaped from a booby-trap of four gigantic bouncing boulders.

7. One assistant was almost crushed by the boulders, but he survived by jumping off a cliff.

8. Before he finds the lost Ark, Jones wants to find the ashes of the Red Heifer.

9. According to one of the Dead Sea Scrolls, the Ark is buried near those ashes.

10. Jones is using the Dead Sea Scrolls and has already found twenty of the reference points leading to the Red Heifer.

B. Write sentences of your own that follow the suggested patterns. Identify each subject (S), helping verb (HV), and main verb (MV).

11. A statement with two subjects and one main verb (S-S-MV):

    The baseball player and his agent decided to
    meet for lunch.

12. A statement with one subject, one helping verb, and one main verb (S-HV-MV):

    _____

    _____

13. A question that begins with a main verb followed by the subject (MV-S):

    _____

    _____

Exercise 1B

continued

14. A statement with a subject, two helping verbs, and one main verb (S-HV-HV-MV):

_____

_____

15. A statement with a subject and main verb followed by ", so" and another subject and main verb (S-MV ", so" S-MV):

_____

_____

Exercise 1C

In the following paragraph, underline all subjects once and complete verbs twice.

1. An unfortunate <u>incident</u> in fifth grade <u><u>was</u></u> one of the most traumatic experiences of my life. 2. It started when both Raymond and I wanted to pitch the ball in a game of kickball. 3. We started to argue about it, but recess ended in the middle of our argument. 4. Ray was still angry, and he expressed his displeasure by striking me in the forehead. 5. He had just hit me and turned to go back to our classroom when someone threw me the kickball. 6. The large ball bounced twice before I caught it. 7. In one motion, I gained control of the ball and lost control of myself. 8. As if in slow motion, I drew back and then hurled the ball at Ray with the bitter words, "You can have the ball!" 9. After leaving my hand and traveling through the air, the ball struck Ray in the back of the neck. 10. He immediately collapsed, holding his neck with both hands. 11. The teacher rushed to his side as Ray shouted, "I can't feel my legs!" 12. I could not believe what I was seeing. 13. As our teacher called for help, I found myself in line with my class-mates watching as though a nightmare were unfolding before my eyes. 14. I pressed my body against a pine tree and thought that I surely would go to jail. 15. Then the sound of the sirens and the sight of the helicopter landing on the distant soccer field made my stomach twist, and a great feeling of sickness came over me.

Modifiers

Although subjects and verbs form the basis of any sentence, most sentences also contain many other words that serve a variety of purposes. One such group of words includes the modifiers, which limit, describe, intensify, or otherwise alter the meaning of other words. The word *modify* simply means "change." Notice how the modifiers change the meaning in each of the following sentences.

The dictator had **total** power.

The dictator had **great** power.

The dictator had **little** power.

The dictator had **no** power.

As you can see, the word *power* is significantly changed by the different modifiers in these sentences.

Although modifiers can change the meaning of words in many different ways, there are basically only two types of modifiers, **ADJECTIVES** and **ADVERBS.** You will be able to identify both types of modifiers more easily if you remember these three points:

1. Sentences often contain more than one modifier.

 EXAMPLE

The **new** moon rose **slowly** over the desert.

In this example, the word *new* modifies *moon;* it describes the specific phase of the moon. The word *slowly* modifies *rose;* it describes the speed with which the moon rose.

2. Two or more modifiers can be used to modify the same word.

 EXAMPLE

The moon rose **slowly** and **dramatically** over the desert.

In this example the words *slowly* and *dramatically* both modify *rose. Slowly* describes the speed, and *dramatically* describes the manner in which the moon rose.

3. All modifiers must modify *something*. You should be able to identify the specific word that is being modified as well as the modifier itself.

 EXAMPLE

Slowly the **new** moon rose over the desert.

In this example, notice that the word *slowly* still modifies *rose,* though the two words are not close to each other. The arrows point from the modifiers to the words being modified.

PRACTICE   Draw an arrow from the underlined modifier to the word it modifies.

1. Merchants <u>once</u> sold <u>pink</u> ducklings at Easter.

2. The fries were <u>hot</u> and <u>crispy</u>.

3. Craig <u>usually</u> has a <u>tuna</u> sandwich for lunch.

4. The <u>tedious</u> movie was <u>mercifully</u> <u>short.</u>

5. <u>Tiny</u> animals ran <u>continually</u> down the path.

---

adjective

An adjective modifies a noun or a pronoun.

Adjectives

An adjective modifies a noun or a pronoun. In English most adjectives precede the noun they modify.

 EXAMPLE

The **young** eagle perched on the **rocky** cliff.

In this example, the word *young* **modifies** *eagle,* and the word *rocky* **modifies** *cliff.*

   Although most adjectives precede the noun or pronoun they modify, they may also follow the noun or pronoun and be connected to it by a linking verb.

 EXAMPLE

Poisonous plants are **dangerous.**

In this example, the word *poisonous* describes the noun *plants.* Notice that it **precedes** the noun. However, the word *dangerous* also describes the noun *plants.* It is **linked** to the noun by the linking verb *are.* Both *poisonous* and *dangerous* are adjectives that modify the noun *plants.*

   Many different types of words can be adjectives, as long as they **modify** a noun or pronoun. Most adjectives answer the questions **which? what kind?** or **how many?** Here are the most common types of adjectives.

1. Descriptive words

 EXAMPLES

I own a **blue** suit.

That is an **ugly** wound.

2. Possessive nouns and pronouns

EXAMPLE   I parked **my** motorcycle next to **John's** car.

3. Limiting words and numbers

EXAMPLES   **Some** people see **every** movie that comes out.

               Two accidents have happened on **this** street.

4. Nouns that modify other nouns

EXAMPLE   The **basketball** game was held in the **neighborhood** gym.

PRACTICE   **A.** In the following sentences, circle all adjectives and draw an arrow to the noun or pronoun each adjective modifies.

1. (Strange) cats have appeared on (our)(front) lawn recently.

2. We attended an unusual concert last Saturday.

3. Our two turtledoves keep fighting with that stupid partridge in the pear tree.

4. My rusty old Honda might give out if it does not see a competent mechanic soon.

5. Kate Chopin wrote many wonderful stories, but most people of her time would not read them.

B. Add two adjectives of your own to each of the following sentences.

6. The garage was filled with *dusty* boxes and *broken* tools.

7. An aardvark wandered into our yard and looked for ants.

8. The writer preferred to use a typewriter for his novels.

9. The turkey on the table was surrounded by vegetables.

10. Officials tried to blame the mess on the birds that lived near the pond.

Adverbs

An adverb modifies a verb, adjective, or another adverb. Adverbs are sometimes more difficult to recognize than adjectives because they can be used to modify three different types of words—verbs, adjectives, and other adverbs. They can either precede or follow the words they modify and are sometimes placed farther away from the words they modify than are adjectives.

 EXAMPLES

V   Adv

The president walked across the room **quickly**.
(adverb modifying a verb)

           Adv   Adj

The president seemed **unusually** nervous.
(adverb modifying an adjective)

        Adv   Adv

The president left **very** quickly after the press conference.
(adverb modifying an adverb)

Because adverbs are often formed by adding "ly" to adjectives such as *quick* or *usual,* many adverbs end in "ly" (*quickly* and *usually*). However, you cannot always use this ending as a way of identifying adverbs because some words that end in "ly" are *not* adverbs and because some adverbs do not end in "ly," as the following list of common adverbs illustrates:

already	now	still
also	often	then
always	quite	too
never	seldom	very
not	soon	well

Here are two ways to help you identify adverbs:

1. Find the word that is being modified. If it is a verb, adjective, or adverb, then the modifier is an adverb.

 EXAMPLES

                  V

Thelma **seriously** injured her finger during the tennis match.

                        Adj

My brother and I have **completely** different attitudes toward Spam.

             Adv

Tuan **almost** always arrives on time for work.

2. Look for words that answer the questions **when? where? how?** or **to what extent?**

EXAMPLES

My grandparents **often** bring gifts when they visit. (**when?**)

The turnips were grown **locally**. (**where?**)

Rachel **carefully** removed the paint from the antique desk. (**how?**)

Homer is **widely** known as a trainer in a flea circus. (**to what extent?**)

NOTE: Adverbs are **not** considered part of the complete verb, even if they come between the helping verb and the main verb. (See page 15 for a list of common adverbs that come between the helping verb and the main verb.)

 EXAMPLE

HV Adv MV
He has **not** failed to do his duty.

 PRACTICE

A. In the following sentences, circle all adverbs and draw an arrow to the word that each adverb modifies.

1. The detective (quietly) stepped into the corridor and (slowly) raised his revolver.

2. The fireman often told the story of that incredibly horrible day.

3. The black widow sometimes gleefully destroys her mate.

4. As Ichabod Crane rode swiftly down the lane, he was already beginning to worry about the headless horseman.

5. Dido was excruciatingly sad as she stood on the rather sheer cliff.

B. Add one adverb of your own to each of the following sentences.

6. The full moon moved *slowly* across the sky.

7. Bill craves a bebop concert.

8. The audience saw the band and applauded.

9. Homer looked into the abyss and stared at the splendid sunset.

10. The boat leaned as the wind from the north filled its sails.

Section Two Review

1. **Modifiers** limit, describe, intensify, or otherwise alter the meaning of other words.

   a. Sentences often contain more than one modifier.

   b. Two or more modifiers can be used to modify the same word.

   c. All modifiers must modify *something*.

2. An **adjective** modifies a noun or a pronoun.

3. Most adjectives answer the questions which? what kind? or how many?

4. Common types of adjectives are the following:

   a. <u>Descriptive words</u>

   b. <u>Possessive nouns and pronouns</u>

   c. <u>Limiting words and numbers</u>

   d. <u>Nouns that modify other nouns</u>

5. An **adverb** modifies a verb, adjective, or another adverb.

6. There are two ways to identify adverbs:

   a. <u>Find the word that is being modified. If it is a verb, an adjective, or an adverb, then the modifier is an adverb.</u>

   b. <u>Look for words that answer the questions when? where? how? or to what extent?</u>

Exercise 2A

A. In the following sentences, identify all adjectives by writing "Adj" above them.

              Adj Adj   Adj
1. Michelle played her favorite Nintendo game.

2. Sam admired his shiny new truck.

3. The corral was empty and quiet when Wyatt Earp opened its rusty gate.

4. Cora's recent discovery was that decent people exist.

5. Your newest hobby is dangerous.

B. In the following sentences, identify all adverbs by writing "Adv" above them.

              Adv   *Adv*
6. The curtain slowly rose, and the actress graciously accepted the roses.

7. Jenna sincerely hoped that her birds would be completely safe in Canada.

8. Carlos soon decided on a rather dangerous plan.

9. The soldiers walked steadily and bravely toward the fort.

10. Homer gratefully loaded his plate with deep-fried Spam but then nearly dropped the

    whole thing.

C. Add one adjective and one adverb to each of the following sentences. Do not use the same adjective or adverb more than once.

                carefully wooden
11. Geppetto worked ∧ on the ∧ shoes all night.

12. The president limped to the stage and spoke to the people of the country.

13. The students were disappointed because they thought the holiday was on Monday.

14. Our parents asked us to meet the stranger in the kitchen and talk to him.

15. On the stage the actors whispered to each other and glanced into the auditorium.

Exercise 2B

In the following sentences, write "Adj" above all adjectives and "Adv" above all adverbs. Underline all subjects once and all verbs twice.

1. According to legend, Betsy Ross sewed the very first American flag in 1776.

2. Betsy's grandson proudly revealed the story in 1870, thirty-four years after her death.

3. Supposedly, George Washington, Robert Morris, and George Ross were members of the congressional flag committee.

4. They gave Betsy a rough sketch and then asked her to design the new flag.

5. She skillfully created a flag with a symmetrical arrangement of five-pointed stars.

6. Her grandson's story quickly spread, and Betsy Ross became a famous historical figure.

7. Many Americans loved the idea that their flag had been cleverly designed by a simple seamstress.

8. Most historians today do not believe the story.

9. Betsy Ross was a seamstress and did actually own an upholstery shop in Philadelphia.

10. She apparently did make some flags, but no evidence supports her grandson's version of history.

11. There is no historical record of Betsy Ross making the flag.

12. There is also no record of a flag committee in 1776.

13. The Second Continental Congress did not even design the Stars and Stripes until 1777.

14. In addition, early American flags often had stars with six or eight points, not the five points that Betsy supposedly designed.

15. Betsy Ross certainly did not live in the historic Flag House in Philadelphia.

Exercise 2C

In the following sentences, identify each of the underlined words as noun (N), pronoun (Pro), verb (V), adjective (Adj), or adverb (Adv).

1. In 1839, the events involving the Cuban ship *Amistad* and its cargo of slaves led to a

       Adj   *N*

<u>significant</u> <u>decision</u> by the United States Supreme Court. **2.** <u>It</u> all began when a group of African

tribesmen from Sierra Leone were kidnapped and <u>sold</u> into slavery. **3.** After they had been sold

and resold several times, the Africans were <u>finally</u> taken to Havana, Cuba, the <u>center</u> of the

illegal slave trade. **4.** In Havana, <u>they</u> <u>were</u> placed in a crowded hold of the slave ship

Amistad. **5.** During <u>their</u> voyage, a captive named Cinque became the leader of the slaves, and

<u>soon</u> he began to plot their escape. **6.** In the middle of the <u>fourth</u> night out, the slaves came on

<u>deck</u>, killed the captain, and took over the ship. **7.** Cinque sent all of the sailors ashore in a

small boat, but he <u>kept</u> the two owners aboard because he needed them to help <u>him</u> sail the ship

home to Africa. **8.** <u>Unfortunately</u>, the <u>owners</u> tricked him and steered the ship toward New

York. **9.** Because they were <u>short</u> of supplies, they anchored the ship off Montauk, New York,

where they sent a <u>party</u> out to look for food. **10.** While <u>they</u> were there, a United States brig

sighted the *Amistad* and <u>promptly</u> boarded it. **11.** Cinque was arrested after a <u>courageous</u>

<u>attempt</u> to escape. **12.** He and the other mutineers were jailed and <u>charged</u> with <u>murder</u> and

piracy, but many Americans came to their defense because the mutineers had been kidnapped

from their own homes in Africa and sold as slaves. **13.** Their <u>case</u> went all the <u>way</u> to the United

States Supreme Court, where John Quincy Adams argued on their behalf. **14.** He accused the

administration of President Van Buren of "utter injustice" in prosecuting people <u>who</u> were fight-

ing <u>valiantly</u> for their freedom. **15.** In February, 1841, the Supreme Court <u>declared</u> the defen-

dants to be <u>free</u> men and innocent of all charges. **16.** Cinque and his <u>fellow</u> former slaves <u>then</u>

traveled to Boston and Philadelphia to speak about their experiences. **17.** <u>Many</u> people donated

money to <u>them</u>, and in December, 1841, they sailed home to Sierra Leone.

Connectors

The final group of words consists of the connectors. These are signals that indicate the relationship of one part of a sentence to another. The two types of connectors are **conjunctions** and **prepositions.**

Conjunctions

> **conjunction**
> A conjunction joins two parts of a sentence.

A conjunction joins two parts of a sentence. The word *conjunction* is derived from two Latin words meaning "to join with." The definition is easy to remember if you know that the word *junction* in English refers to the place where two roads come together.

The two types of conjunctions are **coordinating** and **subordinating.** In Chapter Two we will discuss the subordinating conjunctions. You will find it much easier to distinguish between the two types if you memorize the coordinating conjunctions now.

The **coordinating conjunctions** are *and, but, or, nor, for, yet,* and *so.*

NOTE: An easy way to learn the coordinating conjunctions is to remember that their first letters can spell **BOYSFAN:** (But Or Yet So For And Nor).

Coordinating conjunctions join elements of the sentence that are <u>equal</u> or <u>parallel</u>. For instance, they may join two subjects, two verbs, two adjectives, or two parallel groups of words.

EXAMPLE

   S Conj S   MV Conj   MV
Ernie **and** Bert often disagree **but** never fight.

In this example the first conjunction joins two subjects and the second joins two verbs.

EXAMPLE

   S   MV   Adj Conj   Adj   Conj   MV
Susan often felt awkward **or** uncomfortable **yet** never showed it.

In this example the first conjunction joins two adjectives, and the second joins two verbs.

Coordinating conjunctions may even be used to join two entire sentences, each with its own subject and verb.

EXAMPLE

     S HV MV   S   MV
The rain had fallen steadily all week long. The river was close to overflowing.

     S HV MV   Conj   S   MV
The rain had fallen steadily all week long, **so** the river was close to overflowing.

Notice that the coordinating conjunctions have different meanings and that changing the conjunction can significantly change the meaning of a sentence. *A person should never drink and drive* communicates a very different idea from *A person should never drink or drive.*

- The conjunction *and* indicates **addition.**

EXAMPLE   Jules **and** Jim loved the same woman.

- The conjunctions *but* and *yet* indicate **contrast.**

EXAMPLES   She wanted to go **but** didn't have the money.

I liked Brian, **yet** I didn't really trust him.

- The conjunctions *or* and *nor* indicate **alternatives.**

EXAMPLES   You can borrow the record **or** the tape.

He felt that he could neither go **nor** stay.

- The conjunctions *for* and *so* indicate **cause** or **result.**

EXAMPLES   The plants died, **for** they had not been watered.

Her brother lost his job, **so** he had to find another.

PRACTICE   **A.** In the following sentences, circle all coordinating conjunctions. Underline all subjects once and all complete verbs twice.

1. The cook (or) the dishwasher will clear the tables.

2. Homer loved Spam, but he had misgivings about escargot or sushi.

3. Yeni was glad, for summer vacation was almost here.

4. Scully was not interested in UFO's, nor did she care much for werewolves.

5. Michelle had worked long and hard on her research paper, so she received a good grade on it.

B. In the following sentences, add coordinating conjunctions that show the relationship indicated in parentheses.

6. We can go to the baseball game, _____*or*_____ we can see a movie, but we can't do both. (alternatives)

7. Columbus was convinced he could reach the Orient, _____ very few people agreed with him. (contrast)

8. Uncle Julius tended the vineyard _____ sold grapes to his friends. (addition).

9. Cinderella could not stop to pick up her slipper, _____ the clock had already begun to strike twelve. (cause)

10. The flood was becoming worse, _____ we could not return to our house. (result)

Prepositions

> **preposition**
>
> A preposition relates a noun or pronoun to some other word in the sentence.

A preposition relates a noun or a pronoun to some other word in the sentence. Prepositions usually indicate a relationship of **place** (in, near), **direction** (toward, from), **time** (after, until), or **condition** (of, without).

 EXAMPLE

              Prep
The boy ran **to** the store.

    Notice how the preposition *to* shows the relationship (direction) between *ran* and *store*. If you change prepositions, you change the relationship.

 EXAMPLES

              Prep
The boy ran **from** the store.

              Prep
The boy ran **into** the store.

              Prep
The boy ran **by** the store.

Here are some of the most common prepositions:

about	because of	during	near	to
above	before	except	of	toward
across	behind	for	on	under
after	below	from	onto	until
among	beneath	in	over	up
around	beside	in spite of	past	upon
as	between	into	through	with
at	by	like	till	without

NOTE: *For* can be used as a coordinating conjunction, but it is most commonly used as a preposition. *To* can also be used as part of an infinitive, in which case it is not a preposition.

 PRACTICE

Write "Prep" above the prepositions in the following sentences.

         Prep   *Prep*

1. Mr. Duong sat in the waiting room and thought about his wife.

2. The limousine was parked near the outskirts of town.

3. During the rain storm, Homer lent his umbrella to Hortense.

4. A man from La Mancha had a rather strange obsession with windmills.

5. The Trojans behind the walls looked at the huge wooden horse.

Prepositional Phrases

The word *preposition* is derived from two Latin words meaning "to put in front." The two parts of the word (pre + position) indicate how prepositions usually function. They are almost always used as the first words in **prepositional phrases.**

> **prepositional phrase**
> Preposition + Object (noun or pronoun) = Prepositional Phrase.

    A prepositional phrase consists of a preposition plus a noun or a pronoun, called the object of the preposition. This object is almost always the last word of the prepositional phrase. Between the preposition and its object, the prepositional phrase may also contain adjectives, adverbs, or conjunctions. A preposition may have more than one object.

EXAMPLES

Prep   Obj
after a short **lunch**

Prep   Obj   Obj
with his very good **friend** and his **brother**

Prep Obj   Obj
to you and **her**

Prep   Obj
through the long and dismal **night**

Although prepositions themselves are considered connectors, prepositional <u>phrases</u> actually act as modifiers. They may function as adjectives, modifying a noun or pronoun, or they may function as adverbs, modifying a verb.

EXAMPLES

The cat **(from next door)** caught a gopher.

The burglar jumped **(from the window)**.

In the first example, the prepositional phrase functions as an adjective, modifying the noun *cat*, and in the second example, the prepositional phrase functions as an adverb, modifying the verb *jumped*.

NOTE: If you can recognize prepositional phrases, you will be able to identify subjects and verbs more easily **because neither the subject nor the verb of a sentence can be part of a prepositional phrase.**

In the following sentence it is difficult at first glance to determine which of the many nouns is the subject.

In a cave near the village, a member of the archaeological team found a stone ax from an ancient civilization.

If you first eliminate the prepositional phrases, however, the true subject becomes apparent.

                                         S
(In a cave) (near the village), a member (of the archaeological team)

    MV
found a stone ax (from an ancient civilization).

PRACTICE

Place parentheses around the prepositional phrases and write "Prep" above all prepositions and "Obj" above the objects of the prepositions.

                                    Prep   *Obj* *Prep*   *Obj*

1. Francis Scott Key wrote the words (to the national anthem) (of our country.)

2. However, the music itself came from a popular drinking song.

3.   Francis Scott Key witnessed the British bombardment of Fort McHenry in 1814.

4.   He was inspired by the sight of the American flag flying over the fort.

5.   During the attack, he composed the first stanza of "The Star-Spangled Banner" on the back of an envelope.

6.   The next day Key was told that his poem would go well with a tune that was popular in many taverns.

7.   The original tune, called "Anacreon in Heaven," was probably written by John Stafford Smith in 1780.

8.   Anacreon was a Greek poet who wrote about wine, song, love, and revelry.

9.   "The Star-Spangled Banner" was sung at official ceremonies for many years.

10.   In spite of its popularity, it was not declared the official national anthem until March 3, 1931.

Section Three Review

1. A **conjunction** joins two parts of a sentence.

2. The **coordinating conjunctions** are *and, but, or, nor, for, yet,* and *so.*

3. A **preposition** relates a noun or pronoun to some other word in the sentence.

4. A **prepositional phrase** consists of a **preposition** plus a noun or a pronoun, called the **object of the preposition.**

5. Neither the subject nor the verb of a sentence can be part of a prepositional phrase.

Exercise 3A

A. Combine each pair of sentences into one sentence. Use the coordinating conjunction indicated in the parenthesis.

1. (addition)
   Alice Walker is a well-known African-American novelist.
   Amy Tan is a respected Asian-American writer.

   Alice Walker is a well-known African-American novelist, and Amy Tan is a respected Asian-American writer.

2. (contrast)
   Clarice was kind to her sister.
   Her sister still bullied her.

   _____

   _____

3. (cause)
   Santa's elves were excited that the Christmas season was almost over.
   Santa had promised to take them to Cabo San Lucas in January.

   _____

   _____

4. (alternative)
   The Chargers could punt the ball.
   They could try a trick play.

   _____

   _____

5. (alternative)
   Sir Gawain did not want to lose his honor.
   He did not want to die.

   _____

   _____

continued

6. (result)
The ants and flies would not leave us alone.
We packed up our lunch and left.

_____

_____

B. In each of the following sentences, change the underlined *and* to a coordinating conjunction that expresses the relationship between the ideas in the sentence. If the *and* does not need to be changed, do nothing to it.

7. Ellen loves Kentucky Colonel Fried Chicken, <u>and</u> she ordered a barrel of it for her wedding party.

Ellen loves Kentucky Colonel Fried Chicken, so she ordered a barrel

of it for her wedding party.

8. Ed McBain has written many detective novels, <u>and</u> that is not his real name.

_____

_____

9. If you need more energy, you might try drinking a cup of coffee, <u>and</u> you might try taking a nap.

_____

_____

10. Australian shepherds are smart and loving, <u>and</u> Bill decided to get one.

_____

_____

11. Everyone in our neighborhood was in a bad mood, <u>and</u> a comet was about to destroy the earth.

_____

_____

continued

12. Bill's mother likes *Frasier*, <u>and</u> Bill likes *The Sopranos*.

_____

_____

13. Michelle did not want butter on her popcorn, <u>and</u> she did not want relish on her hot dog.

_____

_____

14. Jonathan Swift wanted to help the Irish children, <u>and</u> not everyone realized that.

_____

_____

15. Andy Warhol stared at the can of Campbell's tomato soup, <u>and</u> to him it seemed like a work of art.

_____

_____

Exercise 3B

Place all prepositional phrases in parentheses and circle all conjunctions. For additional practice, underline all subjects once and all complete verbs twice.

1. <u>Clarise</u> (and) three <u>teammates</u> <u><u>drove</u></u> (to the orphanage.)

2. Sully had been trying to hit a homerun for three seasons.

3. After the trial, Abner talked to his son.

4. In his nose, ears, and tongue were gold and silver rings.

5. Snow White and one of her favorite dwarves have eloped to Magic Mountain.

6. The symbol of the caduceus is often associated with the medical profession.

7. A total of thirty thousand people saw that play, but not one of them liked it.

8. The caduceus was a staff with two entwined serpents, and it was carried by Mercury.

9. The manager took the papers from his desk and placed them in a filing cabinet.

10. Gloria must have arrived by now, for she started in the early morning.

11. The detective took the magnifying glass from his pocket and examined the fingerprints.

12. Hal wanted to be with Falstaff, but his duties called for him to serve the king.

13. Her bookshelves probably contained the finest collection of first editions of Kate Chopin and Emily Dickinson.

14. Everyone admired Beowulf because of his bravery in battle, and he never let them down.

15. Drog had dragged his knuckles in the dirt all day looking for food, but he found nothing except beetles.

Exercise 3C

In the following sentences, identify each of the underlined words as noun (N), pronoun (Pro), verb (V), adjective (Adj), adverb (Adv), conjunction (Conj), or preposition (Prep).

1. According to many Native American legends, the *Adj* animal character Woodpecker was instrumental *Prep* in bringing fire to earth.   2. Long ago, when there was no fire, the chief of the animal people devised a plan to enter the sky country and bring back some fire.   3. He told the animal people to make bows and arrows to shoot at the sky.   4. When they hit the sky, they would make a chain of arrows down to the earth.   5. They would then climb the chain to the sky and steal some fire.   6. Unfortunately, none of them succeeded in hitting the sky with their arrows.   7. Then Woodpecker began to work.   8. He made a bow from the rib of Elk and arrows from the serviceberry bush.   9. He used feathers from Golden Eagle and Bald Eagle and arrowheads from Flint Rock.   10. When the animal people met again, they all laughed at Woodpecker, saying he could not hit the sky with his arrows.   11. However, their own arrows fell short of the sky, so the chief asked Woodpecker to try.   12. When Woodpecker shot his first arrow, it hit the sky.   13. Then each following arrow stuck in the neck of the preceding arrow until there was a chain of arrows down to the earth.   14. One by one, they all ran swiftly up the chain of arrows to the sky.   15. After each one had stolen some fire, they raced to the arrow chain, chased by the sky people, but the chain had broken.   16. To escape, each bird took an animal to earth on its back.   17. When they reached the earth, their chief told them to divide the fire among all people, so Horsefly and Hummingbird carried the fire to all parts of the country.

SECTION four

Sentence Practice: Embedding Adjectives, Adverbs, and Prepositional Phrases

You have now learned to identify the basic parts of a sentence, but this skill itself is not very useful unless you can use it to compose clear and effective sentences. Obviously, you have some flexibility when you compose sentences, but that flexibility is far from unlimited. The following sentence has a subject, a verb, five modifiers, one conjunction, and two prepositional phrases, but it makes no sense at all.

> Architect the quickly president for the drew up building new and plans the them to showed company.

With the parts arranged in a more effective order, the sentence, of course, makes sense.

> The architect quickly drew up plans for the new building and showed them to the company president.

There is no single correct pattern for the English sentence. The patterns you choose will be determined by the facts and ideas you wish to convey. For any given set of facts and ideas, there will be a relatively limited number of effective sentence patterns and an enormous number of ineffective ones. Knowing the parts of the sentence and how they function will help you choose the most effective patterns to communicate your thoughts.

Assume, for example, that you have four facts to communicate:

1. *Moby Dick* was written by Herman Melville.

2. *Moby Dick* is a famous novel.

3. *Moby Dick* is about a whale.

4. The whale is white.

You could combine all these facts into a single sentence:

> *Moby Dick* was written by Herman Melville, and *Moby Dick* is a famous novel, and *Moby Dick* is about a whale, and the whale is white.

Although this sentence is grammatically correct, it is repetitious and sounds foolish.

If you choose the key fact from each sentence and combine the facts in the order in which they are presented, the result is not much better:

> *Moby Dick* was written by Herman Melville, a famous novel about a whale white.

A much more effective approach is to choose the sentence that expresses the fact or idea you think is most important and to use that as your **base sentence.** Of course, the sentence you choose as the base sentence may vary depending upon the fact or idea you think is most important, but, whichever sentence you choose, it should contain the essential fact or idea that the other sentences somehow modify or explain. Once you have found the base sentence, you can **embed** the other facts or ideas into it as **adjectives, adverbs,** and **prepositional phrases.**

For example, let's use "*Moby Dick* is a famous novel" as the base sentence since it states an essential fact about *Moby Dick*—that it is a famous novel. The idea in sentence number one can be embedded into the base sentence as a **prepositional phrase:**

> by Herman Melville
> *Moby Dick* ∧ is a famous novel.

The idea in sentence three can now be embedded into the expanded base sentence as another **prepositional phrase:**

> about a whale
> *Moby Dick* by Herman Melville is a famous novel ∧.

Sentence number four contains an **adjective** that modifies the noun *whale,* so it can be embedded into the sentence by placing it before *whale:*

> *Moby Dick* by Herman Melville is a famous novel
>
> white
> about a ∧ whale.

Thus, your final sentence will read:

> *Moby Dick* by Herman Melville is a famous novel about a white whale.

The same facts could be embedded in a number of other ways. Two of them are:

> *Moby Dick,* a famous novel by Herman Melville, is about a white whale.

> Herman Melville's *Moby Dick* is a famous novel about a white whale.

This process of embedding is called **sentence combining.** The purpose of practicing sentence combining is to give you an opportunity to apply the grammatical concepts you have learned in the chapter. For instance, in the above example the base sentence was expanded into a more interesting sentence by means of prepositional phrases and an adjective. Practicing this process will also help you develop greater flexibility in your sentence structure and will show you how to enrich your sentences through the addition of significant details. After all, the use of specific details is one of the most important ways of making writing interesting and effective.

PRACTICE

a. The farmer was old.
b. The farmer waited in front of the bank.
c. The farmer was in overalls.
d. The overalls were faded.
e. The farmer was patient.

1. In the space below, write the base sentence, the one with the main idea.

   _____

2. Embed the **adjective** from sentence A into the base sentence by placing it before the noun that it modifies.

   _____

3. Embed the **prepositional phrase** from sentence C into the sentence by placing it after the word that it modifies.

   _____

4. Embed the **adjective** from sentence D into the sentence by placing it before the noun that it modifies.

   _____

   _____

5. Change the **adjective** in sentence E into an **adverb** (add "ly") and embed it into the sentence by placing it after the verb that it modifies.

   _____

   _____

Sentence Combining: Exercise A

In each of the following sets of sentences, use the first sentence as the base sentence. Embed into the base sentence the adjectives, adverbs, and prepositional phrases underlined in the sentences below it.

 EXAMPLE

   a. A man strode into the nightclub.
   b. The man was <u>young</u>.
   c. He was <u>in a bright orange bathrobe</u>.
   d. He strode <u>confidently</u>.
   e. The nightclub was <u>fashionable</u>.

A young man in a bright orange bathrobe strode

confidently into the fashionable nightclub.

1. a. The editor fired the reporter.
   b. The editor was <u>enraged</u>.
   c. The reporter was <u>incompetent</u>.

   _____

   _____

2. a. The ambulance swerved.
   b. The ambulance was <u>speeding</u>.
   c. The ambulance swerved <u>because of the couple</u>.
   d. The couple was <u>in the crosswalk</u>.

   _____

   _____

3. a. The town used to be a vacation spot.
   b. The town is <u>empty</u>.
   c. The town is <u>in the middle of the Mojave Desert</u>.
   d. The vacation spot was <u>popular</u>.

   _____

   _____

Sentence Combining: Exercise A

continued

4. a. The bullfighter waved his cape.
   b. The bullfighter was waving <u>at the bull</u>.
   c. The bullfighter was <u>young</u>.
   d. The bullfighter was <u>in the arena</u>.
   e. The bull was <u>angry</u>.

   _____

   _____

5. a. The guard handed the list.
   b. The guard was <u>nervous</u>.
   c. The guard handed the list <u>quietly</u>.
   d. The list was <u>of missing items</u>.
   e. The guard handed the list <u>to the detective</u>.
   f. The detective was <u>frowning</u>.

   _____

   _____

Sentence Combining: Exercise B

First, choose a base sentence and circle the letter next to it. Then, using adjectives, adverbs, and prepositional phrases, embed the other facts and ideas into the base sentence.

 EXAMPLE

    a. The mountains were tall.
    b. The mountains were snow-covered.
    (c.) The mountains towered over the hikers.
    d. There were three hikers.
    e. The hikers were from France.
    f. The hikers were lost.
    g. The mountains towered menacingly.

The tall, snow-covered mountains towered menacingly over the three lost hikers from France.

1. a. The skier was disappointed.
    b. The skier gazed at the mountain.
    c. The mountain was bare.
    d. The mountain was rocky.
    e. The mountain was above her.

_____

_____

2. a. The hikers were starving.
    b. The hikers shouted.
    c. They shouted loudly.
    d. They shouted at the helicopter.
    e. The helicopter was circling.

_____

_____

3. a. They played in the square.
    b. The violinist and his daughter played.
    c. The square was crowded.
    d. They played beautifully.
    e. The violinist was blind.

_____

_____

continued

4. a. The swing was that strong.
    b. It was a swing of the bat.
    c. One swing sent the baseball flying.
    d. It was flying out of the ballpark.
    e. The ballpark was his favorite.

_____

_____

5. a. The ranger was patient.
    b. The plan was dangerous.
    c. The ranger explained the plan.
    d. She explained the plan to the campers.
    e. The campers were eager.

_____

_____

6. a. A person has invented a talking tombstone.
    b. The person is imaginative.
    c. It was invented recently.
    d. The talking tombstone is solar powered.

_____

_____

7. a. The statement is tape-recorded.
    b. The case is Plexiglas.
    c. A statement is placed in a case.
    d. It is a case that sits in an area of the tombstone.
    e. The area is hollowed out.

_____

_____

Sentence Combining: Exercise B

continued

8. a. The speaker is small.
   b. A speaker and a panel are installed.
   c. It is a solar panel.
   d. The speaker and panel are on the tombstone.
   e. It is a three-inch panel.

   _____

   _____

9. a. The recording can be activated with the correct key.
   b. You can activate the recording and listen to a statement.
   c. The recording is in the case.
   d. The statement is from the grave's occupant.

   _____

   _____

10. a. The sunlight must be enough.
    b. With sunlight, the recording will run.
    c. The recording will run for as long as two hours.
    d. The recording is in the tombstone.
    e. The tombstone costs $10,000.

    _____

    _____

Paragraph Practice: Narrating an Event

If you have ever sat for hours before a blank sheet of paper or stared for what seemed like forever at a blank computer screen, you know how difficult and frustrating it can be to write a paper. In fact, some people have such trouble simply <u>starting</u> their papers that for them writing becomes a truly agonizing experience.

Fortunately, writing does not have to be so difficult. If you learn how to use the steps involved in the process of writing, you can avoid much of the frustration and enjoy more of the satisfaction that comes from writing a successful paper. In this section, you will practice using the three general activities that make up the writing process—**prewriting, writing,** and **rewriting**—to produce a paragraph based on the following assignment.

Assignment

Exercises 1C (page 24), 2C (page 33), and 3C (page 45) of Chapter One are about three events: an unfortunate incident on a playground, the kidnapping and eventual freedom of Cinque and his fellow tribesmen, and the bringing of fire to earth by Woodpecker and the other animal people. Although few of us have had experiences as unusual as these, we all have experienced events that were important to us for one reason or another.

For this writing assignment, use the writing process explained below to describe an event that has happened to you. You do not need to have lost your temper or to have been kidnapped. Ask yourself "What events—either from the distant past or from more recent times—have happened to me that I remember well?" Perhaps you remember your first date, your first traffic ticket, or even your first child. Or perhaps you remember the day you won a race in a track meet, performed alone on a stage, or attended your first college class. Often the <u>best</u> event to write about will not be the first one you think of.

Prewriting to Generate Ideas

Prewriting is the part of the writing process that will help you get past "writer's block" and into writing. It consists of <u>anything</u> you do to generate ideas and get started, but three of the most successful prewriting techniques are **freewriting, brainstorming,** and **clustering.**

Freewriting

Freewriting is based on one simple but essential idea: When you sit down to write, you write. You don't stare at your paper or look out the window, wondering what in the world you could write about. Instead, you <u>write down</u> your thoughts and questions even if you have no idea what topic you should focus on. In addition, as you freewrite, you do not stop to correct spelling, grammar, or punctuation errors. After all, the purpose of freewriting is to generate ideas, not to write the final draft of your paper.

Here is how some freewriting might look for the assignment described above.

> To describe an event? What could I write about that? I don't have a lot of "events" that I can think of—but I suppose I must have some. What do I remember? How about recently? Have I gone anywhere or has anything happened to me? I went skiing last month and took a bad fall—but so what? That wouldn't be very interesting. How about something I remember that I didn't like—like what? Death? Too depressing. Besides, I have never been closely involved in death. I was in a car accident once, but that was too long ago, and it doesn't really interest me. How about—what? I'm stuck. How about events I have good memories about—wait—I remember almost drowning when I was practicing for water polo in high school. <u>That</u> was a wild event. I could do it. Any other possibilities? How about good memories—like the time I made that lucky catch in Little League. That would be good. Or the fish I caught with my dad when I was a kid. Lots of good memories there. Any others? Yeah—I joined a softball league recently—that was a real experience, especially because it'd been so long since I'd played baseball. But I can't think of any particular thing I'd write about it.—Of all these, I think I like the drowning one best. I <u>really</u> remember that one and all the feelings that went with it.

You can tell that the above writer was not trying to produce a clean, well-written copy of his paper. Instead, he wrote down his thoughts as they occurred to him, and the result was a very informal rush of ideas that eventually led him to a topic, a near-drowning that occurred when he was in high school. Now that he has his topic, he can continue to freewrite to generate details about the event that he can use in his paper.

Prewriting Application: Freewriting

1. Freewrite for ten minutes about any memories you have of events that were important to you. Don't stop to correct any errors. Just write about as many events as you can remember. If you skip from one event to another, that's fine. If you get stuck, just write "I'm stuck" or something like that over and over—but keep writing for ten minutes.

2. Now re-read your initial freewriting. Is there some event in there that interests you more than the others? Choose one event and freewrite only on it. Describe everything you can remember about the event, but don't stop to correct errors—just write.

Brainstorming

Brainstorming is another prewriting technique that you can use to generate ideas. Brainstorming is similar to freewriting in that you write down your thoughts without censoring or editing them, but it differs in that the thoughts usually appear as a list of ideas rather than as separate sentences. Here is an example of how the above freewriting might have looked as brainstorming.

> An event I remember well—what could I use?
>> recently?
>>> fall while skiing—no
>> things I didn't like
>>> death? too depressing
>>> car accident I was in? too long ago
>>> almost drowned at practice—<u>good one</u>
>> good memories?
>>> lucky catch in Little League
>>> fishing with Dad
> <u>Use the one about almost drowning.</u>

Prewriting Application: Brainstorming

1. Make a brainstorming list of events from your life that were important to you. Include events from as far back as your early childhood to as recently as yesterday.

2. Choose the event that interests you the most. Make a brainstorming list of everything you can remember about it.

Clustering

Clustering is a third prewriting technique that many people find helpful. It differs from brainstorming and freewriting in that it is written almost like an informal map. To "cluster" your ideas, start out with an idea or question and draw a circle around it. Then connect related ideas to the circle and continue in that way. Here is how you might use clustering to find a memorable event to write about.

As you can see, clustering provides a mental picture of the ideas you generate. As such, it can help you organize your material <u>as</u> you think of it.

Prewriting Application: Clustering

1. Develop a "memorable events" cluster of your own. Include as many associations as you can to find the one event that interests you the most.

2. Now choose the event that interests you the most and use it as the center of a new cluster. Write in as many memories of the event as you can.

Freewriting, brainstorming, and clustering are only three of many techniques to help you get started writing. When you use them, you should feel free to move from one to the other at any time. And, of course, your instructor may suggest other ways to help you get started. Whatever technique you use, the point is to <u>start writing</u>. Do your thinking on paper (or at a computer), not while you are staring out a window. Here's a good motto that you should try to follow whenever you have a writing assignment due: **Think in ink.**

Choosing and Narrowing the Topic

Choosing the Topic

Perhaps you have already found the event that most interests you. If you have, continue to prewrite to develop as many details as you can. If you are still undecided about a topic, use the following suggestions to think of possibilities.

1. What experiences of yours have been particularly exciting, happy, or pleasant?

2. What experiences are you most proud of?

3. What events bring you disappointing, unpleasant, or fearful memories?

4. What are your most embarrassing memories?

5. What strange or unusual things have happened to you?

6. What dangerous or frightening experiences have you had?

7. What are the "firsts" in your life? Consider your first day in high school, your first day on a team or as part of a group, your first performance, your first date, your first camping trip, your first traffic ticket.

8. What experiences have inspired you, changed the way you think about life, or made you into a different person?

9. What events do you remember from your early childhood?

10. What events do you remember from elementary school or high school, from vacations or trips?

Narrowing the Topic

Many topics that interest you might be too broad—that is, explaining them might require a much longer paper than has been assigned. And sometimes instructors provide only broad topic ideas when they assign a paper, expecting you to narrow the topic to something appropriate for the length of the assignment. In such cases you need to *narrow* your topic, discussing, perhaps, only part of the event rather than the entire thing. Learning to narrow a topic is an important step in the writing process because broad topics usually lead to general, unconvincing papers.

For example, let's say you have chosen as your topic a high school football game—the championship game in which you scored the winning touchdown. It would be natural to want to cover the entire game because all of it was important to you, but the topic is much too large to be covered in one paragraph. So you must narrow the topic. A successful single paragraph might describe only one play, the one in which you scored the winning touchdown. It would describe everything about the play, from the noise in the stands to the looks on your teammates' faces in the huddle to the smell of the grass to the sound of the quarterback's voice—everything you can think of to provide detail and excitement to the event.

Prewriting Application: Narrowing the Topic

Consider the following events as possible topics for a paragraph. Write "OK" next to any that you think would work. If any seem too broad, explain why and discuss how you might narrow them.

_____ 1. Giving birth to my first child

_____ 2. My vacation to Atlanta

_____ **3.** The car accident that changed my life

_____ **4.** The last time I saw my father

_____ **5.** A day at Disneyland

_____ **6.** Prom night

_____ **7.** Skiing in Aspen

_____ **8.** My first date

_____ **9.** Getting lost in Tijuana

_____ **10.** Moving to Texas

Prewriting Application: Talking to Others

Once you have chosen and narrowed your topic, form groups of two, three, or four and tell your experiences to each other. Telling others about an event is a good way to decide what details to include and how much to say. And listening to someone else's story will help you learn what will keep an audience interested in your own story.

As you describe your event to others, make it as interesting as you can by describing what happened, how you felt, and what you thought. As you listen to the stories of others and as you describe your own experience, consider these questions:

1. What are the time and place of the event? How old were you? What time of day did it occur? What time of year? What was the weather like?

2. Can you visualize the scene? What is the name of the place where the event occurred? What physical features are in the area—trees? buildings? furniture? cars? other people?

3. How did you feel as the event progressed? What were you thinking each step of the way?

4. Did your thoughts and feelings change as the event occurred?

5. What parts of the event would be clearer if they were explained more?

Writing a Topic Sentence

The topic sentence is the one sentence in your paragraph that states both your **narrowed topic** and the **central point** you intend to make about the topic. To find your central point, re-read your prewriting. Look for related details that seem to focus on *one particular reaction* to the event. That reaction is your central point.

College texts and your own college papers describe events in order to make a point. In a psychology text, for example, an airplane crash might be described in detail to help the reader understand how such an event can affect the relatives of those involved. And a history text might describe what happened at the Battle of Gettysburg to help the reader understand why it was a major turning point in the Civil War. Certainly in your own college papers, you will be expected to describe events to illustrate the points you are trying to make.

Although the topic sentence can appear in a variety of places, in college paragraphs you should usually write it as the first sentence so that your central point is clear from the very start. Here are some examples of topic sentences drawn from the exercises in Chapter One. Note that each topic sentence contains a topic and a central point and that each one is the first sentence of its paragraph.

 EXAMPLES

topic   central point
An unfortunate incident in fifth grade was <u>one of the most traumatic</u>

<u>experiences of my life</u>.

                                 topic
In 1839, **the events involving the Cuban ship *Amistad* and its cargo of slaves**

            central point
<u>led to a significant decision by the United States Supreme Court</u>.

                                                         topic
According to many North American Indian stories, the **animal character**

                      central point
Woodpecker was <u>instrumental in bringing fire to earth</u>.

The **central point** of your topic sentence needs to be *limited* and *precise* so that it is not too broad, general, or vague. For example, in the topic sentence *My first date was an interesting experience,* the central idea that the date was *interesting* is much too vague. It could mean the date was the best experience of your life or that it was absolutely horrible. As a general rule, the more precise the topic sentence, the more effective your paragraph will be. Consider the following characteristics of a well-written topic sentence.

1. <u>A topic sentence must include a central point.</u>

 EXAMPLE   (weak)   My paragraph is about my youngest sister's wedding.

In this sentence the topic (my youngest sister's wedding) is clear, but no central point about that wedding is expressed. An improved topic sentence might be:

 EXAMPLE   (improved)   My youngest sister's wedding last year was one of the most hilarious events I have ever experienced.

In this sentence, a central point—that the wedding was hilarious—has been clearly expressed.

2. A topic sentence does not merely state a fact.

EXAMPLE   (weak)   A few months ago I saw a car accident.

This sentence simply states a fact. There is no central point to be explained after the fact is stated. An improved topic sentence might be:

EXAMPLE   (improved)   I will never forget how horrified I was a few months ago when I was an unwilling witness to a major car accident.

This sentence now makes a statement about the accident that causes the reader to want more explanation.

3. A topic sentence must include a narrowed topic and central point.

EXAMPLE   (weak)   My spring break this year was really something.

Both the topic (spring break) and the central point (it was "something") are far too general to describe in detail in one paragraph. Here is a more focused topic sentence:

EXAMPLE   (improved)   On the last day of spring break this year, my vacation in Palm Springs, California, turned from wonderful to absolutely miserable in just one hour.

This sentence now focuses on a specific event—the last day of spring break in Palm Springs—and on a precise central point—it changed from wonderful to miserable.

Prewriting Application: Working with Topic Sentences

In each sentence below, underline the topic once and the central point twice.

1. While driving to Arrowhead Stadium last night, I had a terrifying experience.

2. I don't think I have ever been as embarrassed as I was on the night that I first met my future husband.

3. When I stepped out on the stage at Rancho Buena Vista High School, I had no idea that what was about to happen would change my life.

4. My first scuba diving experience was as exhilarating as it was nerve-wracking.

5. I feel a great sense of pride and satisfaction whenever I think of the day

I decided to take the biggest risk of my life.

Prewriting Application: Evaluating Topic Sentences

Write "No" before each sentence that would not make a good topic sentence and "Yes" before each sentence that would make a good one. Using ideas of your own, rewrite the unacceptable topic sentences into effective ones.

_____ **1.** Last August I visited Lake Ponsett, South Dakota.

_____

_____

_____ **2.** Giving birth to my first child made me wonder if I would ever want to have children again.

_____

_____

_____ **3.** My heart nearly broke the day that I decided it was time to take my dog Jasper on his last ride to the veterinarian's office.

_____

_____

_____ **4.** My first year in college was definitely interesting.

_____

_____

_____ **5.** One of my earliest memories of my father and me spending time together is also one of my most disappointing ones.

_____

_____

_____ **6.** It all happened when I decided to go skiing in Aspen, Colorado.

_____

_____

_____ **7.** My paragraph will be about the time I was in the Rose Parade.

_____

_____

_____ **8.** I was amazed at everything that happened to us while driving from Amarillo, Texas, to Atlanta, Georgia.

_____

_____

_____ **9.** Spooky, strange, weird—these words don't even begin to describe what happened to me that night in the abandoned house on Elm Street.

_____

_____

_____ **10.** A simple ride on the roller coaster in Belmont Park turned out to be one of the most thrilling experiences of my life.

_____

_____

Organizing Details

When describing an event, you will usually present the details in **chronological order.** That is, you will organize them according to how they occurred in time. However, other assignments might require different organizations to present your supporting details effectively. (Other organizational patterns are discussed in future chapters.)

Prewriting Application: Organizing Supporting Details

The following details describe a time a person almost drowned at a water polo practice. Number the details so that they appear in their probable chronological order.

_____ joined water polo

_____ volunteered to try the challenge set

_____ blacked out

_____ two laps underwater

_____ felt okay during the first lap

_____ woke up in coach's arms

_____ choking under water

_____ was sure I could make it

_____ second lap seemed okay at first

_____ determined to make it

_____ everyone around me when I woke up

_____ everything went black

_____ lungs gave out

_____ saw lane markers just before passed out

Writing the Paragraph

Writing a full draft of your paper is the next step in the writing process. The trick to writing your first draft without getting stuck is to remember that what you write now is not your final copy, so you can allow yourself to make mistakes and to write awkward sentences. Don't worry about how "correct" your writing is. Instead, just write your preliminary topic sentence and then describe your experience as thoroughly as you can.

Here is a sample first draft of the paper on drowning. As you read it, notice that the writer has not yet corrected any errors it may contain.

The Challenge Set (First Draft)

An unusual experience happened to me when I was sixteen. It all happened one day at practice for water polo. I was a sophomore on the Kearney High School water polo team. One day I volunteered for the dreaded "Challenge Set." I had just finished the first lap underwater. I still felt good. As I come to the wall, I make the decison to go for another lap, I keep swimming, but my lungs collapse. I took a few more strokes, and then it happened. I blacked out. All I remember was seeing black. I felt completely relaxed. Then I remember hearing voices. Suddenly, starting to cough violently. When I opened my eyes, the first person I saw was my coach. He told me what had happened, I was a little shaken. I couldn't believe that I almost died. This was really a frightening experience that I remember whenever I go for a swim.

The above first draft is far from perfect. It contains writing errors and could use more descriptive details. However, it has accomplished its purpose: *It has given the writer a draft to work with and to improve.*

Writing Application: Producing Your First Draft

Now write the first draft of your paragraph. Remember that your goal is *not* to write an error-free draft. Instead, it is to write a *first* draft that opens with a preliminary topic sentence, a draft that you can then continue to work on and improve.

Rewriting and Improving the Paragraph

Rewriting consists of two stages: **revising** and **proofreading**. In the **revising** stage of the writing process, you improve the "larger" areas of your paper—its content, organization, and sentence structure. Here are some suggestions.

- Improve your preliminary topic sentence.

  You can often improve your topic sentence *after* you have written your first draft because now you really have something to introduce. In fact, if you look at the *concluding* sentences of your first draft, you may find a clearer statement of the central point of your paragraph than the one you have in your preliminary topic sentence. If that is the case, rewrite your topic sentence to include that statement.

- Add more details.

    After you have written the first draft, add any further details that might improve your paper. Look especially for those that will emphasize the central point of your topic sentence.

- Reorganize the details in the first draft.

    There are many ways to organize a paper, but one of the most common ones is to save the most important details for last. Another way to organize details, especially if you are describing an event, is to list the details in chronological order. Whichever way you choose, now is the time to make any changes in the order of your material.

- Combine related sentences and ideas.

    Combine sentences that are obviously related. Where possible, use sentence combining techniques to embed material from one sentence into another. (Sentence combining techniques are discussed in Section 4 of each chapter.)

Improving Supporting Details

The supporting details in many first drafts tend to be vague, colorless, and mediocre. But with just a little work they can be transformed into strong, dramatic sentences. Consider adding details that emphasize specific sights and sounds. Wherever you can, use the precise names of people, places, and things. Look especially for new details and words that will emphasize the central point of your paragraph. Note how the colorless example below is transformed with precise, descriptive details.

EXAMPLE (weak) My father went in one direction while I went in another. I saw a fence covered with all sorts of decorations from local Indians. Inside the fence on the ground was the medicine wheel. I stared at it silently.

EXAMPLE (improved) My father veered off to the west as I continued straight ahead, toward what I perceived to be the main attraction. On this fist of land was a protective, circular chain link fence sixty feet in diameter, festooned with ribbons, scraps of paper, little totem bags made by the local Indian women and girls, eagle feathers and strings of beads: simple poetic offerings and prayers. Inside the fence was the medicine wheel, a fifty-foot spoked wheel etched into the dust of centuries. It was a moment of pause. I stopped and felt the wind and the still sacredness of the view.

Rewriting Application: Improving Supporting Details

Read the following brief paragraphs and identify places where the support could be more descriptive and precise. Then rewrite the paragraphs, adding stronger, more dramatic details.

A. My trip to the grocery store turned into a complete nightmare. When I walked down one of the aisles, I saw a person shoplifting, so I told the manager. She stopped the shoplifter, and they argued. Then the manager said I had to stay to talk to the police. I had some important things to do, so I said I had to leave. As I walked to my car, the manager became really mad at me too.

B. One of the highlights of my short career playing Little League baseball happened when my best friend was at bat. He and I played on opposing teams. I was in the outfield when he hit the ball toward me. It was going to go over my head, so I backed up. When I reached the fence, I stuck up my glove and caught the ball. I looked at the stands and saw people standing and cheering for me. It was a great experience.

Proofreading

Proofreading is the final step in the writing process. It consists of correcting spelling, grammar, and punctuation errors. **Do not skip this step.** A paper focused on an excellent topic and developed with striking details will almost always still receive a poor grade if it is full of distracting writing errors. Here are some suggestions to help you proofread successfully.

- If you use a computer, run the spelling-checker program. (But don't rely only on that program. Read each word carefully yourself.)

- Use a dictionary to check the spelling of any words you are unsure of.

- Watch for incomplete sentences and run-on sentences. (These errors will be discussed in Chapter Two.)

- Look closely at your verbs and pronouns. If you are describing an event from the past, use past tense verbs. (Verb and pronoun errors will be discussed in Chapter Four.)

- Ask someone you trust to read your paper. If your school has tutors available, use them. They can help you find many writing errors that you might have overlooked. **However, please note:** If a friend reads your paper, do not allow him or her to rewrite sentences for you. Most instructors consider that kind of help to be plagiarism.

- When you are satisfied with your paper, print a final copy, and then *read that copy one more time.* You will be surprised how often more errors seem to appear out of nowhere. If you find more errors, fix them and print another copy.

Rewriting Application: Responding to Writing

Reread the first draft of "The Challenge Set" on page 65. Then respond to the following questions:

1. What is the writer's central feeling about his experience? Where is it stated? How would you reword the opening sentence to express that central feeling?

2. Where should the writer add more details? What kind of details would make his paragraph more colorful and descriptive?

3. Should any of the details be reorganized or presented in a different order?

4. What sentences would you combine because they contain related ideas?

5. What changes should the writer make in spelling, grammar, or punctuation?

Here is how the student who nearly drowned revised his first draft. Compare it to his first draft.

The Challenge Set

When I was sixteen, I had a frightening experience that I still remember whenever I go for a swim. This took place when I was a sophomore on the Kearney High School water polo team. One day at practice, I volunteered to try the dreaded "Challenge Set." **It consisted of three to four players attempting to swim fifty yards, two laps of the pool, on a single breath.** I dove into the cool, clear water full of confidence, but I had no idea what was about to happen. When I came to the wall at the end of the first lap, I was well ahead of my teammate, Bryan, who was in the lane to my right. I felt great, as if I could hold my breath forever, so I decided to go for the second lap. I made the flip turn and pushed off the blue tiles. I still felt okay, but without my knowing it, my lungs had started to collapse. I **remember beginning to feel pressure in my chest when I saw the blue hash marks, the halfway markers. I had just a little way to go, but my head was whirling, and my chest felt like it was about to explode. Suddenly everything slowed down. I knew I should stop and take a breath, but I refused to do it.** I took a few more strokes, and then it happened. I started to black out. **All I remember is seeing black and feeling completely relaxed. The next thing I knew, it seemed like someone was shaking me. As I began to hear voices, I started to cough violently. Every time I tried to take a breath, a searing pain shot through me. I was terrified.** When I opened my eyes, the first person I saw was **Coach Leonard, a state beach lifeguard. I was lying in his arms, not knowing where I was or what had happened to me.** When he told me that I had passed out in the pool and that Bryan had pulled me out, I was really shaken. I couldn't believe I had almost drowned. **I got out of the pool, got dressed, and sat in the stands waiting for practice to end.** I don't think I'll ever forget that day.

Revised opening sentence includes reaction to the event.

Added details

Added details

Combined sentences

Added details

Added details

Rewriting Application: Revising and Proofreading Your Own Draft

Now revise and proofread your first draft.

1. Improve your topic sentence.

2. Add more details, especially those that emphasize the central point.

3. Reorganize the details.

4. Combine related sentences and ideas.

5. Once you have revised, <u>proofread</u> for spelling, grammar, and punctuation errors.

As you can tell, thorough revising and editing will involve several new drafts, not just one. Once you have a draft with which you are satisfied, prepare a clean final draft, following the format your instructor has requested.

Chapter One Practice Test

A. In the spaces provided, indicate whether the underlined word is a subject (S), a helping verb (HV), or a main verb (MV). If it is none of these, leave the space blank.

_____ 1. The recent rains <u>have</u> caused many mudslides in our city.

_____ 2. Often they <u>eat</u> at a Thai restaurant near them.

_____ 3. The vampire <u>staring</u> into my window looked absolutely famished.

_____ 4. Katie <u>recently</u> called her friend in Alaska.

_____ 5. In the mountains of Tennessee, <u>Lee</u> was planning his strategy.

_____ 6. Has <u>everyone</u> already heard about the disaster?

_____ 7. From the <u>sky</u> fell a large chunk of space debris that just barely missed Homer's head.

_____ 8. The latest winter Olympics games were <u>held</u> in Utah.

_____ 9. <u>Send</u> these copies of *National Enquirer* to Fox Mulder.

_____ 10. If we had known, we <u>would</u> have turned on our alarm system.

B. Underline all subjects once and all complete verbs twice in the following sentences.

11. Amy and her cousin visited Spain last year.

12. There were only two pieces of bread in the refrigerator.

13. Some of the runners in the marathon wanted to take a shortcut.

14. Don Quixote would just ignore all of the insults and smiles.

15. Someone had left a clue in the desk, but only Cormac could read it.

16. Toby graduated from high school, and then she enrolled in a university.

17. A nearly invisible speck of dust lodged in Ann's eye and scratched her cornea.

18. Do you have a large chip on your shoulder, or are you just weary?

19. Gawain was afraid that he would not survive his meeting with the Green Knight.

20. When I was fighting with my brother, my mother walked through the door.

continued

C. Write sentences of your own that follow the suggested patterns.

21. A statement with one subject, one helping verb, and one main verb (S-HV-MV):

_____

_____

22. A question with one helping verb, one subject, and one main verb (HV-S-MV):

_____

_____

23. A statement with two subjects joined by "and" and two main verbs joined by "and" (S "and" S-MV "and" MV):

_____

_____

24. A statement with one subject, two helping verbs, and a main verb (S-HV-HV-MV):

_____

_____

25. A statement with a subject and a main verb followed by "although" and another subject and main verb (S-MV "although" S-MV)

_____

_____

D. In the following sentences, identify all adjectives by writing "Adj" above them, and identify all adverbs by writing "Adv" above them.

26. Denise looked lovingly at her son in the crib in the nursery.

27. Merle did not know the name of the third planet from the sun.

28. Peter Parker was suddenly bitten by a radioactive spider.

29. Some people truly believe that a monster lives in Loch Ness.

30. Charles sometimes dreams of winning first prize.

continued

E. In the following sentences, place all prepositional phrases in parentheses.

31. Two parakeets with blue wings flew into the house.

32. Suliman wished to finish before dark so that he would not have to drive during the night.

33. In spite of the cold weather, Ruben removed his shirt and headed for the water.

34. Igor opened the door and stared at the package of spiders that had just arrived from Transylvania.

35. The man standing between the two buildings looks a little like my brother.

F. In the following sentences, add coordinating conjunctions that show the relationship indicated in the parentheses.

36. Bertrand washed the dishes, _____ Ali put them away. (addition)

37. Willy could not face the truth, _____ he asked Biff to lie to him. (result)

38. Little Toot did the best he could, _____ the ship seemed too large. (contrast)

39. Eileen might deposit her paycheck in the bank, _____ she might cash it and head for Las Vegas. (alternative)

40. Ulysses was feeling lonesome, _____ he had not been home for almost twenty years. (cause)

G. Identify the underlined words in these sentences by writing one of the following abbreviations above each word: noun (N), pronoun (Pro), verb (V), adjective (Adj), adverb (Adv), conjunction (Conj), or preposition (Prep).

41. The <u>local</u> mountains have more snow this year than <u>they</u> have had in the past five years.

42. The school <u>changed</u> its <u>name</u> to September Eleventh Memorial High School.

43. An ancient mariner watched the <u>albatross</u> drift lazily <u>toward</u> his ship.

44. <u>Fifty</u> volunteers <u>immediately</u> appeared to repair the desecrated synagogue.

continued

45. Putting on his special hog-hide glove, Homer <u>heaved</u> the cow chip <u>over</u> the goal line.

46. Andrea <u>soon</u> forgave Brent, <u>but</u> she never forgot.

47. Last night, <u>someone</u> broke into Jessica's house and stole her entire <u>collection</u> of Elvis Presley records.

48. The trip was <u>enjoyable</u>, <u>so</u> we planned another one just like it.

49. Auden's tooth ached <u>for</u> three days, but he <u>refused</u> to call the dentist.

50. Sheena ran <u>unceasingly</u> for ten miles, and then she paused to give <u>herself</u> a rest.

Understanding
Sentence Patterns

In Chapter One you learned the terms that describe how words function in a sentence. These terms will help you understand how the various word groups operate in a sentence. Understanding these word groups will help you see not only how sentences are put together but also how to revise your writing effectively and systematically. Without some knowledge of these word groups, you really can't even define what a sentence is.

Consider, for example, two common definitions of a sentence:

1. A sentence is a group of words that expresses a complete thought.

2. A sentence is a group of words that contains a subject and a verb.

These definitions may seem adequate, but, if you consider them carefully, you will see that neither of them is really accurate. For example, some sentences do not seem to express "a complete thought." Consider the sentence "*It fell.*" Do these two words really convey a complete thought? In one sense they do: A specific action is communicated, and a subject, though an indefinite one, is identified. However, the sentence raises more questions than it answers. What fell? Why did it fall? Where did it fall to? The sentence could refer to an apple, a star, the sky, or the Roman Empire. If someone walked up to you in the street and said, "*It fell,*" you certainly would not feel that a complete thought had been communicated to you, and yet the two words do form a sentence.

The second definition is no more satisfactory. The words "*Because his father was sleeping*" do <u>not</u> make up a sentence even though they contain both a subject (*father*) and a verb (*was sleeping*). Although it is true that all sentences must contain a subject and a verb, it does not necessarily follow that every group of words with a subject and a verb is a sentence.

The only definition of a sentence that is <u>always</u> correct is the following one: A sentence is a group of words that contains at least one main clause.

---

sentence

A sentence is a group of words that contains at least one main clause.

You will understand this definition easily if you know what a **main clause** is, but it will be incomprehensible if you do not. Thus, it is critical that you be able to identify this word group, for, if you cannot identify a main clause, you cannot be certain that you are using complete sentences in your writing.

Clauses

Main Clauses and Subordinate Clauses

A clause is a group of words that contains at least one subject and at least one verb.

> **clause**
> A clause is a group of words that contains at least one subject and at least one verb.

The two types of clauses are **main clause** and **subordinate clause**.

1. A **main clause** is a group of words that contains at least one subject and one verb and that <u>expresses a complete idea</u>.

2. A **subordinate clause** is a group of words that contains at least one subject and one verb but that <u>does not express a complete idea</u>. All subordinate clauses begin with **subordinators**.

 EXAMPLE

            sub. clause   main clause
[Although he seldom plays,] [Raymond is an excellent golfer.]

This example contains two clauses, each with a subject and a verb. As you can see, the clause *Raymond is an excellent golfer* could stand by itself as a sentence. But the clause *Although he seldom plays* cannot stand by itself (even though it has a subject and a verb) because it needs the main clause to complete its thought and because it begins with the subordinator *although*.

Subordinators

Subordinators indicate the relationship between the subordinate clause and the main clause. Learning to recognize the two types of subordinators—subordinating conjunctions and relative pronouns—will help you identify subordinate clauses.

Subordinating Conjunctions		*Relative Pronouns*	
after	so that	that	who(ever)
although	than	which	whom(ever)
as	though		whose
as if	unless		
as long as	until		
because	when		
before	whenever		
even though	where		
if	wherever		
since	while		

NOTE: Some of the words in the above list of subordinators are underlined (*after, as, before, since, until*). These words are used as prepositions when they do not introduce a subordinate clause.

EXAMPLES

prepositional phrase: *after dinner*

subordinate clause: *after I eat dinner*

The following are examples of sentences containing subordinate clauses. (Note that each subordinate clause begins with a subordinator.)

EXAMPLES

sub. clause   main clause
[**Before** his horse had crossed the finish line,] [the jockey suddenly stood up in his saddle.]

main clause   sub. clause
[Fried Spam is a dish] [**that** few people love.]

main clause   sub. clause
[Antonio won the spelling bee] [**because** he spelled *penicillin* correctly.]

PRACTICE

Identify the following word groups as main clauses (MC) or subordinate clauses (SC) or neither (N).

1. When the moon shone on the river.   *SC*

2. Our car scared the sparrows.   _____

3. Then Circe turned them into pigs.   _____

4. Before the vernal equinox.   _____

5. When the ship rounded the point.   _____

6. Iago was silent. _____

7. Which Ophelia picked by the creek. _____

8. Finally, we could get some sleep. _____

9. That Ishmael kept under his bunk. _____

10. Once every month. _____

PRACTICE Identify the following word groups as subordinate clauses (SC) or prepositional phrases (PP).

1. Since the dampness was harmful. *SC*

2. Since the first semester. _____

3. Since the Battle of Bull Run. _____

4. As a politically correct Snow White. _____

5. As Homer was stirring the black-eyed peas. _____

6. After Paris fell. _____

7. After yesterday's heavy storm. _____

8. After the season's first game. _____

9. Until Vincent saw the sky. _____

10. Until tomorrow morning. _____

PRACTICE Underline the subordinate clauses in the following sentences and circle the subordinators. Not all sentences contain subordinate clauses.

1. A misanthrope is a person (who) does not like people.

2. The yacht returned to the harbor when the sun began to set.

3. After the battle in the lake, Beowulf returned to the hall.

4. Puck gave the potion to Titania, who was sleeping.

5. If the apple feels soft, Chelsea won't eat it.

6. A reformed slave trader wrote "Amazing Grace," which is played at police officers' funerals.

7. The bagpipers played "Amazing Grace" because Chief Martinez had requested it.

8. Sergio tried to help the man whose shoe was caught in the escalator.

9. Darby rested after she had guarded the house all night.

10. Stonewall looked at the mountain where the Yankees were loading their cannons.

Adverb and Adjective Subordinate Clauses

Subordinate clauses may function as adverbs, adjectives, or nouns in their sentences. Therefore, they are called **adverb clauses**, **adjective clauses,** or **noun clauses.** We will be discussing adverb and adjective clauses, but not noun clauses. Although we frequently use noun clauses in our writing, they seldom present problems in punctuation or clarity.

Adverb Clauses

Like single-word adverbs, adverb subordinate clauses can modify verbs. For example, in the sentence *Clare ate a big breakfast because she had a busy day ahead of her,* the adverb clause *because she had a busy day ahead of her* modifies the verb *ate.* It explains <u>why</u> Clare ate a big breakfast.

Another characteristic of adverb clauses is that they begin with a **subordinating conjunction**, not a relative pronoun. In addition, in most cases an adverb clause can be moved around in its sentence, and the sentence will still make sense.

 EXAMPLES

[**When** she ate the mushroom,] Alice grew taller.

Alice grew taller [**when** she ate the mushroom.]

Alice, [**when** she ate the mushroom,] grew taller.

NOTE: When the adverb clause begins the sentence, it is followed by a comma, as in the first example. When the adverb clause ends a sentence, no comma is needed. When the adverb clause interrupts the main clause, it is enclosed by commas.

⟳ **PRACTICE**   Underline the adverb clauses in the following sentences. Circle the subordinating conjunctions.

1. (If) you leave now, you will miss the eruption of Vesuvius.

2. Whenever Homer sees a shelf of Spam cans, his mouth waters.

3. The sprinklers would not work because the water had been shut off.

4. Even though his license had expired, Bill insisted upon driving.

5. Everyone stood and stared as the unicorn stepped on stage.

⟳ **PRACTICE**   Add adverb clauses of your own to the following main clauses in the spaces indicated. Use commas where they are needed.

1. He laid his daughter Regan down for a nap *because she had*

   been acting tired all morning.

2. _____ Mr.

   Jackson posed for the twenty-dollar bill.

3. Georgia liked her place in New Mexico _____

   _____

4. Homer asked for a bag for his leftover black-eyed peas _____

   _____

5. _____

   _____ they threw the hush puppies under the table to their dogs.

Adjective Clauses

Adjective subordinate clauses modify nouns or pronouns just as single-word adjectives do. Adjective clauses follow the nouns or pronouns they modify, and they usually begin with a **relative pronoun**—*who, whom, whose, which, that* (and sometimes *when* or *where*). As you can see in the examples below, relative pronouns sometimes serve as subjects of their clauses. We will discuss the rules for punctuating adjective clauses in Chapter Three.

 EXAMPLES

The horse [that Mr. Lee liked best] was named Traveller. (The adjective clause modifies *horse*.)

On the top shelf was the trophy [**that** Irma had won for her model of the Battle of Shiloh]. (The adjective clause modifies *trophy*.)

Hampton, [**which** is Michelle's hooded rat,] resides at the foot of her bed. (The adjective clause modifies *Hampton*, and the relative pronoun *which* is the subject of the clause.)

NOTE: As you can see in the example above, the adjective clause often appears between the subject and the verb of the main clause. In addition, as you can see in the following example, sometimes the relative pronoun is left out.

 EXAMPLE

The man [I met yesterday] works for the CIA. (Here the adjective clause modifies the noun *man*, but the relative pronoun *whom* is left out.)

A note about relative pronouns:

1. Use *who* or *whom* to refer to people only.

2. Use *which* to refer to nonhuman things only, such as animals or objects.

3. Use *that* to refer to either people or nonhuman things.

 PRACTICE

Underline the adjective clauses in the following sentences and circle the relative pronouns.

1. Holesome Gatherings is the new bagel and jazz place that opened this week.

2. A saxophone player whom we all like was the first act.

3. A drummer who lives next door to us played with her.

4. The Billie Holiday Special, which is my favorite, is a bagel in the shape of a gardenia.

5. A dalmatian that everyone calls Thelonious greets people at the door.

PRACTICE   Add adjective clauses of your own to the following main clauses.

   1. Thelonious often has a bandanna tied around his neck.

   Thelonious often has a bandanna that is red with

   white polka dots tied around his neck.

   2. About 9:00 every evening musicians begin to gather by the coffee bar.

   _____

   _____

   3. The musicians wear colorful clothes.

   _____

   _____

   4. The cats are called Coltrane and Miles.

   _____

   _____

   5. Everyone enjoys the music and food.

   _____

   _____

PRACTICE   In the following sentences, underline the subordinate clauses and identify them as adverb clauses (Adv) or adjective clauses (Adj).

   1. After the bagel shop closes, the musicians sometimes stay

   and play.   *Adv*

   2. Thelonious likes "'Round Midnight" because it is a song

   by Thelonious Monk.   _____

3. The piano player likes to sit below the poster of Duke

   Ellington that is hanging on the back wall. _____

4. When the temperature drops, Coltrane and Miles lie

   by the fire. _____

5. The man who owns the shop once played bass

   with Dizzy Gillespie. _____

(◎) **PRACTICE**   Add subordinate clauses of your own to the following main clauses and indicate whether you have added an adverb clause (Adv) or an adjective clause (Adj).

1. Rupert decided to sell his stamp collection.

   Rupert, who was desperate for extra money, decided

   to sell his stamp collection. (Adj)

2. Michael loaded the motorboat onto the trailer.

   _____

   _____

3. The people sat down, and the meeting started.

   _____

   _____

4. Prometheus warmed his hands by the fire.

   _____

   _____

5. Bill Gates and Steve Jobs began to argue.

   _____

   _____

Section One Review

1. A **clause** is a group of words <u>that contains at least one subject and at least one verb</u>.

2. A **main clause** is a group of words that contains at least one subject and one verb and that <u>expresses a complete idea</u>.

3. A **subordinate clause** is a group of words that contains at least one subject and one verb but that <u>does not express a complete idea</u>.

4. **Subordinate clauses** begin with <u>subordinators</u>.

5. **Adverb subordinate clauses** usually modify verbs and begin with <u>subordinating conjunctions</u>.

6. **Adjective subordinate clauses** modify nouns or pronouns and begin with <u>relative pronouns</u>.

Exercise 1A

Underline all subordinate clauses and circle the subordinators. In the spaces provided, indicate whether the subordinate clause is an adverb clause (Adv) or an adjective clause (Adj). If a sentence contains no subordinate clause, do nothing to it.

1. The chairman suggested a solution (that) he thought would help the homeless

   people in his town. *Adj*

2. As Mr. Hyde made his appearance, Dr. Jekyll disappeared. _____

3. After the disastrous war, they sent the emperor to Elba. _____

4. Homer's plate of spaghetti, which he had covered with Spam meatballs,

   fell to the floor. _____

5. If you pick the dandelions, I will clean them. _____

6. Laura forgave her guest for breaking her glass unicorn even though it was her

   most prized possession. _____

7. The man who had stopped by the woods had miles to go and promises to keep. _____

8. When the storm moved east, it dropped four feet of snow in the mountains. _____

9. Wherever she looked, Dorothy saw lions and tigers and bears. _____

10. Before leaving the party, Bruce performed a hip-hop version of the Macarena. _____

11. Saul and Vinny both want to take Annamaria to the Artichoke Festival,

    which is held every year in Castroville. _____

12. Hortense found a Spam recipe that she had not tried. _____

13. Because sad movies always made him cry, Hector packed his pockets

    with Kleenex. _____

14. You will see the Nike in the Louvre if you look closely. _____

15. Deborah acted with dignity even though Bruce had set fire to her sleeve. _____

A. Join the pairs of sentences below by making one of them either an adverb or an adjective subordinate clause. You may need to delete or change some words.

1. The zookeeper comforted the frightened king cobra.
   The cobra had been attacked by a mongoose.

   The zookeeper comforted the frightened king cobra that had

   been attacked by a mongoose.

2. Steve won the Los Angeles marathon.
   He had suffered from the flu for a week before the race.

   _____

   _____

3. The two of them looked for the feathers.
   The feathers had fallen into the maze.

   _____

   _____

4. The coach was angry at the basketball player.
   The player had tried to strangle him.

   _____

   _____

5. The fire was under control.
   The fire fighters were able to rest.

   _____

   _____

B. Write subordinate clauses (adjective or adverb) in the blanks as indicated in parentheses at the beginning of the sentence. Make sure your clauses have subjects and verbs.

6. (Adv) *Because he was absolutely famished,*

   Homer added some pigs' feet to his casserole.

7. (Adj or Adv) Homer and Hortense visited the Grand Ole Opry _____

   _____

continued

   8. (Adj) The hummingbird is a small bird _____

   _____

   9. (Adv) Henry watched the train pass by _____

   _____

   10. (Adv or Adj) A big brown bear frightened the campers _____

   _____

C. To the main clauses below, add the types of subordinate clauses indicated in parentheses. Add your clause at any place in the sentence that you feel is appropriate. For instance, you may add an adjective clause to any noun in a sentence.

   11. (Adv) Driving your car along the Northwest Coast is a beautiful trip.

   If you take the time to enjoy the view, driving your car along

   the Northwest Coast is a beautiful trip.

   12. (Adj) Andrea attached the skis to the roof of her car.

   _____

   _____

   13. (Adj) Brutus looked for the Ides of March on the calendar.

   _____

   _____

   14. (Adv or Adj) The couple told their butler to chip away certain parts from their classical statues.

   _____

   _____

   15. (Adv) The butler refused to throw away the parts.

   _____

   _____

Exercise 1C

Underline all subordinate clauses and identify the type of clause (adjective or adverb) in the spaces provided.

1. One of my favorite places is San Francisco's Pier 39, <u>which I will always remember for its wonderful blend of unique sights, sounds, and smells.</u> _Adj_ **2.** As I walked down the pier one weekend last summer, I noticed a cook dressed all in white tossing pizza dough to lure hungry customers. _____ **3.** Near him I saw cooks who were roasting and baking all kinds of seafood. _____ **4.** Among the foods that caught my attention were lobster, shark, and clam chowder on sourdough bread. _____ **5.** I soon encountered some people being entertained by hundreds of sea lions making a tremendous racket as they played on the rocks and sunbathed by the pier. _____ **6.** When I turned away from the sea lions, my nose followed an aroma coming from a waffle ice cream stand. _____ **7.** Because I could not resist, I ordered vanilla ice cream with M & Ms mixed in. _____ **8.** The hot waffle cone warmed my hand while the cold ice cream refreshed my throat. _____ **9.** Next I came across a delightful shop, where I found all sorts of posters for children's books like _James and the Giant Peach._ _____ **10.** After I left the poster place, I spotted a chocolate shop and almost swooned in anticipation. _____ **11.** Although I was tempted, I declined the chocolate models of Alcatraz and the Golden Gate Bridge. _____ **12.** Across from the chocolate shop, I saw a restaurant that was built to look like Alcatraz Prison. _____ **13.** People could have their pictures taken in a prison cell while they were waiting to eat. _____ **14.** Close by I saw the tour boat that was taking tourists to Alcatraz Island. _____ **15.** As night fell across San Francisco Bay, I could admire the beauty of the Golden Gate Bridge from the tip of Pier 39. _____ **16.** Before I left, I felt the salty mist of the bay on my skin, a final remembrance of Pier 39. _____

Simple, Compound, Complex, and Compound-Complex Sentences

Sentences are categorized according to the number and types of clauses they contain. The names of the four types of sentences are **simple, compound, complex,** and **compound-complex.** You need to be familiar with these sentence patterns for a number of reasons:

1. **Variety.** Varying your sentence patterns creates interest and avoids monotony. Repeating a sentence pattern endlessly will bore even your most interested reader.

2. **Emphasis.** You can use these sentence patterns to emphasize the ideas that you think are more important than others.

3. **Grammar.** A knowledge of the basic sentence patterns of English will help you avoid the major sentence structure errors discussed in Section Three.

Being able to recognize and use these sentence patterns will help you control your writing and thus express your ideas more effectively.

The Simple Sentence

The introduction to this chapter points out that a sentence must contain at least one main clause. A sentence that contains only one main clause and no other clauses is called a **simple sentence.** However, a simple sentence is not necessarily an uncomplicated or short sentence because, in addition to its one main clause, it may also contain a variety of phrases and modifiers.

The basic pattern for the simple sentence is subject–verb (SV). This pattern may vary in several ways:

⌾ EXAMPLES

                                                     S   V
subject–verb (SV): The plane flew over the stadium.

                                                           V   S
verb–subject (VS): Over the stadium flew the plane.

                                                     S   S   V
subject–subject–verb (SSV): The plane and the helicopter flew over the stadium.

                                                     S   V   V
subject–verb–verb (SVV): The plane flew over the stadium and turned north.

$$\overset{\text{S}}{} \qquad \overset{\text{S}}{} \quad \overset{\text{V}}{}$$

subject–subject–verb–verb (SSVV): The plane and the helicopter flew

$$\overset{\text{V}}{}$$

over the stadium and turned north.

$$\overset{\text{S}}{} \quad \overset{\text{V}}{}$$

A simple sentence can be brief: *It rained.*

$$\overset{\text{S}}{}$$

Or it can be rather long: *Enraged by the taunting of the boys, the huge gorilla*

$$\overset{\text{V}}{} \qquad\qquad\qquad \overset{\text{V}}{}$$

leaped from his enclosure and chased them up a hill and down a pathway to the exit gates.

The important thing to remember about the simple sentence is that it has only one main clause and no other clauses.

PRACTICE

Write your own simple sentences according to the instructions.

1. A simple sentence with the pattern subject–subject–verb:

   Two supermarkets and a department store collapsed in the

   recent earthquake.

2. A simple sentence that begins with a prepositional phrase and has the pattern subject–verb:

   _____

   _____

3. A simple sentence that begins with *Here* and has the pattern verb–subject:

   _____

   _____

4. A simple sentence that expresses a command:

   _____

   _____

5. A simple sentence that has the pattern subject–subject–verb–verb:

_____

_____

The Compound Sentence

Simply put, a **compound sentence** contains two or more main clauses but no subordinate clauses. The basic pattern of the clauses may be expressed subject–verb/subject–verb (SV/SV). The main clauses are always joined in one of three ways:

1. Two main clauses may be joined by a comma and one of the seven coordinating conjunctions (*and, or, nor, but, for, so, yet*).

 EXAMPLE

      S   V   S   V

Maria registered for all of her classes by mail, **but** Brad was not able to do so.

Remember, the two main clauses must be joined by **both a comma and a coordinating conjunction,** and the comma always comes before the coordinating conjunction.

2. Two main clauses may be joined by a semicolon (;).

 EXAMPLE

      S   V   S   V

Maria registered for all of her classes by mail; Brad was not able to do so.

3. Two main clauses may be joined by a semicolon and a transitional word or phrase. Such transitional words or phrases are followed by a comma.

 EXAMPLE

      S   V   S

Maria registered for all of her classes by mail; **however,** Brad

      V

was not able to do so.

Below is a list of the most commonly used transitional words and phrases. Do not confuse these words or phrases with coordinating conjunctions or subordinating conjunctions.

accordingly	hence	next	thus
also	however	nonetheless	undoubtedly
besides	instead	otherwise	for instance
consequently	meanwhile	similarly	for example
finally	moreover	still	on the other hand
further	namely	then	that is
furthermore	nevertheless	therefore	

PRACTICE Write compound sentences of your own according to the instructions.

1. A compound sentence that uses a comma and *but* to join two main clauses:

   I was very hungry after the game, but I decided not to eat anything.

2. A compound sentence that joins two main clauses with a semicolon:

   _____

   _____

3. A compound sentence that joins two main clauses with a semicolon and an appropriate transitional word or phrase followed by a comma:

   _____

   _____

4. A compound sentence that joins two main clauses with a comma and *or:*

   _____

   _____

5. A compound sentence that joins two main clauses with a semicolon followed by the transitional word *nevertheless* or *consequently*:

_____

_____

PRACTICE

In the following sentences, write S above each subject and V above each verb. Then, in the spaces provided, identify each sentence as either **simple** or **compound**.

1. Homer's son Gomer thought about the story of the "Three

   Blind Mice."   *simple*

2. One blind mouse had become lonely, so he had made friends

   with another blind mouse.   _____

3. Then these two found another blind mouse.   _____

4. They had nothing better to do, so they chased a farmer's

   wife.   _____

5. Gomer wondered about the intelligence of these three mice.   _____

6. They had found each other and had formed a group of

   three.   _____

7. He admired the mice for their intelligence; however,

   they should not have run after the farmer's wife.   _____

8. It was not much smarter than chasing one of the farmer's

   cats.   _____

9. Maybe they really did not want to catch her; on the other

   hand, maybe they wanted to live dangerously.   _____

10. They probably enjoyed the chase, yet they lost their tails.   _____

The Complex Sentence

The **complex sentence** has the same subject–verb pattern (SV/SV) as the compound sentence. However, the complex sentence features only one main clause and always contains at least one subordinate clause and sometimes more than one. The subordinate clauses in a complex sentence may occur at any place in the sentence.

 EXAMPLES

Before a main clause: <u>After he retired from the Army,</u> Eisenhower ran for president.

After a main clause: Rugby is a sport <u>that I have played only once</u>.

Interrupting a main clause: Emilio's grandfather<u>, who fought in World War II,</u> told him about his experiences during the war.

Before and after a main clause: <u>When the pianist sat down at the piano,</u> she played a melody <u>that she had written recently</u>.

PRACTICE   Write complex sentences of your own according to the instructions.

1. A complex sentence that includes an adjective clause using the relative pronoun *who:*

    Zelda searched for three days to find the

    person who had lost the German shepherd.

2. A complex sentence that begins with an adverb clause:

    _____

    _____

3. A complex sentence that contains an adjective clause using the relative pronoun *that*:

_____

_____

4. A complex sentence that contains an adverb clause using *because*:

_____

_____

5. A complex sentence that contains one main clause and two adjective clauses:

_____

_____

The Compound-Complex Sentence

The **compound-complex sentence** is a combination of the compound and the complex sentence patterns. It is made up of two or more main clauses and one or more subordinate clauses. Therefore, it must contain a minimum of three sets of subjects and verbs (<u>at least</u> two main clauses and <u>at least</u> one subordinate clause).

 EXAMPLES

                                   main clause   sub. clause
[On the day-long bicycle trip, Ophelia ate the food] [that she had packed,]

                 main clause
[but Henry had forgotten to bring anything to eat.]

            sub. clause   main clause
[Although he was exhausted,] [Ernesto cooked dinner for his mother,]

            main clause
[and after dinner he cleaned the kitchen.]

         main clause   sub. clause
[The travelers were excited] [when they arrived in Paris;]

        main clause
[they wanted to go sightseeing immediately.]

PRACTICE   Write compound-complex sentences of your own according to the instructions.

1. A compound-complex sentence that contains two main clauses joined by *and* and one adjective clause beginning with *who:*

   Murphy, who works at the Mazda dealership, sold ten Miatas

   last month, and this month he plans to sell even more.

2. A compound-complex sentence that contains two main clauses and an adverb clause. Use a semicolon to join the main clauses:

   _____

   _____

3. A compound-complex sentence that contains two main clauses and an adjective clause. Use a semicolon and a transitional word or phrase to join the main clauses:

   _____

   _____

4. A compound-complex sentence that contains two main clauses and two adverb clauses. Use a comma and a coordinating conjunction to join the main clauses:

   _____

   _____

5. A compound-complex sentence about yourself with a pattern of your own choice:

   _____

   _____

◉ PRACTICE   In the following sentences, write S above each subject and V above each verb. Then, in the spaces provided, identify the sentences as simple, compound, complex, or compound-complex.

1. *Cinderella* is a European fairy tale with over five hundred
   versions.   *simple*

2. The oldest versions are from the ninth century; those early
   stories do not give Cinderella glass slippers.   _____

3. The glass slippers appeared when a French version of the
   story was translated incorrectly.   _____

4. In older versions, Cinderella's shoes were made of a rare
   metal or some other valuable covering.   _____

5. The French story used white squirrel fur for the slippers, but
   the French word that meant fur was similar to the word that
   meant *glass*.   _____

6. Charles Perrault, who translated the story in 1697, was the
   first person to describe the slippers as glass.   _____

7. Almost all later versions of the story depict Cinderella as
   wearing glass slippers.   _____

8. In most of the stories, Cinderella is helped by her fairy
   godmother; however, some versions use other characters.   _____

9. Although Cinderella's mother is dead, she magically appears
   in one story, and she takes the place of the fairy godmother.   _____

10. Sometimes cows or goats assist Cinderella, but in the Disney
    version mice come to her aid.   _____

Section Two Review

1. A **simple sentence** contains only one main clause and no other clauses.

2. A **compound sentence** contains two or more main clauses that are joined by a comma and a coordinating conjunction <u>or</u> a semicolon <u>or</u> a semicolon and a transitional word or phrase.

3. A **complex sentence** contains only one main clause and one or more subordinate clauses.

4. A **compound-complex sentence** contains two or more main clauses and one or more subordinate clauses.

Exercise 2A

In the spaces provided, identify the following sentences as simple, compound, complex, or compound-complex.

1. Jazz is often called America's only original art form. *simple*

2. The roots of jazz go back to African-Caribbean music that accompanied work, church, and social events in the early days of this country. _____

3. Because its beginnings are so humble, jazz has not been given as much respect in its own country as European art forms such as classical music. _____

4. In the past one has had to go to smoky saloons and bars to enjoy the best jazz musicians. _____

5. Among the early jazz greats were King Oliver, Eubie Blake, Bessie Smith, and Jelly Roll Morton. _____

6. A typical jazz ensemble includes a drum, bass, piano, saxophone, and trumpet, but many other instruments like banjos, flutes, organs, and accordions are also played. _____

7. Singers have always been a part of jazz, and Billie Holiday, who sang in the forties and fifties, is one of the best loved. _____

8. Her trademark was a white gardenia, which she wore in her hair. _____

9. Billie Holiday sang with most of the great jazz musicians of her time; they include Lester Gordon, Duke Ellington, Benny Goodman, Roy Eldridge. _____

10. One of her most famous songs is "Strange Fruit," which is about the lynchings of African-Americans in the South. _____

11. Duke Ellington was one of the greatest composers of jazz; he had a full jazz orchestra, which was invited to play at Carnegie Hall. _____

12. Count Basie and Duke Ellington, who both led great jazz orchestras, helped to bring more respect to jazz in the second half of the twentieth century. _____

13. The characteristics that set jazz apart from other musical forms are its unique use of rhythm and improvisation combined with its joy and spontaneity. _____

14. Jazz, which is alive and well throughout the world, is practiced today by such players as Sonny Rollins, Joshua Redman, Charlie Haden, and Wynton Marsalis. _____

15. These great musicians stand on the shoulders of people like John Coltrane, Miles Davis, and Thelonious Monk. _____

Exercise 2B

A. Combine each set of sentences to create the sentence type asked for. You may need to delete or change some words.

1. A simple sentence with the pattern verb–subject:
   a. The ship was in the harbor.
   b. The ship was a nineteenth-century three-masted schooner.

   In the harbor was a nineteenth-century three-masted schooner.

   _____

2. A compound sentence:
   a. Homer was feeling romantic toward Hortense.
   b. He decided to bring her a bouquet of beet and spinach greens.

   _____

   _____

3. A complex sentence:
   a. Hortense will take Gomer to the cow chip contest.
   b. Gomer will pay for the tickets.

   _____

   _____

4. A simple sentence (in the form of a question):
   a. Will you clear the table?
   b. Will you empty the garbage?

   _____

   _____

5. A complex sentence:
   a. A violent electrical storm was approaching.
   b. The soccer game was postponed.

   _____

   _____

continued

6. A simple sentence:
   a. Around midnight the cow jumped over the moon.
   b. The spoon jumped over the moon as well.

   _____

   _____

7. A compound sentence:
   a. Leticia Smeg was not impressed with Clyde Merdly's cooking.
   b. She asked him to let her cook the dinner.

   _____

   _____

8. A compound-complex sentence:
   a. The Subreality Cafe is a dark and gloomy place.
   b. It appeals to people who wear black clothing and dark makeup.
   c. It is one of the most popular cafes in the city.

   _____

   _____

9. A compound-complex sentence:
   a. Emily Dickinson spent most of her life alone in her house.
   b. She wrote nearly 1800 poems.
   c. She was not interested in publishing them.

   _____

   _____

B. Following the instructions, construct sentences of your own.

10. A compound-complex sentence that uses a semicolon:

   _____

   _____

11. A complex sentence that includes an adjective clause:

   _____

   _____

continued

12. A compound sentence that uses a semicolon and a transitional word:

_____

_____

13. A simple sentence:

_____

_____

14. A complex sentence that includes an adverb clause at the beginning of the sentence:

_____

_____

15. A compound-complex sentence that does not use a semicolon:

_____

_____

Exercise 2C

Identify the sentences as simple, compound, complex, or compound-complex.

1. After dark, the shore near my cabin is a mysterious place where the absence of light creates a new reality. ___*complex*___ **2.** As I was walking along the beach one night recently, I surprised a snow crab in the beam of my flashlight. _____ **3.** He lay in a pit just above the surface as if he were watching the sea and waiting. _____ **4.** When I turned off the flashlight, I could feel the darkness around me, and I felt alone with the snow crab. _____ **5.** I could hear nothing but the elemental sounds of wind blowing over sand and water and waves crashing on the beach. _____ **6.** When I am on that beach at night, time seems suspended, and I feel alone with the creatures of the shore. _____ **7.** Those creatures, like the sea anemones and the shore birds, have been there since the dawn of time. _____ **8.** As my eyes accustom themselves to the dark, the gulls and sanderlings become shadows. _____ **9.** When I am surrounded by those sights, sounds, and smells, I feel transported into another, older world before humankind. _____ **10.** The rhythm of the sea becomes the rhythm of the whole world, and the smell becomes a fundamental smell. _____ **11.** On that recent night, I sat near that snow crab and watched the sea with him. _____ **12.** Hidden beneath the water before me were patches of bright coral that were the home for blood-red starfish and green sea cucumbers. _____ **13.** All seemed peaceful then, but on the shore the battle for survival rages incessantly. _____ **14.** The largest shark and the smallest plankton must search constantly for the food that sustains them. _____ **15.** In the dim light I saw several hermit crabs scurrying across the sand, and I turned from the dark shore toward the lights of my home. _____

Fragments, Fused Sentences, and Comma Splices

Now that you are combining main and subordinate clauses to write different types of sentences, we need to talk about a few of the writing problems you might encounter. Fortunately, the most serious of these problems—the **fragment**, the **fused sentence**, and the **comma splice**—are also the easiest to identify and correct.

Fragments

The easiest way to identify a **sentence fragment** is to remember that <u>every sentence must contain a main clause</u>. If you do not have a main clause, you do <u>not</u> have a sentence. You can define a fragment, then, like this: A sentence fragment occurs when a group of words that lacks a main clause is punctuated as a sentence.

> **sentence fragment**
>
> A sentence fragment occurs when a group of words that lacks a main clause is punctuated as a sentence.

Using this definition, you can identify almost any sentence fragment. However, you will find it easier to locate fragments in your own writing if you know that fragments can be divided into three basic types.

Three Types of Sentence Fragments

1. <u>Some fragments contain no clause at all.</u> This type of fragment is simple to spot. It usually does not even sound like a sentence because it lacks a subject or verb or both.

 EXAMPLE   The snow in the street.

2. <u>Some fragments contain a verbal but still no clause.</u> This fragment is a bit less obvious because a verbal can be mistaken for a verb. But remember, neither a participle nor an infinitive is a verb. (See Chapter One if you need to review this point.)

 EXAMPLES   The snow **falling** on the street. (participle)

To slip on the snow in the street.   (infinitive)

3. Some fragments contain a **subordinate clause** but no **main clause**. This type of fragment is perhaps the most common because it does contain a subject and a verb. But remember, <u>a group of words without a main clause is not a sentence</u>.

After the snow had fallen on the street.

Because I had slipped on the snow in the street.

Repairing Sentence Fragments

Once you have identified a fragment, you can correct it in one of two ways.

1. Add words to give it a main clause.

(fragment)	The snow in the street.
(sentence)	**I gazed** at the snow in the street.
(sentence)	The snow **was** in the street.
(fragment)	The snow falling in the street.
(sentence)	The snow falling in the street **covered my car.**
(sentence)	The snow **was** falling in the street.
(fragment)	After the snow had fallen in the street.
(sentence)	**I looked for a shovel** after the snow had fallen in the street.

2. Join the fragment to a main clause written before or after it.

(incorrect)	I love to see the ice on the lake. And the snow in the street.
(correct)	I love to see the ice on the lake and the snow in the street.
(incorrect)	My back was so sore that I could not stand straight. Because I had slipped on the snow in the street.
(correct)	My back was so sore that I could not stand straight because I had slipped on the snow in the street.

One final point might help you identify and correct sentence fragments. Remember that we all speak in fragments every day. (If a friend asks you how you are, you might respond with the fragment "Fine.") Because we speak in fragments, you may find that your writing seems acceptable even though it contains fragments. When you work on the exercises in this unit, do not rely on your "ear" alone. Look at the sentences. **If they do not contain main clauses, they are fragments, no matter how correct they may sound.**

PRACTICE Underline any fragment you find. Then correct it either by adding new words to give it a main clause or by joining it to a main clause next to it.

1. The small boy wandered slowly down the street. <u>Stopping sometimes to look into the store windows.</u>

   The small boy wandered slowly down the street, stopping

   sometimes to look into the store windows.

2. The koala that came out during the day because it was hungry.

   _____

   _____

3. Using a lead pipe. Mr. Green committed the crime. While he was in the library.

   _____

   _____

4. Study this chapter carefully. To do well on the next test.

   _____

   _____

5. When the boy had used all of the excuses that he could think of.

   _____

   _____

6. The timer on the oven failed to go off. Probably because I had forgotten to set it.

_____

_____

7. The Chocolate Shoppe owner was locking the door. Even as Rupert was dashing across the street. Begging for her to let him in.

_____

_____

8. Ulysses wanted to hear the Sirens' song. Although he knew he might cause a shipwreck.

_____

_____

9. To remind her of her senior year in high school.

_____

_____

10. Stooping to pick up fallen rocks. My neighbor and I repaired the stone wall. That separates his property from mine.

_____

_____

Fused Sentences and Comma Splices

The **fused sentence** and **comma splice** are serious writing errors that you can correct with little effort. Either error can occur when you write a compound or compound-complex sentence. The fused sentence occurs when two or more main clauses are joined without a coordinating conjunction and without punctuation.

---

fused sentence

The fused sentence occurs when two or more main clauses are joined without a coordinating conjunction and without punctuation.

 EXAMPLE (fused) Raoul drove by his uncle's house he waved at his cousins.

As you can see, the two main clauses in the above example (*Raoul drove by his uncle's house* and *he waved at his cousins*) have been joined without a coordinating conjunction and without punctuation of any kind.

The comma splice is a similar error: The comma splice occurs when two or more main clauses are joined with a comma but without a coordinating conjunction.

---

comma splice

The comma splice occurs when two or more main clauses are joined with a comma but without a coordinating conjunction.

 EXAMPLE (comma splice) The hot sun beat down on the construction workers, they looked forward to the end of the day.

In this example, the two main clauses (*The hot sun beat down on the construction workers* and *they looked forward to the end of the day*) are joined by a comma, but a comma alone is not enough to join main clauses.

NOTE: One of the most frequent comma splices occurs when a writer joins two main clauses with a comma and a transitional word rather than with a semicolon and a transitional word.

 EXAMPLE (comma splice) I wanted a dog for Christmas, however, my parents gave me a cat.

Repairing Fused Sentences and Comma Splices

Because both fused sentences and comma splices occur when two main clauses are joined, you can correct either error using one of five methods. Consider these two errors:

 EXAMPLES

(fused)   Jack left for work early he arrived late.

(comma splice)   Jack left for work early, he arrived late.

Both of these errors can be corrected in one of five ways:

1. Use a comma and a coordinating conjunction.
   Jack left for work early, **but** he arrived late.

2. Use a semicolon.
   Jack left for work early; he arrived late.

3. Use a semicolon and a transitional word or phrase.
   Jack left for work early; **however,** he arrived late.

   NOTE: Do <u>not</u> use a semicolon before a transitional word that does <u>not</u> begin a main clause. For example, in the following sentence, *however* does not need a semicolon.

 EXAMPLE

I have not seen my father, **however,** for ten years.

4. Change one of the clauses to a subordinate clause by beginning it with a subordinator.
   Although Jack left for work early, he arrived late.

5. Punctuate the clauses as two separate sentences.
   Jack left for work early. He arrived late.

NOTE: Sometimes the two main clauses in a fused sentence or comma splice are interrupted by a subordinate clause. When this sentence pattern occurs, the two main clauses must still be connected in one of the five ways.

 EXAMPLES

(fused)   Alma bought a new Mercedes even though she could not afford one she fell behind in her monthly payments.

(comma splice)   Alma bought a new Mercedes even though she could not afford one, she fell behind in her monthly payments.

These errors can be corrected in any of the five ways mentioned above.

 EXAMPLE

Alma bought a new Mercedes even though she could not afford one; consequently, she fell behind in her monthly payments.

⊚ **PRACTICE**   Identify the following sentences as fused (F), comma splice (CS), or correct (C). Then correct the incorrect sentences. Use a different method of correction each time.

CS 1. Butler had wanted to join his brother in New York, his business was going too well for him to leave.

Butler had wanted to join his brother in New York,

but his business was going too well for him to leave.

_____ 2. Gomer looked into the cabinet all he could see was Spam.

_____ 3. When the Ancient Mariner shot the albatross, he knew he was heading for trouble.

_____ 4. Chuck Berry was playing "Hail, Hail, Rock and Roll" on the radio, meanwhile, Gomer and Homer finished the catfish and hushpuppies.

_____ 5. Every day Gilligan searches the horizon he even climbs a tree for a better look.

_____ **6.** Dido begged and begged Aeneas, finally, she gave up and jumped off the cliff.

_____

_____

_____ **7.** Pluto kept feeding Cerberus chocolate turtles even though Cerberus knew they were not good for him he ate them anyway.

_____

_____

_____ **8.** Frances knew, however, that Melvin would never stop eating potato chips.

_____

_____

_____ **9.** Hortense watched *The Fellowship of the Ring* ten times soon the ushers knew her by name.

_____

_____

_____ **10.** Mr. Nosferatu came over for dinner last night, he kept staring at my fiancee's neck.

_____

_____

Section Three Review

1. A **sentence fragment** occurs when a group of words that lacks a main clause is punctuated as a sentence.

2. There are three types of sentence fragments.

   a. Some contain no clause at all.

   b. Some contain a verbal but still no clause.

   c. Some contain a subordinate clause but no main clause.

3. You can correct a sentence fragment in one of two ways.

   a. Add words to give it a main clause.

   b. Join it to an already existing main clause.

4. The **fused sentence** occurs when two or more main clauses are joined without a coordinating conjunction and without punctuation.

5. The **comma splice** occurs when two or more main clauses are joined with a comma but without a coordinating conjunction.

6. You can correct fused sentences and comma splices in one of five ways.

   a. Use a comma and a coordinating conjunction.

   b. Use a semicolon.

   c. Use a semicolon and a transitional word or phrase.

   d. Change one of the clauses to a subordinate clause by adding a subordinator at the beginning of it.

   e. Punctuate the clauses as two separate sentences.

Exercise 3A

Identify each of the following as correct (C), fused (F), comma splice (CS), or sentence fragment (Frag). Then correct each error using any of the methods discussed in this unit.

Frag **1.** Because it was so cold and slimy and ugly that Carl was becoming nauseated just looking at it.

It was so cold and slimy and ugly that Carl was becoming nauseated just looking at it.

_____ **2.** Sonia lost her statistics textbook last week, nevertheless, she passed the test yesterday.

_____ **3.** Please send this chain letter to ten other people.

_____ **4.** Vincent was driving back to Arles suddenly he realized he had forgotten to buy canvas.

_____ **5.** Two professors discussing parallel universes and even parallel lives.

_____ **6.** The unemployment rate has improved this year, the weather has too.

continued

_____ 7. Homer brought a delicious salad of Spam and collard greens to the pot luck, yet no one would eat it.

_____

_____

_____ 8. Most people say that baseball is our national pastime however others say that foot-ball has replaced baseball.

_____

_____

_____ 9. Julio knew that the name of the mythological river started with *L* he couldn't remember its exact name.

_____

_____

_____ 10. The weather was so cold that Garrison's tongue stuck to the pump handle.

_____

_____

_____ 11. Orville loved to square dance, he joined the Grapestompers square dance club in Temecula.

_____

_____

_____ 12. The battle was over, Paris had been liberated.

_____

_____

Exercise 3A

continued

_____**13.** Homer will do anything to please Hortense, in fact, once he went without Spam for a month.

_____

_____

_____**14.** Before putting on his Halloween costume and dyeing his hair bright orange.

_____

_____

_____**15.** The border collie was trying to round up the sheep, although he was fast and clever, some of them escaped.

_____

_____

A. Correct the following sentence fragments by adding words to them to make them complete sentences.

1. Shannon, who had been standing in the rain for two hours.

   Shannon, who had been standing in the rain for two hours,

   finally decided to give up and go home.

2. Even though I had left for the airport in plenty of time.

   _____

   _____

3. Damien, standing at the end of the pier.

   _____

   _____

4. Which Gomer liked to wear to school.

   _____

   _____

5. To the first person who walks through the door.

   _____

   _____

B. Join the following main clauses by using a comma and a coordinating conjunction, a semicolon, a semicolon and a transitional word or phrase, or by making one of the clauses a subordinate clause. Use each of these four methods at least once.

6. Regan asked Cordelia for her third of the kingdom. Eventually, Cordelia gave it to her and left for France.

   Regan asked Cordelia for her third of the kingdom;

   eventually, Cordelia gave it to her and left for France.

continued

7. Hester told their secret to everyone. Dimmesdale would not tell anyone.

_____

_____

8. Manuel used a thesaurus to look up an alternate word. He was quite pleased with the word that he found.

_____

_____

9. Leonardo looked at the new Picasso. The Picasso had just been purchased by the museum.

_____

_____

10. The movie was loud, violent, and full of suspense. Mario slept through the entire thing.

_____

_____

C. Expand each of the following sentences by adding a **clause** to it. Identify the subject and verb of each clause you use and vary the placement of the clauses. (Don't place every clause at the end of its sentence.) When you add the clauses, use each of the following methods at least once: a) use a comma and a coordinating conjunction; b) use a semicolon; c) use a semicolon and a transitional word or phrase; d) make one clause a subordinate clause.

11. Sitting in their patrol car, the police officers tried to comfort the lost child.

    Sitting in their patrol car, the police officers tried to
    comfort the lost child; however, the child would not stop crying.

12. Savion Glover is a contemporary tap dancer.

_____

_____

continued

13. The sun rose over a quiet, peaceful lake high above Denver, Colorado.

_____

_____

14. Amber stood up with a fierce look on her face.

_____

_____

15. The jazz concert was held in the open-air theater.

_____

_____

Exercise 3C

In the following paragraph, correct any fragments, fused sentences, or comma splices.

1. When we entered Canterbury Gardens for the first time, **2.** My mother and I were completely enchanted by the Christmas scene before us. **3.** There were fifteen full-sized Christmas trees, each tree was decorated with its own special theme. **4.** Handmade wreaths adorned the walls antique furniture showed off the rest of the store's wares. **5.** The air was filled with the delicious aroma of vanilla and cinnamon. **6.** Coming from the potpourri pots simmering throughout the store. **7.** Above the laughter and all the "oohs" and "ahs" of the customers. **8.** We could hear the sounds of Christmas music playing softly in the background. **9.** In the center of the store was a twenty-foot-tall Christmas tree decorated with brown teddy bears, cheery-faced Santas, red ribbons, and a carousel of toys that was suspended from the ceiling, going round and round the very top of the tree. **10.** We entered another area of this charming and delightful store we were filled with a new sense of awe. **11.** In one alcove was a dining room scene with an antique dinette set displaying fine china, silverware, and linens, in the hutches were porcelain Santas, Fabergé eggs, Hummel figurines, and other depictions of Christmas. **12.** Another alcove was dedicated entirely to baby's first Christmas. **13.** Each scene had its own Christmas tree to help set it off, my favorite tree was colored pink and decorated with Victorian lace. **14.** We were so intrigued and excited by our first visit to Canterbury Gardens. **15.** That we have made it a yearly tradition to go back each Christmas.

Sentence Practice:
Combining Main and Subordinate Clauses

In this chapter you have learned the basic sentence patterns of English, and you have seen that you can combine the major word groups of a sentence—the clauses—in various ways. Of course, how you present your ideas in your sentences can affect the way a reader perceives your ideas. Take, for instance, the following sentences.

1. Sub-compact cars are economical.

2. Sub-compact cars are easy to handle.

3. Sub-compact cars are simple to park.

4. Full-size sedans are roomier.

5. Full-size sedans are safer.

6. Full-size sedans are quieter.

You can present these ideas in six simple sentences like those above, but doing so makes the writing choppy and simplistic. On the other hand, you can use the sentence patterns discussed in this chapter to combine these six ideas in several ways.

1. You can present these ideas as two simple sentences.

 EXAMPLE   Sub-compact cars are economical, easy to handle, and simple to park. Full-size sedans are roomier, safer, and quieter.

2. Or you can group the ideas into one compound sentence by using a comma and a coordinating conjunction.

 EXAMPLE   Sub-compact cars are economical, easy to handle, and simple to park, but full-size sedans are roomier, safer, and quieter.

Note that the coordinating conjunction *but* allows you to emphasize the contrast between the ideas in the two main clauses.

3. You can also group these ideas into a compound sentence by using a semicolon as a connector.

 EXAMPLE   Sub-compact cars are economical, easy to handle, and simple to park; full-size sedans are roomier, safer, and quieter.

In this sentence the contrast in the ideas is implied rather than directly stated.

4. Of course, you can add a transitional word after the semicolon.

 EXAMPLE

Sub-compact cars are economical, easy to handle, and simple to park; however, full-size sedans are roomier, safer, and quieter.

Note that *however* now signals the contrast between the ideas in the two clauses.

5. Finally, you can group the ideas into a main clause and a subordinate clause by adding a subordinator. Now you have a complex sentence.

 EXAMPLE

Although sub-compact cars are economical, easy to handle, and simple to park, full-size sedans are roomier, safer, and quieter.

Like the other sentences, this sentence shows the reader the contrast between the ideas in the two clauses. However, it also shows the ideas the writer thinks are most important—the ones in the main clause.

Sentence Combining Exercises

Using the knowledge of sentence patterns that you have gained from this chapter, combine the following lists of sentences into longer sentences according to the directions. Be sure to punctuate carefully to avoid comma splices or fused sentences. Remember to look for a base sentence or a main idea to build upon. The most important idea should be in a main clause.

 EXAMPLE   First, combine these ideas into a compound sentence, using one of the three methods presented in Section Two of this chapter. Then form a complex sentence, using a subordinator to make one clause subordinate.

1. New York City often seems dirty.
2. New York City often seems overcrowded.
3. New York City often seems full of crime.
4. New York City has excitement.
5. New York City has charming ethnic communities.
6. New York City has a great variety of cultural attractions.

A. Compound sentence:

New York City often seems dirty, overcrowded, and full of crime; however, it also has excitement, charming ethnic communities, and a great variety of cultural attractions.

B. Complex sentence:

Although New York City often seems dirty, overcrowded, and full of crime, it also has excitement, charming ethnic communities, and a great variety of cultural attractions.

Sentence Combining Exercises

continued

1. Combine the following sentences into one complex sentence. Form sentences b and c into one adjective clause that begins with *who*.

   a. Samuel Wilson was the original "Uncle Sam."
   b. He lived during the Revolutionary War.
   c. He also lived during the War of 1812.

   _____

   _____

   _____

   _____

2. Combine these sentences into one complex sentence. Begin the sentence with a prepositional phrase. Form sentence c into an adjective clause that begins with *who*.

   a. It was the day of Paul Revere's historic ride.
   b. Samuel Wilson alerted the townspeople.
   c. He was the drummer boy for Menotomy, Massachusetts.
   d. He saw the British coming.

   _____

   _____

   _____

   _____

Sentence Combining Exercises

continued

3. Combine these sentences into one complex sentence. Form sentences b and c into one main clause.

   a. He was fourteen.
   b. Sam Wilson joined the army.
   c. He fought against the British.

   _____

   _____

   _____

   _____

4. Combine these sentences into one complex sentence by using sentence d as a subordinate clause starting with *where*.

   a. It was after Sam had served in the Revolutionary War.
   b. He opened a meat-packing company.
   c. It was in Troy, New York.
   d. People soon started to call him "Uncle Sam."
   e. He was like a friendly uncle.

   _____

   _____

   _____

   _____

Sentence Combining Exercises

continued

5. Combine these sentences into one compound-complex sentence. Start the sentence with a prepositional phrase. Form sentence c into an adjective clause that starts with *that*.

    a. It was during the War of 1812.
    b. Sam began to stamp "U.S." on crates of beef and pork.
    c. The crates were to be sold to the United States government.
    d. Those initials were not in common use for "United States."

_____

_____

_____

_____

6. Combine these sentences into one complex sentence.

    a. Government inspectors asked what the initials meant.
    b. The employees joked that they probably referred to their employer.
    c. The employees were at the meat plant.
    d. Their employer was called "Uncle Sam."

_____

_____

_____

_____

Sentence Combining Exercises

continued

7. Combine these sentences into one sentence. Use the most effective pattern you can find. At the end of your new sentence, indicate which type of sentence you have written.

    a. The story of "Uncle Sam" spread.
    b. Soldiers started calling all supplies the property of Uncle Sam.
    c. They began to call themselves Uncle Sam's men.

_____

_____

_____

_____

8. Combine these sentences into one sentence. At the end of your new sentence, indicate which type of sentence you have written.

    a. The first illustrations showed a man in a coat and hat.
    b. The illustrations were of Uncle Sam.
    c. The man was friendly.
    d. The man was clean-shaven.
    e. The coat and hat were black.

_____

_____

_____

_____

Sentence Combining Exercises

continued

9. Combine these sentences into one sentence. At the end of your new sentence, indicate which type of sentence you have written.

   a. Time passed.
   b. Uncle Sam came to be portrayed as a tall figure.
   c. He was white-whiskered.
   d. He wore a jacket.
   e. The jacket was decorated with stars.
   f. He wore pants.
   g. The pants had red and white stripes.
   h. He wore a top hat.
   i. The top hat was covered with stars and stripes.

   _____

   _____

   _____

   _____

10. Combine these sentences into one sentence. At the end of your new sentence, indicate which type of sentence you have written.

    a. The best-known portrait is probably the figure above the caption.
    b. The portrait is of Uncle Sam.
    c. The figure is severe.
    d. The figure is finger-pointing.
    e. The figure appeared on World War I posters.
    f. The caption reads "I Want You for U.S. Army."

    _____

    _____

    _____

    _____

SECTION
five

Paragraph Practice:
Describing a Place

Assignment

In Chapter Two you have read paragraphs that describe a variety of places. Exercise 1C (page 88) describes San Francisco's Pier 39, Exercise 2C (page 103) describes a shore scene at night, and Exercise 3C (page 119) describes a Christmas store named Canterbury Gardens. Your assignment in this writing section is to describe a place that you remember for one particular reason. As you do so, you will practice limiting your paragraph to one idea that is expressed in a topic sentence and developing your paragraph with details that are both specific and concrete.

Prewriting to Generate Ideas

To find a topic, use freewriting, brainstorming, or clustering (or all three) to generate ideas about places that you remember well. Try to develop a list of as many places as you can. Sometimes the most interesting place to describe will be buried deep in your memory, so give prewriting a chance to uncover that memory before you decide on a topic.

Choosing and Narrowing the Topic

As you prewrite, avoid topics that are too broad to cover in one paragraph. For example, a city or an amusement park would be too large of a topic to cover in detail in a brief piece of writing. However, one particular part of a small town or one particular section of an amusement park might work very well.

Prewriting Application: Finding Your Topic

Consider the following questions as you prewrite:

1. What places have you visited in the past several years? Think about vacations you have taken or places you have traveled to.

2. Where have you been in the past two weeks? Make a list of everywhere you have gone.

3. What places from your childhood give you the most pleasant memories?

4. Where do you go to relax, to meditate, or to find peace of mind?

5. Have you ever been somewhere when you felt frightened or concerned for your safety?

6. What are the most beautiful places you have ever seen?

7. What are the most unpleasant ones? What are the strangest ones?

8. Have any places ever made you feel confused or lost?

9. Do you know any places that are particularly chaotic and noisy?

10. Where have you been today? Can you describe an ordinary, everyday place so that a reader sees it in a new way?

Once you have chosen the one place that is most interesting to you, keep prewriting about it. Try to remember as many details as you can about the place. Don't worry about writing well at this point—just brainstorm (make lists) or freewrite to get down as many of the details as you can remember.

Writing a Topic Sentence

After you have written for a while, read over what you have. Look for related details that focus on *one particular impression* of the place. These details and others that give that same impression are the ones you should emphasize in your paragraph. Once you have identified that particular impression, you are ready to write a preliminary **topic sentence.**

Remember, a topic sentence contains both a **topic** and a **central point.** In this writing assignment, your topic will be the place you are describing, and your central point will be the particular impression about the place that your details emphasize and illustrate.

Prewriting Application: Working with Topic Sentences

In each sentence below, underline the topic once and the central point twice.

1. Mammoth Cave, in southwestern Kentucky, is full of eerie, unearthly sights.

2. One of the most confusing places I have ever visited was the Los Angeles International Airport.

3. Snow Summit, in Big Bear, California, is a popular ski resort because it has such a variety of ski runs to choose from.

4. My grandmother's kitchen was one of the few places where I always felt safe and welcome.

5. The artificial decorations and dreary atmosphere were not at all what I had expected when I decided to visit the Excalibur casino in Las Vegas.

Prewriting Application: Evaluating Topic Sentences

Write "No" before each sentence that would not make a good topic sentence and "Yes" before each sentence that would make a good one. Using ideas of your own, rewrite the unacceptable topic sentences into topic sentences that might work.

_____ 1. Last year I spent three days hiking through Yellowstone National Park.

_____

_____

_____ 2. Balboa Island, near Newport Beach, California, is clearly a place designed for the rich and famous.

_____

_____

_____ 3. Whenever I look around at my bedroom, I become thoroughly depressed.

_____

_____

_____ 4. One of my favorite places to visit is the beach.

_____

_____

_____ 5. The waiting area in Dr. Larson's dentist's office is one of the most welcoming, relaxing places that I have ever seen.

_____

_____

_____ 6. Last December 30, we had the opportunity to visit Stone Mountain in Atlanta, Georgia.

_____

_____

_____ 7. My paragraph will describe the Hearst Castle in San Simeon, California.

_____

_____

_____ 8. The undeveloped canyon behind my house is one place where I can feel free and unrestricted.

_____

_____

_____ 9. The most unusual restroom that I have ever seen was the one at the Bahia de Los Angeles Research Station in Baja California, Mexico.

_____

_____

_____ 10. The deep South is one of the most memorable places that I have ever seen.

_____

_____

Prewriting Application: Talking to Others

Before you write your first draft, form groups of two, three, or four people and describe the place that you have decided to write about. Tell the members of your group what central point you are trying to emphasize, and then describe as many details as you can to make that point. As you tell others about the place you have chosen, describe all of the sights, sounds, and smells that contributed to your overall impression of the place. As you listen to the places described by others and as you describe your own place, consider these questions:

1. Where exactly is this place? Has its location been clearly identified? What time of year is it? What time of day? What is the weather like?

2. Can you visualize the place? What physical features are in the area—trees? buildings? furniture? cars? other people? What colors should be included?

3. How did you feel about this place? Is the central point or impression of the place clear?

4. Were there sounds, smells, or physical sensations that should be included in the description of the place?

5. What parts of the scene should be described in more detail?

Organizing Descriptive Details

Writers of descriptive papers use **spatial order** to organize supporting details. Unlike **chronological order,** which describes events as they occur in time, **spatial order** presents details according to their physical placement or characteristics. For example, you might describe the larger, more obvious details of a scene first and then move to the smaller, less obvious details. Or you might mention the details closer to you first and then move to those farther away. Other spatial organizations might involve describing details from left to right or top to bottom or describing the most dominant sense impression first, such as a strong smell, and then moving to other sense impressions.

Descriptions of places often combine spatial and chronological order, especially if you are moving as you describe the place. In such a situation, you might describe what you encounter first in time, then what you encounter second, and so on. If you take such an approach, remember that the purpose of this assignment is to describe the place itself, not to describe what you are doing there.

Prewriting Application: Organizing Supporting Details

Read Exercises 1C, page 88, and 2C, page 103. Examine the details in each paragraph and explain why they are organized as they are.

Writing the Paragraph

Once you have a preliminary topic sentence and a list of related details, it is time to write the first draft of your paragraph. Open your paragraph with your topic sentence and then write out the details that illustrate the central point of your topic sentence. Do <u>not</u> worry about writing a "perfect" first draft. You will have the chance to improve the draft when you revise it.

Rewriting and Improving the Paragraph

1. When you have completed the first draft, read it over to see if your preliminary topic sentence accurately states the central point of your paper. If you can improve the topic sentence, do so now.

2. As you read over your draft, see if you can add still more descriptive details that relate to your central point. Add those that come to mind.

3. Check the words and phrases you have used in your first draft. You will find that many of them can be more descriptive if you make them more **specific** and **concrete**.

Adding Specific and Concrete Details

A **specific** detail is limited in the number of things to which it can refer. For example, the word *poodle* is more specific than the word *dog,* and the word *elm* is more specific than *tree.* A **concrete** detail appeals to one of the five senses. It helps a reader to **see, hear, smell, taste,** or **feel** what you describe. For instance, rather than writing that your grandmother's kitchen smelled "wonderful," you might write that it was always "filled with the aromas of freshly baked bread and my grandfather's cigar smoke."

Unfortunately, most writers—even most professional writers—do not write specific and concrete details naturally. You need to *add* these details to your draft. You do so by reading back through what you have written and changing words from general to specific and from abstract to concrete. As you read, consider these areas.

- Specificity: Which words could be made more specific? Use precise names of people, places, things, emotions, and actions wherever you can.

- Sight: What sights can be included? Consider color, shapes, and sizes.

- Sound: What sounds should be added? Were there loud noises; subtle background sounds; peaceful, relaxing sounds; piercing, metallic, or unpleasant sounds?

- Smell: Were any smells present? Were you in a kitchen, near the ocean, passing by a newly oiled street? Were you at a produce stand or in a gymnasium? Many places have distinctive smells that you should include.

- Taste: Taste might be involved even if you did not eat or drink anything. A strong smell often evokes a taste sensation too. A dusty field as well as dry desert might also elicit a taste reaction.

- Touch: Consider the less obvious touch sensations as well as obvious ones involving pain or pleasure. Were you standing in sand or on hot pavement? Did you touch anything with your hands? Was there a breeze? Was it raining? Did your collar blow up against your face? All of these might involve touch sensations.

Not all senses need to be included, especially if they don't emphasize your central point, but most first drafts have too few specific and concrete details rather than too many.

Rewriting Application: Adding Specific and Concrete Details

In each of the following sentences, identify which words could be made more specific or concrete. Then rewrite the sentence to replace and improve the general, abstract words.

 EXAMPLE   The house was run down.

The three-bedroom tract house on the corner of Elm and Vine had deteriorated into a ruin of broken windows, peeling paint, and splintered, termite-infested walls.

1. The woman walked through the entrance.

_____

_____

_____

2. The food tasted terrible.

_____

_____

_____

3. The man looked angry.

_____

_____

_____

4. Her bedroom walls were colorful.

_____

_____

_____

5. The trees along the driveway smelled wonderful.

_____

_____

_____

Rewriting Application: Responding to Writing

Read the following description of Breaks Interstate Park. Then respond to the questions following it.

Breaks Interstate Park

There is no more beautiful place in the spring than the Breaks Interstate Park. Last year I spent part of the spring with my father and my grandmother in the Smokey Mountains of Virginia. Because the Smokey Mountains are a very remote area, there was not much to do during my vacation until some of my cousins wanted to go to a place called "The Breaks." We drove into the mountains for about an hour. When we got to the entrance, the first thing I noticed was the incredible number of flowers. There were flowers on the ground, flowers in the trees and on the rocks, and there were some on the log cabins and picnic tables. We pulled off the road to one of the campsites and got out of the car. The smell of spring was everywhere. We could smell honeysuckle, strawberry, and the heady scent of wild flowers. All we could hear were bees working the blossoms and birds bathing in the springs trickling out of the mountainside. My cousin Charon came up to me and told me to follow her. We went across the road and down a winding dirt path, past a sign that said "Twin Towers Overlook." I then beheld one of the most striking and magnificent views I have ever seen in my life. I was on an overlook, looking down at a gorge where the river flowing through it makes a horseshoe-shaped bend and the mountains on the other side look like twin towers. I ran back to the car to get my camera. While on my way back, I slipped on a moss-covered rock and skinned my knee. When I got back to the overlook, I sat down on some strawberry vines, ate wild strawberries, and took pictures. I finally ran out of film and deliciously sweet strawberries, not to mention daylight. We packed it up and went back home; however, I will never forget about the Breaks Interstate Park in the springtime.

1. Identify the topic sentence. State its topic and central idea. Is it an effective topic sentence? Why or why not?

2. Identify specific and concrete details. What words do you find particularly effective?

3. Which of the five senses does the writer employ in her description? Identify each of them in the paragraph.

4. What details would you make still more specific or concrete? Would you omit any details because they do not support the central point of the paragraph?

5. What sentences would you combine because they contain related ideas?

Adding Subordinate Clauses

In Chapter Two you have studied main and subordinate clauses and the four sentence types: simple, compound, complex, and compound-complex. As you rewrite papers, look for opportunities to change main clauses to subordinate clauses.

Rewriting Application: Adding Subordinate Clauses

A. Combine the following sentences by changing some of them to subordinate clauses.

1. a. We pulled off the road to one of the campsites and got out of the car.
    b. The smell of spring was everywhere.

2. a. My cousin Charon came up to me and told me to follow her.
    b. We went across the road and down a winding dirt path, past a sign that said "Twin Towers Overlook."
    c. I then beheld one of the most striking and magnificent views I have ever seen in my life.

3. a. Bright, warm sunlight filters through eucalyptus trees and presses against my shoulders.
    b. An old man greets me with a warm smile.
    c. The old man is raking leaves in the middle of the yard.

4. a. My grandfather sits on an old rust-covered metal stool.
    b. The stool used to be painted yellow.
    c. He tells me stories about my father's boyhood.

5. a. I have visited my grandparents' house many times during my childhood.
    b. I have not fully appreciated it until recently.

B. Revise each of the following sentences by changing one of the main clauses to a subordinate clause.

1. I looked to the right, and I could see an astonishingly high water slide.

2. I visited the cemetery in Escondido, California, to attend the funeral of my friend Jake McDonnell, for he had died in a head-on motorcyle accident.

3. The brevity of life was impressed on me, and I read the short accounts of unknown people's lives on the hundreds of tombstones.

4. Each weekend our family visited the Waimanalo Beach Park, and it is surrounded by the evergreen mountain range that towers over the valley below.

5. We took off our jackets and sweaters, but we still felt uncomfortably warm.

C. Now examine your own draft. Identify any main clauses that would work better as subordinate clauses. Consider changing some of your compound sentences to complex sentences. If you have a series of short sentences, combine them by changing some of the short main clauses to subordinate clauses.

Proofreading

When you are finished, proofread your paper. Check the spelling of words you are uncertain about. Examine each sentence closely to be sure it is not a **fragment, comma splice,** or **fused sentence.** If it is, repair the error using the techniques you have studied in this chapter. Once you have a draft you are satisfied with, prepare a clean final draft, following the format your instructor has asked for.

Chapter Two Practice Test

I. Review of Chapter One

A. In the following sentences, identify the underlined words by writing one of the following abbreviations above the words: noun (N), pronoun (Pro), verb (V), adjective (Adj), adverb (Adv), conjunction (Conj), or preposition (Prep).

1. The court <u>ordered</u> the city to remove the cross from <u>public</u> land.

2. The squirrel <u>in</u> the attic was <u>certainly</u> becoming a pest.

3. Hortense showed Gomer the black-eyed <u>peas</u> and hog jowls that she <u>was</u> cooking.

4. The <u>idea</u> of descending into Hades was scary to our leader, <u>but</u> we had gone too far to turn around.

5. The hunters fell <u>into</u> the hidden creek while <u>they</u> were chasing three deer.

6. <u>Everyone</u> gasped when the statue of Venus was discovered <u>under</u> the temple.

7. Dante could <u>not</u> believe Virgil was down there, <u>nor</u> did he believe Virgil could never leave.

8. Bill frowned when he <u>noticed</u> half a <u>worm</u> in the apple he was eating.

9. Assuncion <u>always</u> kept alive her dream of becoming a <u>successful</u> church architect.

10. Herman Munster was disappointed to hear that his <u>only</u> son had called <u>him</u> a "bolthead."

B. For the following sentences, underline all subjects once and all complete verbs twice. Place parentheses around all prepositional phrases.

11. Does anyone want to tour the new museum?

12. The king divided the kingdom among his daughters.

13. The dog with three heads stood before the castle.

14. Before Gettysburg, Lee thought that his army was invincible.

15. There were three football games on television, but only one of them interested Dan.

16. After he saw the ship and crew, Billy should have feared for his life.

17. Some of the pastries had disappeared, but only Diane missed them.

continued

18. Captain Vere and the first mate signaled to the sailors and told them to climb

onto the ship.

19. Chelsea's candy from Halloween is almost gone because her father keeps eating it.

20. Chayo recognized the man who handed her the pamphlet for Greenpeace.

II. Chapter Two

A. Underline the subordinate clauses and identify the type of clause (adjective or adverb) in the space provided.

21. The sculpture that you see above the steps is the Nike of Samothrace. _____

22. Because he wanted a heart so badly, the Tin Woodman was willing

to compromise. _____

23. Homer hoped to visit the bowling alley where he had proposed to Hortense. _____

24. Anne would lose her head if she did not have a good excuse for the king. _____

25. Unless the helicopter arrives soon, it will be too dark to land. _____

B. To the main clauses below, add the types of subordinate clauses indicated in parentheses. Add your clause at any place in the sentence that is appropriate.

26. (adverb clause) Kermit wanted to visit the museum.

_____

_____

27. (adjective clause) The emperor always placed his hand inside his coat.

_____

_____

continued

28. (adjective clause) Brent crossed the street and headed for the basketball court.

_____

_____

29. (adverb clause) Deborah enjoys reading a good novel.

_____

_____

30. (adverb clause) Diem decided to marry Sean anyway.

_____

_____

C. In the spaces provided, identify the following sentences as simple, compound, complex, or compound-complex.

31. If Rocco finds an unusual comic book, he will buy it.   _____

32. The surf was dangerously rough; however, Bruce was determined to finish his swim.   _____

33. Before the ice cream store with the crazy picture of an angel talking to Humphrey Bogart stood Steve with just enough money for a triple decker.   _____

34. Jack promised to wait until Susan got home to watch the movie, but soon he became impatient.   _____

35. It was dark when he left.   _____

D. Compose sentences of your own according to the instructions.

36. Write a simple sentence that contains two prepositional phrases.

_____

_____

continued

37. Write a compound sentence. Use a coordinating conjunction and appropriate punctuation to join the clauses.

_____

_____

38. Write a compound sentence. Use a transitional word or phrase and appropriate punctuation to join the clauses.

_____

_____

39. Write a complex sentence. Use *after* as the subordinator.

_____

_____

40. Write a compound-complex sentence. Use a subordinator *when*.

_____

_____

E. Identify each of the following sentences as correct (C), fused (F), comma splice (CS), or fragment (Frag). Then correct any errors by using the methods discussed in Chapter Two.

_____41. When Angelo ordered a bowl of rattlesnake soup.

_____

_____

_____42. Davy put on his coonskin hat, then he went looking for bears.

_____

_____

continued

_____**43.** Answer the question.

_____

_____

_____**44.** Suzie, standing behind the desk with a smile on her face.

_____

_____

_____**45.** Lindbergh stared at his plane it was named after a famous city.

_____

_____

_____**46.** After the meeting was over, Charlie treated us to kidney pie, it was delicious.

_____

_____

_____**47.** Even though the groundhog did not see its own shadow.

_____

_____

_____**48.** The Honda had been getting very bad gas mileage, however, the dealership could find nothing wrong.

_____

_____

continued

_____**49.** By wearing a hat with candles on it, Goya was able to paint at night.

_____

_____

_____**50.** The doctor could not understand why Homer's tongue was swollen, there-
fore, she consulted a linguologist.

_____

_____

Improving Sentence Patterns

Now you have a fundamental knowledge of the sentence patterns of English. Although sentences may fall into four broad categories according to the number and types of clauses, the ways to express any thought in a sentence are almost infinitely variable.

You may make a sentence short and to the point:

> Eniko sold her netsuke collection.

Or, through the addition of modifying words, phrases, and additional clauses, you can expand it.

> After much soul searching and after seeking the advice of her mother, her brother, and her best friend, Eniko, a person who always carefully considered important decisions, sold her netsuke collection, which was worth several thousand dollars, but she kept one special carving of a frog and a sacred bird.

The essential idea—*Eniko sold her netsuke collection*—is the same for both sentences. Sometimes you will want to be short and to the point, and a five-word sentence will serve your purpose best. But sometimes you will want to be more explanatory, and then you may need more words.

The difference between the five words of the first sentence and the fifty words of the second one is the addition of modifying words, phrases, and clauses. These modifiers can help you write more clearly and vividly. The second sentence, though admittedly a bit overdone, tells a story, paints a picture. Modifying words, phrases, and clauses can be overused and should never be substituted for strong verbs and nouns, but most writers err in the opposite direction, leaving their writing limp and colorless.

You need to follow certain guidelines when you use the various modifying phrases and clauses. First we will discuss the most effective ways to use phrases and clauses in your sentences, and then we will discuss how to avoid the typical errors that writers make in using these devices. We hope that by the end you will have gained an appreciation of the wonderful flexibility of the English sentence and that you will have acquired more tools for making your own writing more interesting and effective.

SECTION

one

Modifying with Participial and Infinitive Phrases

You can use **participial and infinitive phrases** as modifiers in your sentences. These phrases can help you streamline your sentences and achieve sentence variety. In most cases, participial and infinitive phrases take the place of subordinate clauses.

 EXAMPLES

(subordinate clause)   **As he drove to work,** Harry saw a black cat run in front of his car.

(participial phrase)   **Driving to work,** Harry saw a black cat run in front of his car.

As you already know, **a clause is a word group that contains a subject and a verb. A phrase,** on the other hand, **is a word group that does not contain a subject and a verb.** You are already aware of prepositional phrases. Other phrases, generally called verbal phrases, include **present participial phrases, past participial phrases,** and **infinitive phrases.**

Present Participial Phrases

As we mentioned in Chapter One, the present participle is a verbal. It is the form of the verb that ends in "ing" (*running, typing, looking*). Without a helping verb it cannot be used as the verb of a sentence. Instead, it is used as an adjective. For example, you can use it as a one-word adjective.

 EXAMPLE

The **running** man stumbled as he rounded the corner.

In this sentence, the present participle *running* modifies the noun *man*.

You can also use the present participle as part of a phrase that functions as an adjective. Such a phrase is called a **participial phrase,** and it is often used to begin sentences.

 EXAMPLE

Rounding the corner, the running man stumbled.

In this sentence, the present participial phrase *Rounding the corner* is an adjective phrase modifying the noun *man*. The present participle is *Rounding*.

The present participial phrase, then, is an adjective phrase consisting of the present participle plus any other words attached to it. When a present participial phrase introduces a sentence, it is always followed by a comma.

Past Participial Phrases

The past participle is the form of the verb that you use with the helping verbs *have, has,* or *had* (*have eaten, has defeated, had bought*). Like the present participle, the past participle is a verbal when used without a helping verb. And, like the present participle, it is used as an adjective.

You can use a past participle as a single-word adjective.

 EXAMPLE The **defeated** army retreated into the mountains.

In this sentence, the past participle *defeated* modifies the noun *army.*

Or you can use the past participle as part of a past participial phrase.

 EXAMPLE **Pursued by the enemy,** the army retreated into the mountains.

In this sentence, the past participial phrase *Pursued by the enemy* modifies the noun *army.* Notice that it is followed by a comma. As with the present participial phrase, when the past participial phrase introduces a sentence, you should place a comma after it.

Participial phrases make good introductions to sentences, but you can use them anywhere. To avoid confusion, though, you should place them as closely as possible to the words they modify.

 EXAMPLES All of the students **submitting essays for the contest** used word processors.

The man **bitten by the rattlesnake** walked ten miles to the hospital.

The present participial phrase *submitting essays for the contest* modifies the noun *students.* The past participial phrase *bitten by the rattlesnake* modifies the noun *man.*

 PRACTICE Underline the participial phrases in the following sentences and circle the words they modify.

1. Put into the game in the last ten minutes, Zoila scored twelve points for her team.

2. The server apologized to the customers sitting by the front door.

3. Swimming silently under the ship, Nessie avoided the monster hunters.

4. Standing alone on the beach, Robinson stared at the footprint in the sand.

5. Henrietta will not watch any movies produced by that studio.

6. The Spam hidden under Homer's bed had started to mold.

7. The old grouch yelled at the children selling Girl Scout cookies in his

   neighborhood.

8. Angered by his rude response, Barb headed for his front door.

9. Walking past the lingerie counter, Byron brooded about his sore foot.

10. The coach, confused by the umpire's call, asked for a time out.

Infinitive Phrases

The infinitive is a verbal that you can use as a noun, an adjective, or an adverb. You form the infinitive by adding *to* to the present tense form of the verb (*to write, to run, to listen*).

You can use the infinitive by itself.

 EXAMPLE   **To fly,** you must first take lessons and get a license.

Or you can use the infinitive to form an infinitive phrase.

 EXAMPLE   To play the saxophone well, you must practice often.

Notice that the infinitive phrase consists of the infinitive plus any words attached to it. Like the two participial phrases, it is followed by a comma when it introduces a sentence. However, when you use the infinitive as a noun, it can act as the subject of a sentence. In this case, you do not use a comma.

 EXAMPLE   **To be a good husband** was Clint's ambition.

The infinitive phrase *To be a good husband* is the subject of the verb *was*.

Generally, like the two participial phrases, the infinitive phrase can appear in a variety of places in a sentence.

 EXAMPLE   Carla's motives were hard **to understand at first.**

Here the infinitive phrase *to understand at first* acts as an adverb to modify the adjective *hard*.

 EXAMPLE   Eduardo liked having a sister **to talk to** even though she teased him constantly.

Here, the infinitive phrase *to talk to* acts as an adjective to modify the noun *sister*.

PRACTICE   Underline the modifying participial and infinitive phrases in the following sentences and circle the words they modify.

1. Mahdieh finally found a (pot) to hold her geraniums.

2. Sailing across the Pacific, Cameron and Peter wondered if their supplies would last.

3. Luckily, William Tell knew the correct way to aim a crossbow.

4. Bitten by a radioactive spider, Peter Parker dreamed about houseflies.

5. Ellen's obsessive desire to make money drove away many of her friends.

6. Jack traded his cow for some magic beans to plant in his garden.

7. Yelling loudly, the Rebels charged up the hill toward the Yankees.

8. Frustrated by the rainy weather, Sarah stayed home and watched television.

9. Ruben could not decide which flower to give to his wife.

10. Once the basketball game started, Brent completely forgot about his promise to arrive home early.

Section One Review

1. The **present participle** is a verbal that ends in "ing" and that is used as an adjective. (When the "ing" form is used as a noun, it is called a **gerund.**)

2. A **present participial phrase** consists of the present participle plus any words attached to it.

3. A comma follows a **present participial phrase** that introduces a sentence.

4. The **past participle** is the form of the verb used with the helping verbs *have*, *has*, and *had*.

5. The **past participle** is a verbal used as an adjective.

6. A **past participial phrase** consists of the past participle plus any words attached to it.

7. A comma follows a **past participial phrase** that introduces a sentence.

8. An **infinitive** is formed by adding *to* to the present tense of a verb.

9. The **infinitive** is a verbal that can be used as a noun, an adjective, or an adverb.

10. An **infinitive phrase** consists of the infinitive plus any words attached to it.

11. A comma follows an **infinitive phrase** that introduces a sentence and acts as a modifier.

Exercise 1A

Underline all participial and infinitive phrases. Circle the words that they modify. In the spaces, identify the phrase as present participle (Pres P), past participle (Past P), or infinitive (Inf).

Inf 1. In Roman times, the intersection of three roads was used as a (place) to stop and talk.

_____ 2. Sharing the events of the day, Roman travelers would rest for a few minutes.

_____ 3. Farmers, concerned about their crops, would discuss the weather or the land.

_____ 4. This kind of place was called a *trivium,* meaning a "three-road intersection."

_____ 5. Found in words like *triple, trinity,* and *tricycle, tri* means "three."

_____ 6. A common Spanish word to refer to a street or road is *via* (from the Latin *vium*).

_____ 7. "Trivial" conversation, referring to discussions of unimportant matters, really

means "three-road" conversation.

_____ 8. Placing their lost teeth under their pillows at night, children throughout the United

States wait eagerly for the tooth fairy.

_____ 9. The tooth fairy will take any tooth hidden by a child.

_____ 10. The tooth taken by the fairy is replaced with money or a gift.

_____ 11. The tooth fairy tradition might have originated with a desire to protect lost pieces

of the body.

_____ 12. Hiding teeth or nail clippings, the people of some ancient cultures believed that lost

body parts were linked to the owner.

_____ 13. The Pony Express, founded by three entrepreneurs in 1860, is a part of American

history.

_____ 14. Galloping across the frontier with mail in their saddlebags, the riders of the Pony

Express braved many dangers.

_____ 15. Unfortunately, the Pony Express was a financial disaster, costing its owners over

two hundred thousand dollars in nineteen months.

In the places indicated by ^, add your own participial or infinitive phrases to the following sentences. Use the verbs in parentheses. Be sure to place a comma after any phrase that introduces a sentence.

1. ^ Jalayne checked the tires, the oil level, the coolant, and the amount of gas in her car. (prepare)

   To prepare for her trip across the country, Jalayne checked the tires,

   the oil level, the coolant, and the amount of gas in her car.

2. Whenever Randy visits the orphanage, he takes extra clothing ^ . (give)

   _____

   _____

3. The man ^ lit one more cigarette and then moved on. (stand)

   _____

   _____

4. ^ Sisyphus decided to try one more time. (frustrate)

   _____

   _____

5. At the poetry reading, we were surprised to find Billy Collins and Richard Wilbur ^. (argue)

   _____

   _____

6. A fast-food restaurant is sometimes the best place ^. (get)

   _____

   _____

7. ^ Galileo wondered if the sun really did circle the earth. (stare)

   _____

   _____

Exercise 1B

continued

8. ^ Prufrock kept the bottoms of his trousers rolled. (walk)

_____

_____

9. The treasure ^ was discovered two hundred years later by a local surfer. (hide)

_____

_____

10. ^ Brent listened to his favorite oldies station. (drive)

_____

_____

11. The governor ^ promised that he would never raise taxes. (elect)

_____

_____

12. ^ The dwarfs headed down the hall toward Jack's office. (whistle)

_____

_____

13. The circus audience stared in disbelief at the baby elephant ^ . (fly)

_____

_____

14. ^ Avoid drinks that contain caffeine or desserts that are full of sugar. (sleep)

_____

_____

Exercise 1B

continued

15. The clothing and food ^ were distributed to the homeless. (donate)

_____

_____

Exercise 1C

Underline all infinitive and participial phrases and circle the words that they modify.

1. Jackie Robinson, the first (African-American) to play baseball in the major leagues, has been honored in many cities across the United States and Canada. 2. For instance, a statue honoring Jackie stands outside Olympic Stadium in Montreal, Quebec, where Jackie played for a Dodger farm club. 3. In addition, Daytona, Florida, is home to Robinson Stadium, named after this great player. 4. Jersey City, New Jersey, has also honored Robinson, dedicating a bronze plaque to him at Society Hill. 5. Of course, New York, home of the Brooklyn Dodgers, showed its appreciation to Jackie when it made the decision to change the name of Interboro Parkway to Jackie Robinson Parkway. 6. In Los Angeles, UCLA has honored Jackie, who was the first UCLA athlete to star in four sports. 7. UCLA baseball teams now play at Jackie Robinson Stadium, named after the legendary player. 8. Erected at the stadium in 1985, a statue of Robinson was generously paid for by Jackie's brother, Mack Robinson. 9. Pasadena, California, is another city showing its appreciation for Jackie's accomplishments. 10. Moving to the city when they were young, Jackie and Mack grew up in Pasadena. 11. On New Year's Day, 1997, the grateful city honored Robinson with a beautiful Rose Parade float donated by the Simon Wiesenthal Center. 12. Naming a youth center, a post office, a park, and a baseball field after Jackie, Pasadena further showed its respect for the famous baseball player. 13. Lately, the school board of Grady County, Georgia, which is near Jackie's birthplace, unanimously passed a motion to change the name of the Cairo High School baseball field to Jackie Robinson Field. 14. Featuring a granite marker and bronze plaque, the field is dedicated to Jackie. 15. Jackie Robinson, recognized by all as a brave man and gifted player, richly deserves all of these honors.

SECTION

two

Modifying with Adjective Clauses and Appositives

Adjective Clauses

We discussed adjective clauses earlier in a section on subordinate clauses. An adjective clause is an important option when you want to modify a noun or pronoun in a sentence. Using an adjective clause instead of single-word adjectives or modifying phrases tends to place more emphasis on what you are saying about the noun or pronoun you are modifying. Consider the following sentences, for instance.

 EXAMPLES

(adjective)   My **insensitive** neighbor plays his trombone all night long.

(adjective clause) My neighbor, **who is insensitive,** plays his trombone all night long.

Using the adjective clause *who is insensitive* places more importance on the neighbor's insensitivity. Sometimes you need only single-word modifiers, but it is good to be aware of all of your choices for modifying words.

Here is a brief review of adjective clauses.

1. Adjective clauses follow the noun or pronoun they modify.

2. Adjective clauses begin with the relative pronouns *who, whom, whose, which, that* (and sometimes *when* or *where*).

 EXAMPLES

We returned the money to the *person* **who had lost it.** (*Who* introduces an adjective clause that modifies the noun *person.*)

I remember the *time* **when Homer and Hortense were married at the Spam factory.** (*When* introduces an adjective clause that modifies the noun *time.*)

Sidney decided to move to *Colorado,* **where his family used to spend summer vacations.** (*Where* introduces an adjective clause that modifies the noun *Colorado.*)

3. If the adjective clause provides information that is necessary to identify the noun or pronoun, do not set it off with commas.

 EXAMPLE

The man **who was sitting next to my uncle at the banquet** is a famous sportswriter.

The information in this adjective clause is necessary to identify which man at the banquet is the famous sportswriter.

4. If the adjective clause provides information that is merely descriptive and is not necessary to identify the noun or pronoun, then set the clause off with commas.

 EXAMPLE   Merlin Olsen, **who was an all-pro football player,** became a famous sportscaster.

Merlin Olsen's name already identifies him, so the adjective clause contains added but unnecessary information. Therefore, you need the commas.

We will discuss the rules for the use of commas with adjective clauses again in Chapter Five.

 PRACTICE   Underline all adjective clauses and circle the words they modify. For further practice, try to determine which clauses need commas and add them where necessary.

1. The (woman) who developed the new microchip was from Vietnam.

2. *The Tunnel* which was written by William Gass was a labor of thirty years.

3. Everybody who attended last night's baseball game received a free yo-yo.

4. Zen Buddhism which is an ancient religion is practiced by many people who live in the United States.

5. Maurice Ravel who was a famous French composer wrote *Bolero* which became one of the most popular concert pieces of the twentieth century.

6. The frustrated contestant could not name the planet that was third from the sun.

7. Toots was looking for a place where he could play his tuba in peace.

8. The women who were arguing about the baby decided to ask Solomon for advice.

9. The train that left the station at noon had to stop for a cow that was standing on the railroad tracks.

10. Wolf Moonglow who was an exceptionally hirsute man was telling us about the time when he first began to study lycanthropy.

Appositives

Appositives give you another option for adding descriptive detail. An **appositive** is a noun or pronoun, along with any modifiers, that **renames** another noun or pronoun. The appositive almost always follows the word it refers to, and it is usually set off with commas.

Note how the following two sentences can be combined not only by adding an adjective clause but also by adding an appositive:

My neighbor plays the trombone all night long.

He is an insensitive man.

EXAMPLES   (adjective clause)   My neighbor, **who is insensitive,** plays his trombone all night long.

(appositive)   My neighbor, **an insensitive man,** plays his trombone all night long.

In the appositive, the noun *man* renames the noun *neighbor.*

EXAMPLES   The wedding <u>ring</u>, **a <u>symbol</u>** of eternal love, dates back to 2800 B.C. in Egypt. (The noun *symbol* renames the noun *ring.*)

The huge <u>trout</u>, **the <u>one</u> still in the river,** would have made an impressive trophy on the wall of Harold's den. (The pronoun *one* renames the noun *trout.*)

The <u>honeymoon</u>, **a popular marriage <u>custom</u>,** comes from an ancient Northern European practice of stealing brides. (The noun *custom* renames the noun *honeymoon.*)

PRACTICE   Underline the appositives and circle the nouns or pronouns that the appositives rename.

1. The cell (phone,) <u>a product of modern technology,</u> is an indispensable tool of many businesses.

2. Gothic cathedrals are often ornamented with gargoyles, grotesque sculptures of evil spirits.

3. Homer and Hortense were asked to endorse Spam Lite, a new product.

4. Harry Houdini, a famous American escape artist and magician, spent many years exposing fraudulent mediums and mind readers.

5. The one-armed man, Richard Kimble's elusive enemy, was recently seen playing the slot machines in Las Vegas.

6. Patrick Stewart, the former Captain Picard of the *U.S.S. Enterprise,* has also starred as Captain Ahab of the *Pequod.*

7. Christopher picked up his favorite instrument, a handcrafted classical guitar, and began to play.

8. Thomas had always wanted to visit Utopia, a city not found on most maps.

9. Diamonda, a jeweler from Switzerland, collects antique clocks.

10. Bill Liscomb was a pioneer in hang gliding, a popular sport among the Peter Pan crowd.

 PRACTICE   Add an appositive or an adjective clause to each of the following sentences. Use commas when they are needed.

1. The sports car was parked near the school.

   The sports car that had been stolen last week was

   parked near the school.

2. Amelia Earhart vanished while flying over the Pacific Ocean.

   _____

   _____

3. Professor Emerson asked me to write a report on Edgar Allan Poe.

   _____

   _____

4. Wile E. Coyote carefully constructed the trap.

   _____

   _____

5. An angry old man barged into the office and headed toward the dentist.

_____

_____

6. The pilot flew fearlessly into the Bermuda Triangle.

_____

_____

7. Buffy was honored when Count Dracula invited her to dinner.

_____

_____

8. The librarian hopped into his car and drove to his fishing spot.

_____

_____

9. Homer smiled in delight as Hortense brought out his favorite dessert.

_____

_____

10. Mount Vesuvius still smolders over the ruins of Pompeii.

_____

_____

Section Two Review

1. **Adjective clauses** modify nouns and pronouns.

2. **Adjective clauses** follow the nouns or pronouns they modify.

3. **Adjective clauses** begin with *who, whom, whose, which, that* (and sometimes *when* or *where*).

4. **Adjective clauses** that contain information necessary to identify the words they modify are not set off with commas.

5. **Adjective clauses** that do not contain information necessary to identify the words they modify are set off with commas.

6. **Appositives** are words or word groups containing a noun or pronoun that renames another noun or pronoun in a sentence.

7. **Appositives** usually follow the nouns or pronouns they rename.

8. **Appositives** are usually set off with commas.

Exercise 2A

Underline all adjective clauses and appositives. Circle the words they modify or rename. Indicate whether the modifier is an appositive (AP) or an adjective clause (Adj). Add commas where necessary.

Adj   **1.** The body of (Abraham Lincoln) who was assassinated in 1865 was almost stolen from its grave in 1876.

_____   **2.** Big Jim Kenealy the leader of an Illinois counterfeiting gang had recently been put out of business by the U.S. Secret Service.

_____   **3.** Secret Service agents had arrested key members of his gang as well as the engraver who did Kenealy's most important work.

_____   **4.** Kenealy developed a plan that would force the government to release his men.

_____   **5.** He decided to kidnap Lincoln's body which was buried two miles outside of Springfield, Illinois.

_____   **6.** After his death, Mary Todd Lincoln had taken her husband's body to Oak Ridge Cemetery where he was buried in an unguarded grave.

_____   **7.** Kenealy who knew there was no Illinois law against stealing a body considered his plan foolproof.

_____   **8.** However, Kenealy made one blunder a very serious mistake.

_____   **9.** To steal the body, he recruited a helper an undercover agent of the Secret Service.

_____ **10.** He decided upon November 7 the night after the national elections as the best time to dig up Lincoln's body.

_____ **11.** He planned to use the excitement that accompanies all elections to cover his activities.

_____ **12.** On November 8 his arrest was reported in the *Chicago Tribune* which ran the full story of his plot.

Exercise 2A

_____ **13.** Robert Todd Lincoln the President's oldest son hired attorneys to prosecute Jim Kenealy.

_____ **14.** The only crime that they were able to charge him with was conspiracy to steal a coffin.

_____ **15.** Kenealy who almost succeeded in stealing the body of President Lincoln received a sentence of one year in the state penitentiary.

A. Add adjective clauses of your own to each of the sentences below. Make sure you use commas where necessary.

1. Chris likes to work on his old motorcycle.

   Chris likes to work on his old motorcycle, which he

   purchased last year from his brother.

2. A briefcase has disappeared from my office.

   _____

   _____

3. Pocahontas did not marry Captain John Smith of the Jamestown colony.

   _____

   _____

4. Next Saturday, Carlos will drive to Tupelo, Mississippi.

   _____

   _____

5. The eagle flew over the lake looking for fish for its mate.

   _____

   _____

6. Lake Tahoe is famous for the clarity of its water.

   _____

   _____

7. A man stood in the middle of the freeway and held up a sign.

   _____

   _____

8. After meeting his sons, Willy Loman planted seeds.

   _____

   _____

Exercise 2B

continued

B. Add appositives of your own to the sentences below. Make sure you use commas where necessary.

9. The pilot landed the burning airplane in a muddy field.

The pilot, an eighty-five-year-old grandmother, landed the

burning airplane in a muddy field.

10. The sedan had been parked in front of the store since Friday.

_____

_____

11. The musician smiled when she looked at her new instrument.

_____

_____

12. Lex Luthor wondered why he had never even met Batman.

_____

_____

13. This evening Carlton plans to stay at home and watch his favorite television show.

_____

_____

14. The biologist developed a plan to clone an important bug.

_____

_____

15. The tree toppled onto the nearby building and nearly injured a child.

_____

_____

Underline all adjective clauses and circle the words they modify. Underline all appositives and circle the words they rename. Add commas where necessary.

1. Many English-speaking people are surprised when they discover the number of everyday (words) that are drawn from different mythologies. **2.** For example, the names of several of our weekdays—Tuesday, Wednesday, Thursday, and Friday—derive from Norse mythology. **3.** Tuesday and Thursday refer to Tiu the Norse god of war and Thor the Norse god of thunder. **4.** Wednesday refers to Woden who was the king of the Norse gods and Friday refers to Frigga the Norse goddess of love. **5.** Other common words are derived from Greek mythology. **6.** For instance, the word *tantalize* refers to Tantalus who was a king condemned to Hades as a punishment for his crimes. **7.** In Hades he was forced to stand below fruit that was just beyond his reach and in water that he could not drink. **8.** Another common Greek word in our language is *atlas* which refers to a map of the world. **9.** As a mythological figure, Atlas was a Titan who was condemned to support the heavens on his shoulders. **10.** Finally, Roman mythology which in many ways parallels Greek mythology is another source of many English words. **11.** For example, the month of January is named after Janus the Roman god with two faces. **12.** Janus whose two faces allowed him to watch two directions at once was the Roman god of doorways. **13.** June another of the many months that refer to Roman mythology is named after Juno the goddess of marriage and childbirth. **14.** These examples are just a few of the hundreds of English words that reflect the many mythologies of the world.

SECTION

three

Misplaced and Dangling Modifiers

In Chapter Two, when you combined clauses to form various sentence types, you learned that joining clauses improperly can lead to comma splices and fused sentences. As you can probably guess, adding modifiers to sentences leads to an entirely new set of problems. In some cases, these problems are a bit more complicated than those caused by comma splices and fused sentences, but with a little practice, you should have no trouble at all handling them.

Misplaced Modifiers

Misplaced modifiers are exactly what their name says they are—modifiers that have been "misplaced" within a sentence. But how is a modifier "misplaced"? The answer is simple. If you remember that a modifier is nearly always placed just before or just after the word it modifies, then a misplaced modifier must be one that has been mistakenly placed so that it causes a reader to be confused about what it modifies. Consider the following sentence, for example:

 EXAMPLE

Albert said **quietly** to move away from the snake.

Does the modifier *quietly* tell us how Albert said what he said, or does it tell us how we should move away from the snake? Changing the placement of the modifier will clarify the meaning.

 EXAMPLES

Albert **quietly** said to move away from the snake. (Here, the word modifies the verb *said*.)

Albert said to move **quietly** away from the snake. (Here the word modifies the verbal *to move*.)

Sometimes finding the correct placement of a modifier can be a bit difficult. Let's look at a few other typical examples.

Misplaced Words

Any modifier can be misplaced, but one particular group of modifiers causes quite a bit of trouble for many people. These words are *only, almost, just, merely,* and *nearly.* Consider, for example, the following sentences:

 EXAMPLES

By buying her new computer on sale, Floretta **almost** saved $100.

By buying her new computer on sale, Floretta saved **almost** $100.

As you can see, these sentences actually make two different statements. In the first sentence, *almost* modifies *saved*. If you *almost* saved something, you did *not* save it. In the second sentence, *almost* modifies *$100*. If you saved *almost* $100, you saved $85, $90, $95, or some other amount close to $100.

Which statement does the writer want to make—that Floretta did *not* save any money or that she *did* save an amount close to $100? Because the point was that she bought her computer on sale, the second sentence makes more sense.

To avoid confusion, be sure that you place all of your modifiers carefully.

EXAMPLES

(incorrect)	Her piano teacher encouraged her **often** to practice.
(correct)	Her piano teacher **often** encouraged her to practice.
(correct)	Her piano teacher encouraged her to practice **often.**
(incorrect)	Sophia **nearly** drank a gallon of coffee yesterday.
(correct)	Sophia drank **nearly** a gallon of coffee yesterday.

PRACTICE   Underline and correct any misplaced words in the following sentences. Some of the sentences may be correct.

1. During breakfast, Marshall ~~nearly~~ drank ^*nearly*^ a whole quart of orange juice.

2. Mr. Martinez asked me often to eat dinner with him.

3. After the battle, Stonewall wanted only to lie down and rest.

4. The commando who had been approaching silently signaled to me.

5. By the time he had almost eaten the entire case of Spam, Homer was feeling a little woozy.

6. Peyton Farquhar nearly crept to the edge of the trees before he saw the Union soldiers.

7. Although Charlene had many relatives in the area, she decided just to visit her aunt Mary.

8. The counselor advised Fred frequently to attend the meetings.

9. Vernon was disappointed to see that the menu only offered two side dishes.

10. Frodo almost slept twenty hours once he got rid of that stupid ring.

Misplaced Phrases and Clauses

The phrases and clauses that you studied earlier in this chapter are as easily misplaced as individual words. Phrases and clauses often follow the words they modify.

 EXAMPLES

(prepositional phrase)	The driver **in the blue sports car** struck an innocent pedestrian.
(present participial phrase)	The dog **chasing the car** barked at the bewildered driver.
(past participial phrase)	They gave the bicycle **donated by the shop** to the child.
(adjective clause)	Lucia gave the money **that she had borrowed from her sister** to the homeless woman.

In each of the above sentences, the modifier follows the word it modifies. Notice what happens when the modifier is misplaced so that it follows the wrong word.

 EXAMPLES

The driver struck an innocent pedestrian **in the blue sports car.**

The dog barked at the bewildered driver **chasing the car.**

They gave the bicycle to the child **donated by the shop.**

Lucia gave the money to the homeless woman **that she had borrowed from her sister.**

Obviously, misplaced phrases and clauses can create rather confusing and sometimes even humorous situations. Of course, not all phrases and clauses follow the words they modify. Many occur before the word they refer to.

 EXAMPLES

(past participial phrase)	**Angered by the umpire's poor call,** Dana threw her bat to the ground.
(present participial phrase)	**Hoping to win the debate,** Cyrus practiced three hours every day.

Regardless of whether the modifier appears before or after the word it modifies, the point is that you should place modifiers so that they clearly refer to a specific word in the sentence.

⊚ **PRACTICE**   Underline and correct any misplaced phrases and clauses in the following sentences. Some of the sentences may be correct.

1. The doctor set the leg of the dog ~~that had been broken in the accident.~~

   The doctor set the dog's leg that had been broken in

   the accident.

2. Vera gave a cake to her boyfriend soaked in rum.

   _____

   _____

3. Scratchy Wilson yelled at the stray dog dressed in his colorful Sunday shirt.

   _____

   _____

4. Consuelo introduced her daughter to the surgeon who had just entered second grade.

   _____

   _____

5. Sabrina gave the fruit to her mother-in-law full of worm holes.

   _____

   _____

6. Claude took his rifle to the gun shop that had a broken trigger.

   _____

   _____

7. Homer daydreamed about Hortense chewing on his plug of tobacco.

_____

_____

8. The two border collies growled at the teenagers with their tails wagging.

_____

_____

9. Anse Bundren drove the cart carrying the coffin of his dead wife complaining the entire way about his bad luck.

_____

_____

10. Amber showed her pond full of koi to her class, which had bright orange and black markings.

_____

_____

Dangling Modifiers

A **dangling modifier** is an introductory phrase (usually a verbal phrase) that lacks an appropriate word to modify. Since these modifiers usually represent some sort of action, they need a **doer** or **agent** of the action represented.

For example, in the following sentence the introductory participial phrase "dangles" because it is not followed by a noun or pronoun that could be the doer of the action represented by the phrase.

 EXAMPLE

Driving madly down the boulevard, the horse just missed being hit and killed.

The present participial phrase *Driving madly down the boulevard* should be followed by a noun or pronoun that could logically do the action of the phrase. Instead, it is followed by the noun *horse,* which is the subject of the sentence. Was the horse "driving"? Probably not. Therefore, the modifying phrase "dangles" because it has no noun or pronoun to which it can logically refer. Here are some more sentences with dangling modifiers.

 EXAMPLES

Nearly exhausted, the game was almost over.
(Was the *game* exhausted?)

After studying all night, the test wasn't so difficult after all.
(Did the *test* study all night?)

To impress his new girlfriend, Dominic's Chevrolet was polished.
(Did the *Chevrolet* want to impress Dominic's girlfriend?)

As you can see, you should check for dangling modifiers when you use introductory phrases.

PRACTICE

In the following sentences, indicate whether the modifying phrases are correctly used by writing either C for correct or D for dangling modifier in the spaces provided.

_____*D*_____ **1.** Hurrying to work, Ofelia's briefcase fell into a puddle.

_____ **2.** Hissing and rattling its tail, Howard turned and ran from the snake on the path.

_____ **3.** Frightened by the sound of the thunder, Rocco began to tremble.

_____ **4.** To get a good seat at the concert, arriving an hour ahead of time is a good idea.

_____ **5.** Wanting to get to the play on time, Sven's taco was eaten very quickly.

Correcting Dangling Modifiers

You can correct a dangling modifier in one of two ways.

1. Rewrite the sentence so that the introductory modifier logically refers to the subject of the sentence it introduces.

EXAMPLES

Nearly exhausted, **I** hoped the game was almost over.
(*I* was nearly exhausted.)

After studying all night, **Lucilla** passed the test easily.
(*Lucilla* studied all night.)

To impress his new girlfriend, **Dominic** polished his Chevrolet.
(*Dominic* wanted to impress his girlfriend.)

2. Change the introductory phrase to a clause.

EXAMPLES

Because I was nearly exhausted, I hoped the game was almost over.

After Lucilla had studied all night, she passed the test easily.

Dominic wanted to impress his girlfriend, so he polished his Chevrolet.

NOTE: Do not correct a dangling modifier by moving it to the end of the sentence or by adding a possessive noun or pronoun to a sentence. In either case, it will still "dangle" because it lacks a **doer** or **agent** that could perform the action of the modifier.

EXAMPLES

(incorrect)	**After searching for three weeks,** the lost watch was finally found. (There is no doer for *searching*.)
(still incorrect)	The lost watch was finally found **after searching for three weeks.** (There still is no logical doer.)
(still incorrect)	**After searching for three weeks,** Alfredo's lost watch was finally found. (Adding the possessive form *Alfredo's* does not add a doer of the action.)
(correct)	**After searching for three weeks,** Alfredo finally found his watch. (The noun *Alfredo* can logically perform the action—*searching*—of the modifying phrase.)
(correct)	**After Alfredo had searched for three weeks,** he finally found his watch. (Here again, the doer of the action is clear.)

PRACTICE

Underline and correct any dangling modifiers in the following sentences. Some of the sentences may be correct.

1. Delighted by the victory, the champagne and caviar were quickly

consumed.

Delighted by the victory, the coach and her team quickly

consumed the champagne and caviar.

2. Waiting for the game to begin, Michael's stomach was upset.

_____

_____

3. After telling the lie, Pinocchio's nose began to grow.

_____

_____

4. To make his ideas clear, Plato decided on the cave metaphor.

_____

_____

5. Running swiftly up the hill, the flag was raised by the warrior.

_____

_____

6. Attempting a comeback in the Daytona 500, Darryl's driver's license was revoked.

_____

_____

7. To join the choir, a sign-up sheet is on the wall.

_____

_____

8. Huffing and puffing as hard as he could, the house of bricks would not blow down.

_____

_____

9. Burned in the explosion, a bandage was placed on Curt's right hand by the paramedic.

_____

_____

10. To show remorse, Mary received flowers and an apology.

_____

_____

Section Three Review

1. A **misplaced modifier** is a modifier that has been mistakenly placed so that it causes the reader to be confused about what it modifies.

2. Commonly misplaced words are *only, almost, just, merely,* and *nearly.*

3. Place modifying phrases and clauses so that they clearly refer to a specific word in a sentence.

4. A **dangling modifier** is an introductory phrase (usually a verbal phrase) that lacks an appropriate word to modify. Since these modifiers usually represent some sort of action, they need a **doer** or **agent** of the action represented.

5. You can correct a dangling modifier in one of two ways.

   a. Rewrite the sentence so that the introductory modifier logically refers to the subject of the sentence it introduces.

   b. Change the introductory phrase to a clause.

6. Do not correct a dangling modifier by moving it to the end of the sentence or by adding a possessive noun or pronoun.

A. Underline and correct any misplaced words in the following sentences. Some sentences may be correct.

1. After <u>nearly</u> chasing Trigger for four hours, Roy was almost out of breath.

   After chasing Trigger for nearly four hours, Roy was almost out of breath.

2. Abdul only asked for one favor.

3. Gregor had planned to order steak and lobster for dinner, but instead he merely ordered a small salad.

4. The drill sergeant told the marines that they nearly had marched fifty miles that day.

5. Liza wanted a week to practice for the concert, but she just had one day.

B. Underline and correct any misplaced phrases or clauses in the following sentences. Some of the sentences may be correct.

6. As Elise sat down in the bus, she looked over at the man in the next seat <u>with the huge ears.</u>

   As Elise sat down in the bus, she looked over at the man with the huge ears in the next seat.

continued

7. My friend gave a rabbit to her new husband that had big floppy ears and a white tail.

_____

_____

8. Yolanda jumped into the river when she saw the bear screaming for help.

_____

_____

9. Rebecca watched the ducks as they paddled across the pond wondering if she should buy a new car.

_____

_____

10. While driving to the mall, I saw the thirteen-year-old girl with the minister who had run away from home.

_____

_____

C. Underline and correct any dangling modifiers in the following sentences. Some of the sentences may be correct.

11. <u>Angered by the booing of the fans,</u> bats and helmets came flying out of the Dodger dugout.

<u>Angered by the booing of the fans, the Dodger players</u>

<u>threw bats and helmets out of the dugout.</u>

_____

Exercise 3A

continued

12. After finishing the marathon, cool off slowly by walking around a bit and drinking lots
    of fluids.

    _____

13. Visiting Graceland for the tenth time, Homer's belief that Elvis was still alive grew
    even stronger.

    _____

    _____

14. To do well in this class, the assignments should be read.

    _____

    _____

15. Thinking about the message from the ghost, a plan was devised by Hamlet.

    _____

    _____

Underline and correct any misplaced or dangling modifiers in the following sentences. Some of the sentences may be correct.

1. <u>Before leaving for their cross-country trip,</u> the silver was placed in their safety deposit box.

   Before leaving for their cross-country trip, the McDonalds put their silver in their safety deposit box.

2. Marvin put down his board and introduced his friend that he had bought at the surf shop.

3. Homer only flosses his teeth if he knows he is going to see a dentist.

4. Looking at the territory from the top of the mountain, Lewis and Clark were worried.

5. Overwhelmed by the good news, Phoebe's eyes filled with tears.

6. One band member walked onto the stage and picked up his guitar with a skull and bones tattoo.

Exercise 3B

continued

7. After looking forward to the snowstorm, the skiers merely saw a few gray clouds.

_____

_____

8. When returning merchandise, bring the receipt to the store with you.

_____

_____

9. The Boy Scouts stopped to look at the snake hiking down the mountain.

_____

_____

10. Refusing to give up her seat, Rosa Parks's actions helped to start the civil rights movement of the 1950s and 1960s.

_____

_____

11. Ed gave the fishing rod to his granddaughter that he had bought at the bait shop.

_____

_____

12. To get to the cabin, you only need to follow a few simple directions.

_____

_____

13. After hiking for three days, my back began to ache.

_____

_____

continued

14. Because the hike in the desert was so long, Cody almost consumed a gallon of Gatorade.

_____

_____

15. The player bouncing the ball with a bald head looked at the stands.

_____

_____

Exercise 3C

Correct any dangling or misplaced modifiers in the following paragraph.

1. We almost put fifteen hundred miles on our SUV on our trip to the Four Corners area in the Southwest, but it was worth it because of the adventures we had. 2. Reading about this part of the country, books told us that Four Corners is where four states—Arizona, New Mexico, Utah, and Colorado—come together. 3. Driving through a rugged part of Colorado, our first adventure occurred when our battery gave out. 4. We had to walk for two hours before we were finally given a ride without any food or water. 5. While we were walking, I pointed out a mule deer to my friend with huge antlers. 6. Traveling around the Four Corners, our next adventure began when we had the chance to visit the ancient Native American ruins of the Anasazi. 7. We were able to drive to their remote cliff dwellings in our SUV, which had been abandoned hundreds of years ago. 8. The Hopis and Navajos believe the Anasazi are their ancestors who inhabit the Four Corners now. 9. Living successfully and peacefully in the Four Corners area, no one has a good explanation of why the Anasazi civilization suddenly abandoned its home. 10. Finally, visiting a local museum, hundreds of articles that had been found in the ruins were on display. 11. As I wandered through the museum, I almost felt as if I had stepped back in time. 12. A beautiful piece of pottery was shown to us by one of the museum employees that had been left when the Anasazi abandoned one of their villages. 13. This trip was a very special one, and I can now see why New Mexico is called "The Land of Enchantment," which is one of the four corners.

Sentence Practice: Using Participial and Infinitive Phrases, Appositives, and Adjective Clauses

In this chapter, you have become aware of the many choices you have when you want to modify words in your sentences. Your options range from single-word modifiers to modifying phrases to subordinate clauses. Let's explore some of the possibilities with the following sentence.

> The beautiful dalmatian looked hungrily at the thick steaks cooking on the grill and quietly begged the chef for a bite.

By changing various modifiers, you can express the sentence in several other ways. For instance, *The beautiful dalmatian,* with its single-word modifier *beautiful* describing *dalmatian,* could be changed into an appositive.

> The dog, **a beautiful dalmatian,** looked hungrily at the thick steaks cooking on the grill and quietly begged the chef for a bite.

This version tends to emphasize the beauty of the dog.

If you change the part of the sentence that contains the verb *looked* to a present participial phrase, you will get a different effect.

> **Looking hungrily at the thick steaks cooking on the grill,** the beautiful dalmatian quietly begged the chef for a bite.

This version places a bit more emphasis on the dog's hungry look.

Another alternative is to change the present participial phrase *cooking on the grill* to an adjective clause.

> The beautiful dalmatian looked hungrily at the thick steaks **that were cooking on the grill** and quietly begged the chef for a bite.

As you can see, the choices are many, and good writers often try several versions of a sentence before deciding on the one that best expresses their ideas. Experimenting with your sentences in this way is part of the fun and the challenge of writing.

The exercises in this section are designed to give you practice in using various types of modifiers when you compose your sentences.

Sentence Combining Exercises

Using your knowledge of modifying phrases and clauses, combine the following lists of sentences according to the directions. Avoid dangling and misplaced modifiers. Add commas where necessary.

 EXAMPLE   Combine these sentences into one sentence. Use sentence a as a present participial phrase. Use sentence b as an appositive.

   a. Elvira hoped to win the Los Angeles Marathon.
   b. Elvira is a world-class runner.
   c. Elvira practiced running on the sand dunes.
   d. The sand dunes were in the deserts of Southern California.

   Hoping to win the Los Angeles Marathon, Elvira, a world-class runner, practiced running on the sand dunes in the deserts of Southern California.

1. Combine the following sentences into one sentence. Use sentence a as an appositive. Use sentence c as an adjective clause.

   a. Charles Stilwell was the inventor of the brown paper grocery bag.
   b. Charles Stilwell called his invention "S.O.S."
   c. "S.O.S." stood for "self-opening sack."

   _____

   _____

   _____

2. Combine the following sentences into one sentence. Use sentence a as an appositive. Use sentence e as a past participial phrase.

   a. Felina was an inept burglar.
   b. Felina was arrested.
   c. She was stealing a cat suit.
   d. She was going to wear it to the police officers' ball.
   e. The ball was held each October 30.

   _____

   _____

   _____

Sentence Combining Exercises

continued

3. Combine these sentences into one sentence. Use sentence b as an adjective clause. Use sentence c as an appositive. Use sentence d as an adjective clause.

   a. The Barbie doll was named after Barbie Handler.
   b. Barbie Handler was the daughter of Ruth and Elliot Handler.
   c. Ruth and Elliot Handler were toy manufacturers.
   d. Ruth and Elliot Handler founded Mattel Toy Co. in 1945.

   _____

   _____

   _____

4. Combine these sentences into one sentence. Use sentences c and d as appositives.

   a. Goldfish swallowing was started by Lothrop Withington, Jr.
   b. It was started in 1939.
   c. It was one of the most unusual fads of the 20th century.
   d. Lothrop Withington, Jr., was a Harvard freshman.

   _____

   _____

   _____

5. Combine the following sentences into one sentence. Use sentence a as an introductory adverb clause. Use sentence b as an adjective clause. Use sentence d as an infinitive phrase.

   a. Withington boasted to friends that he had once eaten a live fish.
   b. His friends attended college with him.
   c. His friends dared him.
   d. The dare was to eat another one.

   _____

   _____

   _____

Sentence Combining Exercises

continued

6. Combine the following sentences into one sentence. Use sentence a as a present participial phrase. Use sentence d as an adjective clause.

    a. Withington accepted the challenge.
    b. He agreed to meet on March 3.
    c. He would meet them in the student dining hall.
    d. He would eat a live goldfish.

_____

_____

_____

7. Combine the following sentences into one sentence. Use sentence c as an appositive phrase. Use sentence d as an adjective clause.

    a. The date arrived.
    b. Withington stood before a crowd of students.
    c. Withington was a natural actor.
    d. The students had heard about the challenge.
    e. Withington grabbed a goldfish from a bowl.

_____

_____

_____

8. Combine the following sentences into one sentence. Use sentence a as a present participial phrase.

    a. He held the fish by its tail.
    b. Withington slowly lowered it into his mouth.
    c. He chewed it for a moment.
    d. He then swallowed it.

_____

_____

_____

Sentence Combining Exercises

continued

9. Combine these sentences into one sentence. Use sentence a as an infinitive phrase. Use sentence c as an adjective clause.

    a. He completed his performance.
    b. Withington pulled out a toothbrush.
    c. He used it to clean his teeth.
    d. Then he said, "The scales caught a bit on my throat."

_____

_____

_____

10. Combine the following sentences into one sentence. Use sentence a as an introductory prepositional phrase. Use sentence c as a past participial phrase.

    a. It was that spring.
    b. College students across the country were gulping down goldfish.
    c. The students were worried about exams.
    d. They were ready for any diversion.
    e. They were gulping as many as forty-two goldfish at one sitting.

_____

_____

_____

SECTION

five

Essay and Paragraph Practice: Using Examples

Assignment

In the first two chapters of this text, you have written paragraphs about an event and a place. Such writing is usually called "narrative" or "descriptive" because it either narrates (tells about) an event or describes a place. In this chapter you will write an **expository** paragraph or essay (your instructor will decide which one). Expository writing **explains** a topic or idea to a reader, or it **informs** the reader about a topic or idea. The topic of an expository paragraph or essay can range from explaining how to conduct an experiment in chemistry to analyzing the causes of World War II. In fact, most of the writing you will do in college classes will be expository.

One common type of expository writing is the paragraph or essay that relies upon examples to make its point. If you look at Exercises 1C, 2C, and 3C of Chapter Three, you will see that they all rely on examples to support the statements made in the topic sentences. Exercise 1C gives examples of cities that have honored Jackie Robinson. Exercise 2C gives examples of English words that are drawn from mythology. And Exercise 3C gives examples of adventures experienced on a trip to the Four Corners area of the United States.

Supporting your ideas with examples is a powerful way to help your readers understand your point. Examples allow your readers to see your topic at work in real-life situations, and they show your readers that your topic is based on reality. Of course, examples are also important when you take tests. Your ability to back up general answers with specific examples can show an instructor that you have understood and mastered the material you have been studying.

For this chapter, your assignment is to write a paper that uses several *specific examples* to support a statement made in a topic sentence or a thesis statement. Develop your paper from one of the following prewriting suggestions or from an idea suggested by your instructor.

Prewriting to Generate Ideas

Whether you are writing a paragraph or an essay, the prewriting techniques are the same. Use freewriting, brainstorming, and clustering to develop ideas from the topic suggestions that follow. Look for topics that you can illustrate with specific, detailed examples of your own.

Prewriting Application: Finding Your Topic

Read the following topic suggestions before you begin to prewrite. Not all of them will apply to you. Find the suggestions that interest you the most and then spend five or ten minutes freewriting on each of them. Try not to settle for a topic that seems only mildly interesting. Instead, look for that "Aha!" experience, the emotional reaction that identifies a topic that really moves you.

1. Give examples of *one* particular personality characteristic of your own. Are you a hard-working, "Type A" personality? Do you overeat when you experience stress, anger, or boredom? Are you sometimes too outspoken? Are you overly impulsive? Choose <u>one</u> personality characteristic of your own and illustrate it with examples.

2. Give examples of *one* particular personality characteristic of someone you know. Choose someone close to you—a family member, a close friend, or someone you work with or have known for a while. Identify *one* of that person's personality characteristics, and then illustrate it with examples.

3. Have you ever found that at times telling a lie is the ethical, responsible thing to do? Have you ever told a lie to protect someone from danger or from unnecessary pain? Use specific examples to illustrate times when lying seemed to you to be the correct, responsible behavior.

4. Take any simple statement that you know to be true and illustrate it with specific examples. Consider ideas like these:

   Last year's rains damaged many homes in my hometown.

   The food served in some restaurants can have appalling things happen to it while it is still in the kitchen.

   At last year's comic convention I was introduced to some of the weirdest people that I have ever seen.

   The Sun City Senior Center is full of people who have led exciting, adventurous lives.

   Some people treat their pets as if they were people.

5. Have you ever experienced intolerance or bigotry because of your race, gender, religious beliefs, or age? Write a paragraph in which you use specific examples to illustrate what has happened to you.

6. People sometimes say that the simplest things in life are the most valuable. If you agree, use specific examples to illustrate the truth of that statement in your own life.

7. Choose a sport, activity, or hobby with which you are familiar. Use specific examples to illustrate something that you know to be true about it.

8. Use examples to illustrate an idea about something that you own: your car, an animal, your computer, your clothing.

9. Choose a statement that people commonly believe to be true and use examples to show why it is or is not true in your life. Here are some examples:

Whatever can go wrong will go wrong.

Sometimes help can come from the most unlikely places.

If you try hard enough, you will succeed.

You can't tell who your real friends are until you need help.

10. Choose a technological device—the computer, cell phone, answering machine, fax machine, etc.—and use examples to illustrate your attitude toward it.

Choosing and Narrowing the Topic

As you choose your topic, remember that a more specific focus will result in a better paper than a more general focus. For example, don't try to give examples of a topic as general as *problems in the United States*. There are hundreds of possible examples of such a general topic, so all you would be able to do is briefly list a few of them, without going into detail about any. On the other hand, a more focused topic, such as *problems caused by my father's excessive drinking,* could certainly be supported by several detailed, descriptive examples.

Writing a Topic Sentence

If your assignment is to write a single paragraph, use your prewriting to decide upon a narrowed topic and a limited central point. Then write a topic sentence that can be supported with examples. Examine your topic sentence closely. Not all statements suggest that examples will follow. Consider the following sentences. Which would cause a reader to expect examples as support? Which would not?

 EXAMPLES

1. Last summer I had a chance to visit Toronto, Canada.

2. Many people on the corner of Queen and Peter Streets in Toronto, Canada, looked as if they had stepped directly out of the 1960's.

Sentence 1 merely states a fact. It does not cause one to expect examples. Sentence 2 would cause a reader to expect examples of the people on Queen and Peter streets.

 EXAMPLES

3. Some of my best friends today used to be some of my worst enemies.

4. One of my best friends recently made a very unwise decision.

Sentence 3 causes one to expect examples of friends who used to be enemies. Sentence 4 would cause a reader to expect an explanation of the decision and why it was unwise, but it does not suggest that several examples will follow.

Prewriting Application: Working with Topic Sentences

Identify the topic sentences in Exercises 1C (page 155), 2C (page 166), and 3C (page 183). Then identify the topic and the central point in each topic sentence.

Prewriting Application: Evaluating Topic Sentences

Write "No" before each sentence that would not make a good topic sentence *for this assignment.* Write "Yes" before each sentence that would make a good one. Using ideas of your own, rewrite the unacceptable topic sentences into topic sentences that might work.

_____ **1.** I have many different personality characteristics.

_____ **2.** Computers are supposed to be convenient, time-saving machines, but mine has brought me nothing but trouble.

_____ **3.** People who believe that money can't buy happiness have obviously never met my uncle.

_____ **4.** Basketball has been my favorite sport for as long as I can remember.

_____ **5.** After having owned a horse for ten years, I have decided that my particular horse has to be one of the stupidest animals alive.

_____ **6.** Whenever I go to a garage sale or a swap meet, I end up buying some absolutely useless item.

_____

_____

_____ **7.** My paragraph is about why Idaho holds such pleasant memories for so many people.

_____

_____

_____ **8.** My best friend's parties always seem to turn into near riots.

_____

_____

_____ **9.** Our country is a wonderful place to live, but it has many serious problems that need to be resolved.

_____

_____

_____ **10.** My father believes that we should never lie, but sometimes his honesty is so painful it is almost cruel.

_____

_____

Prewriting Application: Talking to Others

Once you have decided upon a topic and a preliminary topic sentence, you need to develop your examples. A good way to do so is to tell three or four other members of your class why your topic sentence is true. Think of yourself as an attorney before a jury. You must provide the evidence—the examples—to support the central idea in your topic sentence.

For example, if your topic is that your father's honesty borders on cruelty, convince the other people in your group with brief, specific examples. Consider these questions as you discuss your topics.

1. Exactly where and when does each example occur? Has the place and time of each instance been clearly identified?

2. Can you visualize the examples? Are the people mentioned in the example identifed by name or by relationship? Are physical features specifically named or described?

3. What point do these examples reveal? Should the topic sentence be revised to express that point more clearly?

4. Are you convinced? Have enough examples been provided to illustrate the topic idea? Should any of the examples be more convincing?

5. Which example should be used first in the paper? Last?

Organizing Examples

Examples can be organized a number of ways. Sometimes a **chronological order** is best, arranging examples according to *when* they occurred. Sometimes a **spatial order** would work well, arranging examples by *physical location*. Many times an **emphatic order** should be used, arranging examples from *least to most important* (or, sometimes, from most to least important).

Prewriting Application: Organizing Examples

First, arrange the following examples in chronological order, numbering them 1, 2, 3, 4, 5. Then arrange them in spatial order. Then arrange them in emphatic order. If you prefer one arrangement over another, explain why.

Topic Sentence: My father thinks that the junk he buys at swap meets and garage sales makes terrific household decorations.

_____   He bought a warped wooden tennis racket a few months ago for five dollars and nailed it above our front door. He thinks it makes our house look "sporty."

_____   On the hallway wall is a cuckoo clock that he bought last Saturday. The bird is missing one of its wings, and the clock will not keep correct time anymore. He thought it was a real bargain because he got the clock for one dollar.

_____   Upstairs in our guest bedroom is a faded velvet picture of Elvis Presley and another one of some dogs playing poker. He bought them last year for ten dollars each.

_____   When we used to live in Big Bear, California, he spent $75 for a huge moth-eaten moose head that turned out to be crawling with bugs that infested our whole house. It's now mounted over the fireplace in the living room.

_____   Two plastic pink flamingos are stuck into our front lawn. Dad bought them the weekend we moved into this house. He says they add "character" to our home.

Writing the Paragraph

Write the first draft of your paragraph. Your first sentence should be your preliminary topic sentence. After writing the topic sentence, write the examples that illustrate your point. Devote several sentences to each example and be as specific and as detailed as you can in each of those sentences.

Using Transitions

Transitions are words, phrases, or clauses that let the reader know when you are moving from one idea or example to another. They are essential for clear writing because they help your readers follow your train of thought. Since you will be writing several examples in one paragraph for this assignment, you need to let your readers know when one example has ended and another is beginning. Use common transitional phrases such as those below to introduce each new example:

for example   to illustrate
for instance   another example of

Notice how transitional words and phrases are used to introduce examples in Exercise 2C, page 166.

 EXAMPLES

For example, the names of several of our weekdays—Tuesday, Wednesday, Thursday, and Friday—derive from Norse mythology.

Other common words derive from Greek mythology.

For instance, the word *tantalize* refers to Tantalus, who was a king condemned to Hades as a punishment for his crimes.

Finally, Roman mythology, which in many ways parallels Greek mythology, is another source of many English words.

For example, the month of January is named after Janus, the Roman god with two faces.

Writing Application: Identifying Transitional Sentences

Examine Exercises 1C (page 155) and 3C (page 183). In each paragraph, identify the transitions that introduce each example.

Rewriting and Improving the Paragraph

1. Once your first draft is complete, read it over to determine how you can improve the examples you have used. In particular, try to make the examples as specific and as concrete as you can. Use actual names of people and places and refer to specific details whenever possible.

2. As you read your draft, make sure you can tell where each of your examples ends and the next begins. Revise your transitional sentences as needed to make them clearer.

3. If your preliminary topic sentence can be improved so that it more accurately states the central point of your paragraph, change it now.

4. Examine your draft for sentences that can be combined using participial phrases, appositives, infinitive phrases, or adjective clauses. Combine such sentences the way you did in the Sentence Combining Exercises.

Rewriting Application: Responding to Writing

Read the following paragraph. Then respond to the questions following it.

I Enjoy H_2O to Relax

Whenever I feel stressed, I find that I can relax best if I am near the water. For example, as a teenager living in San Bernardino, I would drive many miles into the local foothills of the mountains, where a small river or a large stream called Lytle Creek was located in the little town of Apple-white. I would walk down between the trees and then over all of the rocks to find a place where I would sit for hours. I enjoyed watching the water rush by because it made me become very relaxed. Then, in the late 1980s, I moved to San Diego County. My first apartment was in Escondido, and times were troubled and stressful nearly every day, yet I was able to find comfort by driving to Lake Dixon. After several weekend trips I began taking this drive at all different times of the week. Usually alone, but sometimes with my boys, I would go to the lake and feed the ducks or just fish from the shore. Now, living in San Marcos, I prefer the ultimate water experience by relaxing at the beach. During most of my quick trips, I drive down Del Dios Highway and across the railroad tracks into Solana Beach parking lot. I walk down the large ramp and sit on the sand or walk along the shoreline to the cave. Watching the water really washes away any troubles that I brought with me. It seems to clear my head and to bring a warm feeling of contentment to my soul. In conclusion, no matter whether the water is a stream, lake, or ocean, its appearance and its soothing sounds take away all of my stress and troubles.

1. Identify the topic sentence. State its topic and central idea. Is it an effective topic sentence? Why or why not?

2. Identify the transitional sentences that introduce each example.

3. Are the examples specific? Point out which words in each example identify specific places or things.

4. Which words in each example would you make still more specific?

5. Which example is the most effective? Why? Which one would you improve? How?

Proofreading

Before you do the final editing of your paper, revise it one more time. If the topic sentence needs work, improve it now. Check the examples. Are they as specific and descriptive as they can be? Add transitional sentences between examples. Wherever you can, combine related sentences using subordinate clauses as well as participial and infinitive phrases.

Now edit the paper. Check your draft for any of the following errors:

■ Sentence fragments

■ Comma splices

■ Fused sentences

■ Misplaced modifiers

■ Dangling modifiers

■ Misspelled words

Prepare a clean final draft, following the format your instructor has requested. Before you turn in your final draft, proofread it carefully and make any necessary corrections.

Moving from Paragraph to Essay

All of the assignments so far have asked you to write single paragraphs, but most college classes will ask you to produce essays consisting of several paragraphs.

Writing an essay is not really much different from writing a paragraph. An essay focuses on and develops one central idea, just as a paragraph does. The central idea of an essay is called its **thesis statement.**

The main difference between an essay and a paragraph is that the supporting material in an essay is longer and more complicated, so it needs to be separated into different body paragraphs, each with its own **topic sentence.**

Recognizing Essay Form

An essay consists of an introductory paragraph, one or more body paragraphs, and a concluding paragraph.

■ The *introductory paragraph* includes the **thesis statement** (usually as the last sentence of the first paragraph).

■ Each *body paragraph* starts with a **topic sentence** that supports the thesis statement. The central idea of each body paragraph is supported with **facts, examples, and details.**

■ The *concluding paragraph* brings the essay to a close, often by restating the central idea of the essay.

Introductory Paragraph

Introductory sentences

ending with a

thesis statement

Body Paragraphs

Topic sentence

supported with

facts, examples, and details

Topic sentence

supported with

facts, examples, and details

Topic sentence

supported with

facts, examples, and details

Concluding Paragraphs

Concluding sentences

bringing the essay

to a close

Choosing and Narrowing a Thesis Statement

A **thesis statement** states the topic and the central idea of an entire essay, just as a topic sentence states the topic and central idea of a paragraph. Like a topic sentence, a thesis statement needs to be narrowed and focused so that it does not try to cover too much material in a short essay.

Consider the following sentences. Which is narrowed enough to function as a thesis statement in a brief essay?

 EXAMPLES

1. Many people have problems when they move to a new place.

2. Immigrants face many obstacles when they move to the United States.

3. Immigrants who do not yet speak English will encounter several obstacles when they try to get a job in the United States.

Sentence 1 is much too broad for any essay at all. Both sentences 2 and 3 could work as thesis statements, but sentence 3 will work better in a brief essay because it is narrowed to the topic of *Immigrants who do not yet speak English,* and its central point is focused on *obstacles when they try to get a job.* An essay with this thesis statement would devote a separate body paragraph to each obstacle to getting a job. Each body paragraph would then include examples of one or more immigrants who encountered that obstacle.

Writing the Essay

An essay takes more time to write than a paragraph, but the writing process itself is very similar.

- Generate topic ideas as well as supporting material by freewriting, brainstorming, and clustering.

- Focus your material on one central idea, expressed in a thesis statement.

- Divide your supporting material (examples, facts, details) into separate body paragraphs.

- Arrange your body paragraphs into a logical order, such as a chronological, spatial, or emphatic order.

- Write your first draft without worrying too much about the quality of your writing. Focus more on getting your ideas onto paper. You can improve them later.

Rewriting and Improving the Essay

Once you have a complete draft, consider these questions as you revise your paper.

■ Do your opening sentences introduce the topic in a way that will interest a reader?

■ Is your thesis sufficiently narrowed? Is it placed at the end of the introductory paragraph?

■ Does each paragraph open with a topic sentence that clearly supports the thesis statement?

■ Are the supporting facts and examples in each paragraph specific and clear?

■ Does each paragraph contain enough examples?

■ Are transitions used to move clearly from one idea to another?

■ Does the conclusion close the essay in an interesting way?

Application: Working with Essay Form

Read the following student essay and answer the questions at the end.

Lying

My parents are two of the most honest people I have ever met. Ever since I can remember, they have told me that "Honesty is the best policy." My father says that lying only leads to more lying and that telling the truth is exactly the right thing to do. The problem is that I don't think they are right. There are times when the right thing to do is to tell a lie.

For example, sometimes lying can mean the difference between survival and disaster. I have a friend with two daughters, ages three and five. When her husband deserted her, she needed to find a job fast. But there was one problem. Every place where she applied asked if she had ever been convicted of a crime. She told the truth that she had been convicted of selling marijuana years ago, and she was politely shown out the door at Sears, Target, and Wal-Mart. It didn't matter that she hasn't used drugs or alcohol now for over seven years. She needed to feed her children, so on her next job application she lied and got the job. I would have lied too.

Lying is also the right thing to do when you need to spare people any unnecessary pain in an emotional time. For instance, when I was in high school, a friend of mine named Melody died in a car accident, and the police believed drugs were involved. The parents refused to believe that their little girl would ever have taken drugs, but they didn't know everything about their daughter. Several of her friends and I knew that Melody had been using marijuana for a while. She had even tried cocaine a few times, but when her parents talked to us, we told them that she had never tried drugs. What good would telling the truth have done? It would only have hurt her parents more. So we lied.

I've also found that telling the truth can sometimes cause trouble among friends. There have been plenty of times when I have prevented a fight by not telling one friend what another one said about him or her. I've prevented these situations when I felt that the argument between the two was not worth fighting over.

I know that lying is not usually the right answer to a problem. But sometimes honesty isn't either. It seems to me that a person has to think about each situation and not live his life by general rules that don't always apply.

1. Underline the thesis statement. Is it sufficiently narrowed for a brief essay? Explain your response.

2. Now underline each topic sentence. Each topic sentence should clearly refer to and support the thesis statement. Explain how each one does so.

3. Look at the introductory sentences before the thesis statement. What function do they serve?

4. Look at the examples in each body paragraph. Which examples are the strongest? Why? Which are the weakest? Why?

5. Consider the organization of the three body paragraphs. Should it be changed at all? Explain why or why not.

6. Look at the concluding paragraph. Does it close the essay effectively? Why or why not?

Proofreading

As with all of your papers, proofread your essay carefully before you submit it.

Chapter Three Practice Test

I. Review of Chapters One and Two

A. In the following sentences, identify the underlined words by writing one of the following abbreviations above the words: noun (N), pronoun (Pro), verb (V), adjective (Adj), adverb (Adv), conjunction (Conj), or preposition (Prep).

1. After ten <u>minutes</u> on the job, Elmer <u>knew</u> he would have to quit.

2. Huck had <u>never</u> liked rafting, <u>but</u> he did not tell Jim.

3. Whenever Butch flexed his muscles, his <u>snake</u> tattoo moved <u>menacingly</u>.

4. Almost <u>no one</u> visits Jim Morrison's grave <u>in</u> France.

5. Mrs. Hemingway <u>probably</u> disliked all of the animal heads <u>on</u> the wall.

B. In the following sentences, underline the subjects once and the complete verbs twice. Put parentheses around all prepositional phrases.

6. Two foxes moved silently into the forest.

7. Are the McCoys and the Hatfields coming to the wedding?

8. The Montagues walked across the street and confronted the Capulets.

9. Hortense wept during the wedding, but Homer merely munched on his Spam sandwich.

10. After Thetis dipped her son in the river, she dried him with a towel.

C. Compose sentences of your own according to the instructions.

11. Write a simple sentence with one subject, two verbs, and at least one prepositional phrase.

_____

_____

12. Write a compound sentence. Use a coordinating conjunction and appropriate punctuation to join the two clauses.

_____

_____

continued

13. Write a complex sentence that starts with a subordinate clause. Use appropriate punctuation.

_____

_____

14. Write a complex sentence that uses the subordinator *who*.

_____

_____

15. Write a compound-complex sentence. Use the conjunction *so* and the subordinator *while*.

_____

_____

D. Identify the following items as being correct (C), fused (F), comma splice (CS), or fragment (Frag). Then correct the errors. If a sentence is correct, do nothing to it.

_____ **16.** The Lion King looked at the mouse, then he asked for help.

_____

_____

_____ **17.** Seymour Seahorn, a man who had always believed in telling the truth and in admitting his mistakes.

_____

_____

_____ **18.** When he saw the burning bush, Moses was overcome with awe.

_____

_____

continued

_____ **19.** King Kong had always admired Godzilla, however Godzilla thought King Kong was just a big ape.

_____

_____

_____ **20.** Ahab came on deck he wanted to talk to Starbuck.

_____

_____

II. Chapter Three

A. Underline all infinitive and participial phrases and circle the words that they modify.

21. Rounding the tip of South America, Magellan headed into the Pacific.

22. Before he entered the arena, the gladiator chose a weapon to use against the lion.

23. Homer worried that Hortense would find the Spam hidden at the bottom of his sock drawer.

24. The sword hanging on the wall once belonged to King Arthur.

25. The person to see about your overdue tax bill has just entered the building.

B. Add infinitive or participial phrases to the following sentences at the places indicated. Use the verbs in parentheses.

26. The money ^ was not his own. (spend)

_____

_____

27. ^ Blanche dimmed all of the lights. (conceal)

_____

_____

continued

28. The firefighters ^ were determined to save the kitten. (climb)

_____

_____

29. Clyde thought that Bonnie's plan ^ was a good one. (steal)

_____

_____

30. ^ Suzanne stood in a long line in front of the theater. (hope)

_____

_____

C. Underline the adjective clauses and appositives in the following sentences and circle the words they modify.

31. Dr. Nguyen, a well-known physicist, will discuss chaos theory tonight in the

auditorium.

32. The arrow that William Tell shot split the apple.

33. Cochise, who was a great Apache leader, resisted attempts to move his tribe from

Arizona to New Mexico.

34. Cranberry, my mother's cat, was missing yesterday.

35. In the morning they sail aboard the *Ancient Mariner,* which had been built in

Baltimore.

D. Add adjective clauses or appositives to the following sentences and punctuate them correctly.

36. Romeo drove his new car to the costume party.

_____

_____

continued

37. Jack's warm, gooey cinnamon roll fell onto his stack of student papers.

_____

_____

38. The police officer watched the three men enter the bank.

_____

_____

39. Daisy frowned when she saw Donald and Minnie dancing at the Academy Awards ceremony.

_____

_____

40. Sophocles discussed his new play with his wife.

_____

_____

E. Underline and then correct any dangling or misplaced modifiers in the following sentences. Do nothing if a sentence is correct.

41. Sylvio was not very impressed with the food in the new restaurant that he had just

eaten.

_____

_____

42. Running out the door, Cynthia almost forgot her briefcase.

_____

_____

continued

43. Taking a deep breath, the air was fresh and clean.

_____

_____

44. To enter the museum, a special pass was needed.

_____

_____

45. The toy poodle only had one goal—to get even with the Doberman pinscher next door.

_____

_____

46. Living on a fixed income, there was often not enough food for the children.

_____

_____

47. A horde of killer bees attracted by the smell of sweet potato pie chasing Homer and

Hortense flew into our house.

_____

_____

48. Climbing up the tall bean stalk, the giant's head began to ache.

_____

_____

continued

49. Drifting down the river at night and hiding during the day, Huck and Jim wondered

if they would ever reach Cairo.

_____

_____

50. Two of the men who had entered the room secretly wanted to assassinate the senator.

_____

_____

Lining Up the Parts
of a Sentence

The Careful Writer

As you have probably already noticed, effective writing is less a matter of inspiration and more a matter of making innumerable choices and paying careful attention to detail. Strictly speaking, every word in each of your sentences represents a specific choice on your part. Good writers carefully choose words and their positions in sentences, not only to be grammatically correct but also to make their writing clear and concise.

Although close attention to detail alone will not ensure good writing, it does have a number of advantages. The most important reason for you to take care in your writing is to make certain that you communicate your ideas clearly. As you can see from having worked through the last chapter, if your sentences contain misplaced or dangling modifiers, your reader will sometimes be confused about what you mean. In addition, a clear and careful piece of writing in itself creates a good impression, just as a well-tended lawn does. You have probably already found that people are often judged by their writing. If your writing is carefully thought out and presented with an attention to correctness and detail, it will be taken seriously.

Making sure that your sentences are correctly constructed and checking to see that your modifiers clearly and logically modify the right words are two ways of taking care in your writing. In this chapter we will discuss a few others: paying attention to the special relationship between those two most important parts of your sentences, the subjects and verbs; making sure that the pronouns you use are in their correct forms; and checking the connection between your pronouns and the words they stand for.

Subject–Verb Agreement

One reason you need to be able to identify subjects and verbs accurately is that the form of the verb often changes to match the form of its subject. If the subject of your sentence is singular, your verb must be singular. If the subject is plural, your verb must be plural. This matching of the verb and its subject is called **subject–verb agreement.**

You need to pay special attention to subject–verb agreement when you use present tense verbs. **Most present tense verbs that have singular subjects end in "s." Most present tense verbs that have plural subjects do not end in "s."** Here are some examples.

Singular	*Plural*
The dog barks.	The dogs bark.
He walks.	They walk.
It is.	They are.
The man has.	The men have.
She does.	They do.

Notice that in each case the verb ends in "s" when the subject is singular. This rule can be confusing because an "s" at the end of a <u>noun</u> almost always means that the noun is plural, but **an "s" at the end of a <u>verb</u> almost always means it is singular.**

 PRACTICE   Change the subjects and verbs in the following sentences from singular to plural or from plural to singular. You may need to add *a, an,* or *the* to some of the sentences.

1. At night, the mockingbirds sing too loudly.

At night, the mockingbird sings too loudly.

2. The dog next door has barked all day.

_____

3. My friends often visit me at school.

_____

4. Soldiers sometimes write several letters each day.

_____

SECTION one

5. A low grade always makes me feel unhappy.

Identifying Subjects: A Review

1. <u>Make sure you accurately identify the subject.</u> Sentences usually contain several nouns and pronouns.

 EXAMPLE

The **boys** from the private **school** on the other **side** of **town** often use our **gymnasium.**

This sentence contains five nouns, but only *boys* is the subject.

2. <u>Remember that a noun or pronoun that is part of a prepositional phrase cannot be the subject.</u>

 EXAMPLE

Each of the children takes a vitamin with breakfast.

The subject is *Each*, not *children*, because *children* is part of a prepositional phrase.

3. <u>Indefinite pronouns can be subjects.</u> The indefinite pronouns are listed on page 5.

 EXAMPLE

Everyone sitting at the tables under the trees has a picnic lunch.

Subject–Verb Agreement: Points to Know

1. <u>Two subjects joined by *and* are plural.</u>

 EXAMPLES

S   S   V
The **boy** <u>and</u> his **dog were** far from home.

S   S   V
Ham <u>and</u> **rye make** a delicious combination.

2. <u>However, if a subject is modified by *each* or *every*, it is singular.</u>

 EXAMPLES

S   S   V
<u>Every</u> **boy** and **girl** at the party <u>**was**</u> given a present to take home.

S   S   V
<u>Each</u> **envelope** and **piece** of paper <u>**has**</u> the name of the company on it.

3. The following indefinite pronouns are singular.

(◎) **EXAMPLES**

anybody	either	neither	one
anyone	everybody	nobody	somebody
anything	everyone	no one	someone
each	everything	nothing	something

(◎) **EXAMPLES**

S   V

Each of the band members **has** a new uniform.

S   V

Everyone sitting under the trees **is** part of my family.

4. A few nouns and indefinite pronouns, such as *none, some, all, most, more, half,* or *part* may sometimes be considered plural and sometimes singular, depending on the prepositional phrases that follow them. If the object of the preposition is singular, treat the subject and verb as singular. If the object of the preposition is plural, treat the subject and verb as plural.

(◎) **EXAMPLES**

                    S   V

(singular)   **None** of the cake **is** left.

                    S   V

(plural)   **None** of the people **are** here.

(◎) **PRACTICE**

Place an "S" above the subjects and underline the correct verb form in the parentheses.

                    S   S

1. In the writing lab, a teacher and a student (was <u>were</u>) working on a piece

of writing.

2. An old bicycle with two flat tires (does do) seem to be a strange gift.

3. Every surfer and skateboarder in Pacific Beach (thinks think) that the new

law is unfair.

4. A Spam omelette and a glass of buttermilk always (starts start) Homer's day well.

5. Some of the corn (was were) harvested too early.

6. Since he had started to speak, every soldier and archer (was were) listening

to Agamemnon.

7. Somebody from one of our local schools (has have) won the prestigious

Peacock scholarship.

8. The car's upholstery and paint job (make makes) it look almost new.

9. Some of the fans in the audience (was were) standing and cheering.

10. A squirrel with two cats chasing it (is are) running down the street.

---

5. When subjects are joined by *or* or *nor,* the verb agrees with the closer subject. If one subject is singular and one is plural, place the plural subject closer to the verb to avoid awkwardness.

 EXAMPLES

(singular subjects)
S   S V
Neither **Alberto** nor his **brother knows** what to do.

(plural subjects)
S   S   V
Either the **actors** or the **screenwriters have decided** to strike.

(singular and) (plural subjects)
S   S V
Neither **Alberto** nor his **sisters were** at last night's concert.

NOTE: When you have helping verbs in a sentence, the helping verb—not the main verb—changes form.

 EXAMPLE

HV   S   S   MV
Does Alberto or his **brother** want to go fishing?

HV   S   S   MV
Have the actors or **screenwriters** decided to strike?

6. Collective nouns usually take the singular form of the verb. Collective nouns represent groups of people or things, but they are considered singular. Here are some common collective nouns.

audience	crowd	herd
band	family	jury
class	flock	number
committee	government	society
company	group	team

 EXAMPLES

S   V
The **audience was** delighted when the curtain slowly rose to reveal the orchestra already seated.

S   V
My **family goes** to Yellowstone National Park every summer.

7. The relative pronouns *that, which,* and *who* may be either singular or plural. When one of these pronouns is the subject of a verb, you will need to know which word it refers to before you decide whether it is singular or plural.

 EXAMPLES

(singular)   I bought the <u>peach</u> **that was** ripe.

(plural)   I bought the <u>peaches</u> **that were** ripe.

(plural)   Colleen is one of the <u>students</u> **who are** taking flying lessons.

(singular)   Colleen is the only <u>one</u> of the students **who is** taking flying lessons.

PRACTICE   Place an "S" above the subjects and underline the correct verb forms in the parentheses.

1. Neither the money nor my excuses for the accident (pleases please)

   Mr. Hernandez.

2. A flock of geese (has have) just landed in my backyard.

3. Rory is one of the dogs that (plays play) Frisbee so well.

4. Neither the first officer nor the seamen (wants want) Captain Vere to hang

   Billy.

5. Her trip to Disneyland or her two vacations to Nepal (seems seem) to be all

   that Amanda thinks about.

6. The mob in Paris (loves love) to watch the executioner at work.

7. Henry is the only citizen in Concord who (refuses refuse) to pay taxes.

8. (Has Have) your mother or your brother arrived yet?

9. The debate team that Ray coaches (wins win) every year.

10. Henrietta is one of the women who (has have) recently joined our lawn

    bowling club.

8. A few nouns end in "s" but are usually considered singular; they take the singular form of the verb. These nouns include *economics, gymnastics, mathematics, measles, mumps, news, physics,* and *politics.*

 EXAMPLES

                S   V

World **economics** <u>has</u> **been** an important international issue for years.

      S   V

Gymnastics <u>is</u> one of the most popular events in the Olympics.

9. When units of measurement for distance, time, volume, height, weight, money, and so on are used as subjects, they take the singular verb form.

 EXAMPLES

            S   V

Two **teaspoons** of sugar **was** all that the cake recipe called for.

        S   V

Five **dollars** **is** too much to pay for a hot dog.

10. In a question or in a sentence that begins with *there* or *here,* the order of the subject and verb is reversed.

 EXAMPLES

      V   S

Was the **bus** on time?

      V   S

Is there a squeaking **wheel** out there somewhere?

        V   S

There **is** an **abundance** of wildflowers in the desert this spring.

        V   S

Here **are** the **keys** to your car.

11. The verb must agree only with the **subject**.

 EXAMPLE

                S   V

Our biggest **problem** **is** termites in the attic.

The singular verb form *is* is correct here because the subject is the singular noun *problem.* The plural noun *termites* does not affect the form of the verb.

 PRACTICE

Place an "S" above the subjects and underline the correct verb forms in the parentheses.

      S

1. Mathematics (<u>remains</u> remain) one of the hardest subjects for students.

2. Fifteen inches of rain (fall falls) in Murrieta every winter.

3. One of Charlie's favorite British dishes (is are) bangers.

4. According to Bruce, the news of his lottery winnings (was were) exaggerated.

5. (Has Have) the mumps ever seemed like a serious disease to you?

6. After deliberating for three days, the jury in the Mallory trial (has have) not yet reached a verdict.

7. Barbara says that two hundred pounds of tuna (is are) too much for her freezer.

8. There still (are is) people who believe that the earth is flat.

9. Randall's only source of income (is are) his stocks and bonds.

10. Ten miles of unpaved road (lies lie) between my house and the beach.

Section One Review

1. In the present tense, when the subject is a singular noun or a singular pronoun, the verb form usually will end in "s."

2. Subject–verb agreement: points to know

   a. Two subjects joined by *and* are plural.

   b. If a subject is modified by *each* or *every,* it is singular.

   c. Indefinite pronouns are usually singular.

   d. Sometimes indefinite pronouns like *some, half,* or *part* are considered plural, depending on the prepositional phrases that follow them.

   e. When subjects are joined by *or* or *nor,* the verb agrees with the closer subject. If one subject is singular and one is plural, place the plural subject closer to the verb to avoid awkwardness.

   f. When a collective noun, such as *family* or *group,* is the subject, the singular form of the verb is used.

   g. The relative pronouns *that, which,* and *who* may be either singular or plural, depending upon the word the pronoun refers to.

   h. A few nouns, such as *economics* or *news,* end in "s" but are usually considered singular.

   i. When the subject is a unit of measurement, such as distance, weight, or money, the singular form of the verb is used.

   j. In a question or in a sentence that begins with *there* or *here,* the verb will often come before the subject.

   k. The verb must agree only with the **subject.**

Exercise 1A

Circle the subjects and underline the correct verb forms in the parentheses.

1. (Anyone) with plaid pants and pink shoes (was were) let into the golf tournament free.

2. Either my neighbor's German shepherd or her two toy poodles (make makes) a mess on my lawn every morning.

3. Both his mother and his uncle (has have) been puzzled by Hamlet's behavior.

4. The last team to enter the stadium (was were) the Japanese.

5. Of all the subjects Angela is studying, economics (interest interests) her the most.

6. A colorful mallard with its seven ducklings (waddle waddles) down this road each evening.

7. Six hundred tons of wheat (was were) not enough to feed the victims of the drought.

8. A good used car with a sound engine and good tires (costs cost) about five thousand dollars.

9. (Has Have) the committee decided what to do about that troll under the bridge?

10. Every knife, fork, and spoon in the restaurant (was were) washed and polished last night.

11. According to the report, high school gymnastics (cause causes) more injuries than football.

12. Everybody around the cows (was were) asking Homer to autograph a chip.

13. Two weeks with his daughter Regan (was were) too much for Lear and his men.

14. (Does Do) the witch or the warlock have any idea where the ogre is?

15. Everyone from both baseball teams (is are) invited to the party after the game.

Exercise 1B

Correct any subject–verb agreement errors in the following sentences. If a sentence is correct, do nothing to it. To check your answers, circle the subjects.

1. Neither (Horatio) nor (Fortinbras) ~~want~~ *wants* to clean up the mess.

2. Last night, everybody visiting from New York and California was asked to leave the room.

3. Each mountain and river were surveyed by Lewis and Clark.

4. The recent news say that Odysseus has left for Ithaca.

5. A mouse with big round ears and a duck in a sailor suit makes an unusual pair.

6. Mrs. Hutchinson is one of the villagers who supports the lottery.

7. That large herd of aardvarks always take two hours to cross the creek.

8. Do Robin Hood or William Tell wish to participate in the archery tournament?

9. Benvolio and another member of the Montague family has decided to go to the party.

10. Mallory's new motorboat, as well as Marie's thirty-two foot sailboat, have been vandalized recently.

11. Homer and his cowchip-pitching team helps clean the barn out each month.

12. As the time approached, everyone near the falls were looking for the barrel.

13. Five hundred feet of kite string have been found tangled in Charlie Brown's tree.

14. Brent's proposal to boycott steak houses seem unreasonable to us carnivores.

15. Half of the people living on the third floor near my sister knows who broke into her apartment.

Exercise 1C

Correct all subject–verb agreement errors. Not all sentences will contain errors.

    1. Sometimes I have a hard time believing the effects that chocolate ~~have~~ *has* on my mother. **2.** For instance, her craving for chocolate have reached the point that all of her thoughts is focused on chocolate. **3.** When she goes to the grocery store, chocolate pudding or chocolate ice cream always sit at the very top of her list. **4.** And everyone at her work know that she keep the bowl on her desk filled with chocolate candies for them to munch on. **5.** She even hide chocolate in her purse and around the house. **6.** Another way chocolate affect my mother is that it changes her personality. **7.** The actions of Doctor Jekyll and Mr. Hyde seems mild compared to her mood swings. **8.** When she eat chocolate, her disposition is upbeat, and she act as if all is well with the world. **9.** When she doesn't have any chocolate, everybody need to watch out. **10.** She says that pieces of chocolate even appears in her dreams. **11.** Unfortunately, my mom's chocolate addiction come with one major drawback—it causes her to gain weight. **12.** Every time she gains a few pounds, she goes on a diet, and the whole family suffer. **13.** Her attitude and temper is terrible, and she becomes very emotional at any little thing. **14.** Then when any holiday arrive, how can she be expected to resist all the sweet temptations? **15.** My mother says that trying to avoid all the chocolates have made her very depressed during some holidays. **16.** I hope that anyone who have an addiction like my mother's has more success resisting it than she has.

SECTION two

Pronoun Agreement and Reference

Pronoun–Antecedent Agreement

Because pronouns stand for or take the place of nouns, it is important that you make it clear in your writing which pronouns stand for which nouns. The noun that the pronoun takes the place of is called the **antecedent. Pronoun–antecedent agreement** refers to the idea that a pronoun must match or "agree with" the noun that it stands for in **person** and in **number.**

Person

Person in pronouns refers to the relationship of the speaker (or writer) to the pronoun. There are three persons: **first person, second person,** and **third person.**

1. **First person** pronouns refer to the person speaking or writing:

Singular	*Plural*
I	we
me	us
my, mine	our, ours

2. **Second person** pronouns refer to the person spoken or written to:

Singular	*Plural*
you	you
your	your
yours	yours

3. **Third person** pronouns refer to the person or thing spoken or written about:

Singular	*Plural*
he, she, it	they
him, her, it	them
his, her, hers, its	their, theirs

Because nouns are always in the third person, pronouns that refer to nouns should also be in the third person. Usually this rule poses no problem, but sometimes writers mistakenly shift from third to second person when they are referring to a noun.

EXAMPLE   When a new **student** first enters the large and crowded registration area, **you might** feel confused and intimidated.

In this sentence, *you* has mistakenly been used to refer to *student*. The mistake occurs because the noun *student* is in the third person, and the pronoun *you* is in the second person. There are two ways to correct the sentence:

1. You can change the second person pronoun *you* to a third person pronoun.

 EXAMPLE   When a new **student** first enters the large and crowded registration area, **he or she** might feel confused and intimidated.

2. You can change the noun *student* to the second person pronoun *you*.

 EXAMPLE   When **you** first enter the large and crowded registration area, **you** might feel confused and intimidated.

Here's another incorrect sentence.

 EXAMPLE   Most **people** can stay reasonably healthy if **you** watch **your** diet and exercise several times a week.

One way to correct this sentence is to change *you* to *they* and *your* to *their* so that they agree with *people*.

 EXAMPLE   Most **people** can stay reasonably healthy if **they** watch **their** diets and exercise several times a week.

PRACTICE   Correct any errors in pronoun person in the following sentences. When you correct the pronoun, you also may need to change the verb.

1. When a person wants to get a driver's license, ~~you~~ *he or she* really need*s* to take a test at the Department of Motor Vehicles.

2. Most people are very nervous even if you have studied for the test.

3. An applicant should get a good night's sleep if you want to do well on the test.

4. When I drove my daughter to her first test, you could see that she was worried.

5. During my driving test, you needed to drive on the freeway for three miles.

Number

Errors in number are the most common pronoun–antecedent errors. To make pronouns agree with their antecedents in **number,** use singular pronouns to refer to singular nouns and plural pronouns to refer to plural nouns. The following guidelines will help you avoid errors in number.

1. Use plural pronouns to refer to words joined by *and* unless the words are modified by *each* or *every.*

 EXAMPLE

General Ulysses S. Grant and General Dwight D. Eisenhower led **their** armies to victory.

2. Use singular pronouns to refer the following indefinite pronouns.

anybody	either	neither	one
anyone	everybody	nobody	somebody
anything	everyone	no one	someone
each	everything	nothing	something

 EXAMPLES

Everything was in **its** place.

Neither of the girls wanted to give up **her** place in line.

One of the fathers was yelling loudly at **his** son throughout the game.

NOTE: In spoken English, the plural pronouns *they, them,* and *their* are often used to refer to the antecedents *everyone* or *everybody.* However, in written English the singular pronoun is still more commonly used.

 EXAMPLE

Everybody at the game cheered for **his** favorite team.

3. In general, use singular pronouns to refer to collective nouns.

 EXAMPLE

The **troop** of soldiers had almost reached **its** camp when the blizzard started.

4. When antecedents are joined by *or* or *nor,* use a pronoun that agrees with the closer antecedent.

 EXAMPLE

Neither **Chris** nor **Craig** wanted to spend his Saturday mowing the lawn.

NOTE: If one antecedent is singular and one is plural, place the plural antecedent last to avoid awkwardness. If one antecedent is female and one is male, rewrite the sentence to avoid awkwardness.

EXAMPLES

(awkward)	Either the **members** of the council or the **mayor** will send **his** regrets.
(rewritten)	Either the **mayor** or the **members** of the council will send **their** regrets.
(awkward)	Either **Mary** or **Ruben** will lend you **his** watch.
(rewritten)	You may borrow a watch from either Mary or Ruben.

PRACTICE

Correct any pronoun–antecedent errors in the following sentences. When you correct a pronoun, you may also need to change the verb.

1. If an accountant wants to do a good job, *he or she needs* ~~you need~~ to be careful and precise.

2. Everybody who wanted to attend the meeting had to say the secret password before they were let in the door.

3. When visitors tour the local dairy, you should watch where you step.

4. One team from Ohio has won all of its games for the past five years.

5. Neither Galileo nor Copernicus could keep their eyes focused on the ground.

6. Someone from the Halloween party left their giraffe costume on the couch.

7. No one could tell us where the dog had misplaced its tail.

8. Once a skier tries snowboarding, you will never go back to skiing.

9. Either Croesus or the Rockefellers left their dinner plates in my sink.

10. A camper in these woods will often see a bear wander through their campsite.

Sexist Language

In the past it was traditional to use masculine pronouns when referring to singular nouns whose gender could be either masculine or feminine. A good example is the sentence *A **person** should stop delivery of **his** newspaper before **he** leaves on a trip of more than a few days.* Although the noun *person* could be either masculine or feminine, masculine pronouns like *he* or *his* tended to be used in a case like this one.

Because women make up over fifty percent of the English-speaking population, they have been justifiably dissatisfied with this tradition. The problem is that the English language does not contain a singular personal pronoun that can refer to either sex at the same time in the way that the forms of *they* can.

The solutions to this problem can prove awkward. One of the solutions is to use feminine pronouns as freely as masculine ones to refer to singular nouns whose gender could be masculine or feminine. Either of the following sentences using this solution is acceptable.

 EXAMPLES

A **person** should stop delivery on **her** newspaper before **she** leaves on a trip of more than a few days.

A **person** should stop delivery on **his** newspaper before **he** leaves on a trip of more than a few days.

Another solution is to change *his* to *his or her* and *he* to *he or she*. Then the sentence would look like this:

 EXAMPLE

A **person** should stop delivery on **his or her** newspaper before **he or she** leaves on a trip of more than a few days.

As you can see, this solution does not result in a very graceful sentence. An alternative is to use *her/his* and *she/he*, but the result would be about the same. Sometimes a better solution is to change a singular antecedent to a plural one and use the forms of *they*, which can refer to either gender. That would result in a sentence like this:

 EXAMPLE

People should stop delivery of **their** newspapers before **they** leave on a trip of more than a few days.

This sentence is less awkward and just as fair. Finally, in some situations, the masculine pronoun alone will be appropriate, and in others the feminine pronoun alone will be. Here are two such sentences:

 EXAMPLES

Each of the hockey players threw **his** false teeth into the air after the victory. (The hockey team is known to be all male.)

The last runner on the relay team passed **her** opponent ten yards before the finish line. (All members of the relay team are female.)

Whatever your solutions to this problem, it is important that you be logical and correct in your pronoun–antecedent agreement in addition to being fair.

Unclear Pronoun Reference

Sometimes, even though a pronoun appears to agree with an antecedent, it is not clear exactly which noun in the sentence is the antecedent. And sometimes a writer will use a pronoun that does not clearly refer to any antecedent at all. The following two points will help you use pronouns correctly.

1. A pronoun should refer to a specific antecedent.

EXAMPLE

Mr. Mellon told **Larry** that **he** could take a vacation in late August.

In this sentence, *he* could refer to *Mr. Mellon* or to *Larry*. To correct this problem, you can eliminate the pronoun.

EXAMPLE

Mr. Mellon told Larry that **Larry** could take his vacation in late August.

Or you can revise the sentence so that the pronoun clearly refers to only one antecedent.

EXAMPLES

Mr. Mellon told **Larry** to take **his** vacation in late August.

OR

Mr. Mellon told Larry, "Take your vacation in late August."

Here is another example:

EXAMPLE

Every time **Patricia** looked at the **cat, she** whined.

In this sentence, the pronoun *she* could refer to *Patricia* or the *cat*. The pronoun reference needs to be clarified.

EXAMPLES

Patricia whined every time **she** looked at the cat.

OR

The **cat** whined every time Patricia looked at **her.**

PRACTICE

Revise the following sentences so that each pronoun refers to a specific antecedent.

1. Julio told his roommate that his new contact lenses were at the optometrist's office.

   Julio said to his roommate, "Your new

   contact lenses are at the optometrist's office."

2. When Tom told Huck about finding the lost treasure, he became very excited.

_____

_____

3. I tried to help in the dispute between my mother and my sister, but she would not give in.

_____

_____

4. When Gary introduced his in-laws to his parents, he hoped they would not reveal his secret.

_____

_____

5. When Seymour found a cockroach in his soup, he refused to eat it.

_____

_____

2. Pronouns should not refer to implied or unstated antecedents. Be especially careful with the pronouns *this, that, which,* and *it.*

EXAMPLE   My baseball coach made us go without dinner if we lost a game; **this** was unfair.

In this sentence, there is no specific antecedent for the pronoun *this* to refer to. The following sentence clarifies the pronoun reference.

EXAMPLE   My baseball coach made us go without dinner if we lost a game; **this punishment** was unfair.

Sometimes a pronoun refers to a noun that is only implied in the first part of the sentence.

EXAMPLE   Mrs. Brovelli is a poet, **which** she does some of every day.

In this sentence, *which* apparently stands for "writing poetry," which is implied in the noun *poet*; however, there is no specific noun for the pronoun *which* to stand for. The faulty pronoun reference can be cleared up in several ways.

EXAMPLES   Mrs. Brovelli is a poet, and **she writes** poetry every day.

Mrs. Brovelli is a poet **who writes** poetry every day.

PRACTICE   Revise the following sentences so that each pronoun refers to a specific, not an implied or unstated, antecedent. To correct the sentence, you may have to eliminate the pronoun altogether.

1. I have always resisted learning how to serve oysters, which annoys my roommate.

   My resistance to learning how to serve oysters annoys

   my roommate.

2. Zeda had always wanted to visit the San Diego Zoo, but this wasn't possible on her last trip to San Diego.

   _____

   _____

3. There were empty M & M wrappers all over the couch, but Randy said that he had not eaten them.

   _____

   _____

4. Dan is a sailor, which he does every weekend.

   _____

   _____

5. Daniel loved the snow, and he was an avid skier. This made him decide to move to Colorado.

   _____

   _____

Reflexive and Intensive Pronouns

The reflexive and intensive pronouns are those that end in *self* or *selves*. The singular pronouns end in *self,* and the plural ones end in *selves.*

Singular	*Plural*
myself	ourselves
yourself	yourselves
himself	themselves
herself	
itself	
oneself	

These are the only reflexive and intensive forms. Avoid nonstandard forms like *hisself, ourselfs, theirselves,* or *themselfs.*

The **reflexive pronouns** are used to reflect the action of a verb back to the subject.

 EXAMPLE   Amos gave **himself** a bloody nose when he tried to slap a mosquito.

The **intensive pronouns** emphasize or intensify a noun or another pronoun in the sentence.

 EXAMPLE   Let's have **Estella Cordova herself** show us how to cross-examine a witness in court.

To help you use intensive and reflexive pronouns correctly, remember these three points.

1. Do not use a reflexive pronoun unless it is reflecting the action of a verb back to a subject.

2. Do not use an intensive pronoun unless the sentence contains a noun or pronoun for it to emphasize or intensify.

3. In general, do not use a reflexive or intensive pronoun where a personal pronoun is called for. For example, reflexive and intensive pronouns are never used as subjects.

 EXAMPLES   (incorrect)   Tim's mother and **myself** often go shopping together on Saturdays.

(correct)   Tim's mother and **I** often go shopping together on Saturdays.

(incorrect)   The other employees at the restaurant gave Carmen and **myself** large bouquets of flowers on the anniversary of our first year there.

(correct)   The other employees of the restaurant gave Carmen and **me** large bouquets of flowers on the anniversary of our first year there.

PRACTICE   Correct any errors in the use of reflexive or intensive pronouns in the following sentences.

ourselves.

1. We decided to redecorate the den ~~ourself.~~

2. Alberto and myself knew that we were the best snowboarders on the mountain.

3. Homer and Hortense sent a dehydrated Spam omelet to ourselves for Christmas.

4. Even though Jerry and herself were tired, they stayed up for *The Late Late Show.*

5. Cecilia and Ebony were sure that they could drive to Yellowstone by themself.

 PRACTICE   Correct any errors in pronoun reference or in the use of reflexive and intensive pronouns in the following sentences.

painting them

1. I used to paint landscapes, but I do not like ~~it~~ anymore.

2. The Gallo family and myself will visit the winery next week.

3. My accountant filled in my tax return in pencil, and he took a large deduction for jelly doughnuts. This made the government suspicious.

4. Sherri asked her mother if her clock was right.

5. The faculty voted to give a $25,000 bonus to Bill and herself.

6. I would like to listen to a CD on the stereo, but I don't have one.

7. I have always enjoyed the genius of Picasso, which I saw two of at the museum.

8. They decided to treat themself to a weekend by the seashore.

9. Bean stuck a peppermint stick in his nose and broke it.

10. Madame Bovary told Edna Pontellier that her husband was a bore.

SECTION 2 REVIEW

Section Two Review

1. The **antecedent** is the word a pronoun stands for.

2. A pronoun must agree with its **antecedent** in **person** and in **number.**

3. Use a plural pronoun to refer to antecedents joined by *and.*

4. Use a singular pronoun to refer to an **indefinite pronoun.**

5. Use a singular pronoun to refer to a **collective noun.**

6. When antecedents are joined by *or* or *nor,* use a pronoun that agrees with the closer antecedent.

7. Make sure a pronoun refers to a specific antecedent in its sentence or in the previous sentence.

8. Be sure that your pronoun does not refer to an implied or unstated antecedent.

9. A **reflexive pronoun** reflects the action of a verb back to the subject.

10. An **intensive pronoun** emphasizes or intensifies a noun or pronoun in the sentence.

11. Do not use a reflexive or intensive pronoun when a personal pronoun is called for.

Exercise 2A

Underline the correct pronouns in the parentheses.

1. Ms. Pelican likes to watch the eleven o'clock news, but Mr. Pelican doesn't consider (<u>it</u> them) interesting.

2. Barb and Rob told everyone who arrived at the party to put (his or her their your) umbrella in the back room.

3. After the convoy passed Cuba, (it they) turned toward South America.

4. Either the *Niña,* the *Pinta,* or the *Santa Maria* had used up all of (its their) fresh water.

5. Anyone who wants to be considered for this promotion must notify (his or her their) manager by this afternoon.

6. Crossing the equator, we found (ourselfs ourselves) becalmed.

7. If a driver hears an ambulance or a police siren, (you he or she) should pull over to the right.

8. After pulling the dogsled all day, the lead dog was eagerly gobbling (its it's) supper.

9. Someone had told us that Mammoth Mountain was situated near a volcano, but we did not take (her their) warning seriously.

10. Each new member of the committee had a bright blue badge given to (him or her them).

11. When Homer had tried every method he knew, he asked (himself hisself) if he would ever find a way to serve okra and beets.

12. When a traveler passes the House of Usher (you he or she they) should ignore the horrible shrieks coming from the second-story windows.

13. The wooden horse had lost one of (it's its) front wheels.

14. As the boat crossed the River Lethe, one of the passengers lost (his their) memory.

15. Every person who visits the local Spam factory is given a six-pack of Spam to take home with (him or her them you).

Exercise 2B

Correct all errors in pronoun usage in the following sentences. Do nothing if the sentence is correct.

1. When a player has lost three games in a row, ~~you~~ *he or she* can become rather frustrated.

2. Last year the meat packing company in our town gave all of its employees a side of beef for Christmas.

3. Anyone in their right mind would avoid that place.

4. At halftime, the school band gave their best performance ever.

5. Neither Pinocchio nor Cyrano knew if their nose would keep growing.

6. Whenever a fan hears the National Anthem, you should stand and take off your hat.

7. Huck and Jim wanted to eat by theirself, but Tom would not let them.

8. Kobe Bryant is a great basketball player, which is my favorite sport.

9. Hortense showed my brother and myself how Homer chooses his cow chips.

10. Priscilla told Rosalie that her mother had just been announced as this week's lottery winner.

11. Many neighbors complained about his messy yard, but this did not bother Michael.

12. Mr. Borden's organization was mentioned in the local paper because they had organized a food drive to help needy families.

13. If a person quietly approaches that cave, you might see a monster with one eye.

14. Cezanne, Manet, and Van Gogh agreed on what color to paint the house, which was unbelievable.

15. When Dante saw the sign above the entrance, he knew that Virgil and himself were in trouble.

Exercise 2C

Correct any errors in pronoun agreement or reference in the following paragraph.

1. Until recent years, a common practice of a newly married man was to lift his bride over the threshold of their new home. **2.** Few people know that this results from a number of ancient traditions. **3.** Perhaps the most ancient of them all is the tradition of marriage-by-capture. **4.** In many primitive societies, when a man wanted a woman from another tribe, you would seize them if they wandered too far from the protection of home. **5.** He would then force her to accompany himself back to his own tribe, and you would do battle with members of her tribe who tried to stop you. **6.** In this case, the connection to the bridegroom who picks up their bride and carries her into a new home is clear. **7.** This also comes from Roman times, when people believed that the threshold was guarded by both a good spirit and an evil spirit. **8.** The Romans believed that it would try to trip the bride as she stepped across the threshold, thus bringing bad luck to the groom and herself. **9.** To prevent this, each newly married man would carry their bride over the threshold. **10.** Finally, the practice of lifting your bride over the threshold was influenced by one other Roman tradition. **11.** Many Romans believed that something evil would happen if the bride placed their left foot across the threshold first. **12.** Since neither the groom nor the bride wanted to start the marriage out on the wrong foot, the groom would lift you over the threshold. **13.** Today, many newly married couples still practice this.

SECTION
three

Pronoun Case

Pronouns, like verbs, can appear in a variety of different forms, depending on how they function in a sentence. For example, the pronoun that refers to the speaker in a sentence may be written as *I, me, my,* or *mine.* These different spellings are the result of what is called **pronoun case.**

The three pronoun cases for English are the **subjective,** the **objective,** and the **possessive.**

Subjective Case

Singular	Plural
I	we
you	you
he, she, it	they
who	who

Objective Case

Singular	Plural
me	us
you	you
him, her, it	them
whom	whom

Possessive Case

Singular	Plural
my, mine	our, ours
your, yours	your, yours
his, her, hers, its	their, theirs
whose	whose

Subjective Pronouns

The subjective pronouns are *I, we, you, he, she, it, they,* and *who.* They are used in two situations.

1. Subjective pronouns are used as subjects of sentences.

 EXAMPLES

    s
I will return the car on Monday.

    s
They are trying to outwit me.

2. Subjective pronouns are used when they follow linking verbs. Because the linking verb identifies the pronoun after it with the subject, the pronoun must be in the same case as the subject.

EXAMPLES

                    S

It was **she** who won the award for being the best-dressed mud wrestler. (The subjective pronoun *she* is identified with the subject *it* by the linking verb *was*.)

        S

That was **I** you saw rowing across the lake yesterday.

    S

It was **they** who caused the huge traffic jam.

Objective Pronouns

The **objective pronouns** are *me, us, you, him, her, it, them,* and *whom*. They are used in three situations.

1. Objective pronouns are used as objects of prepositions.

EXAMPLES

Sally loved the chrysanthemums that Mr. Kim had given <u>to her</u>.

The difficulties <u>between Samantha and me</u> continued into the fall.

2. Objective pronouns are used as direct objects of action verbs. The noun or pronoun that receives the action of the action verb is called the **direct object**.

For example, in the simple sentence *Tuan visited Serena yesterday,* the verb is *visited,* an action verb. The direct object of *visited* is *Serena* because *Serena* receives the action of the verb *visited*. If you substitute a pronoun for *Serena,* it must be the objective pronoun *her*—*Tuan visited **her** yesterday.*

EXAMPLES

Brenda married **him** on March 7, 1987.

Last summer Joan beat **me** at tennis every time we played.

Both classes helped clean up the park, and the city rewarded **them** with a picnic.

3. Objective pronouns are used as indirect objects. The **indirect object** indicates **to whom or for whom (or to what or for what)** an action is directed, but the prepositions *to* and *for* are left out.

EXAMPLES

(prepositional phrase)   He threw the ball **to her.**

(indirect object)   He threw **her** the ball.

In the first sentence, *her* is the object of the preposition *to*. In the second sentence, the *to* is omitted and the pronoun is moved, making *her* the indirect object. In both sentences, the direct object is *ball*. Here are other examples.

 EXAMPLES

She had already given **me** two chances to make up for my mistakes.

The architect showed **them** a picture of how the new city hall would look.

PRACTICE

In the blanks, identify the underlined pronouns as subjective (sub) or objective (obj).

*sub* **1.** On Saturday, <u>we</u> will leave for our trip to the Mardi Gras.

_____ **2.** Willy told <u>him</u> to mind his own business.

_____ **3.** Was it <u>she</u> who saved these seats for us?

_____ **4.** It would be the third win in the dog sled race for <u>her</u>.

_____ **5.** The chimpanzee stared at <u>them</u> from its cage.

_____ **6.** The Loch Ness Monster was on their minds as <u>they</u> submerged.

_____ **7.** That was John <u>whom</u> you saw admiring the Titian.

_____ **8.** For three years, the father searched for <u>her</u>.

_____ **9.** Because <u>he</u> was a quadruped, he had to buy two pairs of shoes.

_____ **10.** The police officer told <u>me</u> to drive slower.

Possessive Pronouns

The **possessive pronouns** are *my, mine, our, ours, your, yours, his, her, hers, its, their, theirs,* and *whose.* They are used in two situations.

1. Possessive pronouns are used as adjectives to indicate possession.

 EXAMPLES

The old sailor had turned up **his** collar against the wind.

The weary travelers shuffled off to **their** rooms.

The polar bear constantly paced up and down **its** enclosure.

NOTE: The contraction *it's* means "it is." The word *its* is the only possessive form for *it*. (In fact, you do not use apostrophes with any of the possessive pronouns.)

2. <u>Some possessive pronouns indicate possession without being used as adjectives.</u> In this case, they may be used as subjects or objects.

EXAMPLE   I had to borrow Zan's flashlight because **mine** was lost.

Here the possessive pronoun *mine* is the subject of its clause.

EXAMPLE   The Chin house is large, but **yours** is cozy.

In this example, *yours* is the subject of its clause.

EXAMPLE   He didn't have any change for a phone call because he had given **his** to the children begging on the street.

Here the possessive pronoun *his* is a direct object.

Common Sources of Errors in Pronoun Case

Compound Constructions

Compound subjects and objects often cause problems when they include pronouns. If your sentence includes a compound construction, be sure to use the correct pronoun case.

EXAMPLES

(compound subject)	**Sandra and <u>she</u>** will return the car on Monday.
(compound after linking verb)	That was **my friend and <u>I</u>** whom you saw on the news.
(compound object of a preposition)	They awarded first place trophies **to both Dolores and <u>me</u>.**
(compound direct object)	Julio's boss fired **Mark and <u>him</u>** yesterday.
(compound indirect object)	She had already given <u>**him and me**</u> two chances to make up our minds.

In most cases, you can use a simple test to check whether you have chosen the right pronoun case when you have a compound construction. Simply remove one of the subjects or objects so that only one pronoun is left. For example, is this sentence correct? *Our host gave **Erin and I** a drink.* Test it by dropping **Erin and.** *Our host gave I a drink.* Now you can see that the *I* should be *me* because it is an object (an indirect object). The correct sentence should read: *Our host gave **Erin and me** a drink.*

PRACTICE   Underline the correct pronoun in the parentheses.

1. My brother and (I me) enjoy our dune buggies.

2. Let's keep this information just between you and (I me).

3. For the class and (she her), the ascent to the top had been thrilling.

4. Gary was glad that Karen and (him he) had made it to the top.

5. When Dorothy told Auntie Em and (I me) her story, we started to laugh.

6. Charlie and John showed Bruce and (I me) the new computers.

7. The vice squad stopped Manuela and (he him) for interdigitation.

8. Ms. Matusan said that it was Mary and (she her) at the door.

9. Chuck Berry smiled when Keith Richards and (she her) asked him for an autograph.

10. Homer and (they them) have decided to enter the Spam sculpture contest.

Who and Whom

When to use *who* or *whom* is a mystery to many writers, but you should have no problem with these pronouns if you remember two simple rules.

1. Use the subjective pronoun *who* or *whoever* if it is used as the subject of a verb.

2. Use the objective pronoun *whom* or *whomever* if it is not used as the subject of a verb.

 EXAMPLES   After leaving the airport, I followed the man **who** had taken my bags. (*Who* is the subject of *had taken*.)

The letter was sent to the person **whom** we had decided to hire. (*Whom* is not the subject of a verb.)

Please give the money to **whoever** needs it. (*Whoever* is the subject of *needs*.)

PRACTICE   Underline the correct pronoun in the parentheses.

1. The people (who <u>whom</u>) we saw at the concert were having a good time.

2. Leonardo is painting a woman (who whom) has a very subtle smile.

3. The banquet was for the person (who whom) had created the longest palindrome.

4. Tonight's grand prize will go to (whoever whomever) sold the most tickets.

5. Mr. Murlin always dislikes (whoever whomever) his daughter brings home.

Comparisons

When a pronoun is used in a comparison, you often need to supply the implied words in order to know what pronoun case to use. For example, in the sentence *My brother cannot skate as well as I*, the implied words are the verb *can skate: My brother cannot skate as well as I [can skate].*

EXAMPLE   The police officer allowed my friend to leave the scene sooner than **me.**

You can tell that *me* is the correct case in this sentence when you supply the implied words:

The police officer allowed my friend to leave the scene sooner than **[she allowed]** me **[to leave].**

PRACTICE   Underline the correct pronoun in the parentheses.

1. Oscar never drives as fast as (<u>I</u> me).

2. Even though our tax returns were identical, the IRS sent me a larger refund than (she her).

3. Chris thought she was as triskaidekaphobic as (he him).

4. Homer worried that others would not savor the Spam puree as much as (he him).

5. When they won the lottery, our parents told Melinda the news sooner than (I me).

Appositives

As you will remember from Chapter Three, an appositive is a word group containing a noun or pronoun that renames another noun or pronoun. When the appositive contains a **pronoun** that does the renaming, be sure that the pronoun is in the same case as the word it renames.

 EXAMPLE   Some team members—Joe, Frank, and **I**—were late for practice.

Here *I* is in the subjective case because the appositive *Joe, Frank, and I* renames the word *members*, the subject of the sentence.

 EXAMPLE   When the show is over, please send your review to the producers, Mark and **her.**

Here *her* is in the objective case because the appositive *Mark and her* renames *producers*, the object of the preposition *to.*

 PRACTICE   Underline the correct pronoun in the parentheses.

1. Alejandro was disappointed when the authors—Elena, Serena, and (<u>he</u> him)—were not paid well.

2. You should have your car repaired by the two best mechanics in town, Brent and (I me).

3. Kalisha was disappointed that her teammates, Cameron and (he him), had given up.

4. The most dangerous stunt was performed by the oldest skaters, Sergei and (she her).

5. The last people to arrive—Celeste, Annamaria, Lawrence, and (I me)—were told to sit in the back of the room.

 PRACTICE   Underline the correct pronoun form in the parentheses.

1. The tape will be broken by (<u>whoever</u> whomever) crosses the finish line first.

2. Do you really think that she can swim as fast as (I me)?

3. The only two people in the theater, Sheila and (I me), watched *Attack of the Killer Tomatoes* for the fourteenth time.

4. Will Prunella and (she her) join us at the fruit bar?

5. Petra decided that she would marry (whoever whomever) her astrologer recommended.

6. The long wait exhausted some of the elderly people, especially Mr. Rivera and (he him).

7. Include Risa and (she her) on the list of probables.

8. When we arrived home early, my parents praised my sister more than (I me).

9. Homer made a Spam sculpture of Elvis Presley, (who whom) he has always admired.

10. When the forest started to burn, Smokey and (she her) knew that they should not have been playing with matches in the first place.

Section Three Review

1. The **subjective pronouns** are used in two ways:

   a. As the subjects of sentences

   b. After linking verbs

2. The **objective pronouns** are used in three ways:

   a. As objects of prepositions

   b. As direct objects of action verbs

   c. As indirect objects

3. The **possessive pronouns** are used in two ways:

   a. As adjectives to modify nouns to indicate possession

   b. As subjects and objects

4. Some common sources of errors in pronoun case:

   a. Pronouns in compound constructions

   b. The use of the pronouns *who, whom, whoever,* and *whomever*

   c. Pronouns in comparisons

   d. Pronouns in appositives

Exercise 3A

Underline the correct pronoun form in the parentheses.

1. The baby seal was barking because it could not find (<u>its</u> it's) mother.

2. Between you and (I me), we have only five dollars to spend on lunch.

3. The $64,000 challenge for Eric and (she her) was to name the thirteen original colonies.

4. Was it (he him) (who whom) sold your house?

5. No one was more surprised than (I me) to see Neptune rise from the waves in Ocean Beach.

6. Inform Ulysses and (they them) that the pointed stick did its job.

7. The fellows (who whom) the Earps met at the OK Corral were soon sorry they had come.

8. Have Carlos and (she her) arrived with the decorations yet?

9. Walking through the maze, the Minotaur lost (its it's) way.

10. Was it (they them) who broke into your house and stole your bottlecap collection?

11. The prize goes to (whoever whomever) throws a cow chip the farthest.

12. Peter McGarr told Noreen that he would meet his daughter and (she her) at the Tickled Trout.

13. Scottie hired two sub-contractors, Dennis and (she her), to remodel his house.

14. The gorilla leapt from (its it's) enclosure and charged Ferdinand and (I me).

15. When they heard the buzz of the fly, Emily and (he him) started closing the windows.

Correct any pronoun errors in the following sentences. Some sentences may not contain errors.

1. Alice likes mushrooms and white rabbits more than ~~me~~. *I*

2. Do you think that Mephistopheles and he will reach an agreement?

3. Was that Madonna and child who I saw with you in church?

4. Babar gave Robin and I keys to his kingdom for our kindness.

5. When he heard the news, Oscar advised the two accountants, Jeremy and he, to leave town.

6. The club had lost it's lease for the building.

7. Plato smiled philosophically at Bill and I as we stared at the shadows flickering across the screen.

8. By this time next year, you and he will have moved to another town.

9. The children who Homer visited in the hospital asked to see his cow chip award.

10. After taking square dance lessons, Tex and Lynette could do-si-do and allemande-left better than them.

11. Between Horace and me was a deep chasm.

12. If it's screeching at every stop, your car might need it's brakes relined.

13. The first and second place ribbons for hallway whistling were awarded to Bruce and him.

14. The iconoclasts whom were bothering Pollyanna and her were finally asked to leave.

15. In the doughnut shop, my daughter and me decided to buy a maple bar and a glazed twist.

Exercise 3C

Correct any errors in pronoun case in the following paragraph.

1. Urban legends—ironic, supernatural, or unbelievable accounts of real life events—may be

the result of the ordinary human emotions of the people ~~whom~~ *who* tell them. **2.** For example, one of

my favorite urban legends clearly finds it's origin in the desire to get something for nothing. **3.** It

was originally told to my brother and I by a local bank manager. **4.** Someone whom she knows

has a friend who says that his wife and him paid only $1500 for a $50,000 Porsche Targa.

5. They paid so little because it had sat in the Mojave Desert for two weeks with the body of it's

owner in it. **6.** My brother is more skeptical than me, but even he would like to believe that such

an event could happen to him. **7.** Another urban legend is probably caused by our fear of the

unknown, especially in dark, lonely places. **8.** According to this legend, a boy and a girl whom

have parked in the woods are talking about a rumor that a one-armed man has been seen

nearby. **9.** Friends have told the boy and she that he has attacked several people with his hook in

the past few weeks while frothing at the mouth and yelling, "Bloody murder!" **10.** Frightened,

the two leave the woods, but when they arrive home and get out of the car, they find a hook dan-

gling from it's right front door. **11.** They are both terrified, but the boy is determined to find the

man who tried to attack his girlfriend and he. **12.** He drives back to the woods and is never

heard from again. **13.** Finally, an urban legend that my wife and me have heard several different

versions of must be caused by a need to see people get what they deserve. **14.** In this one, an

elderly woman whom lives in a downtown apartment with her blind husband finds her beloved

cat dead one day. **15.** The old woman puts the body into a shopping bag, and her husband and

her tearfully take a bus across town to a pet cemetery. **16.** On the trip, a teenage gang member,

who is much stronger than them, grabs the bag, laughs at the woman, and jumps off the

bus. **17.** According to almost every version told to my wife and I, when the thief looks into the

bag, he is so startled that he falls backward into the path of a car. **18.** Clearly, urban legends like

these are repeated because they express many of our unspoken desires and fears.

Sentence Practice: Using Transitions

Writers use certain words and phrases to indicate the relationships among the ideas in their sentences and paragraphs. These words and phrases provide links between ideas, leading a reader from one idea to another smoothly. They show relationships like time, addition, or contrast. Consider this paragraph from Rachel Carson's *Edge of the Sea:*

> **When** the tide is rising the shore is a place of unrest, with the surge leaping high over jutting rocks **and** running in lacy cascades of foam over the landward side of massive boulders. **But** on the ebb it is more peaceful, **for then** the waves do not have behind them the push of the inward pressing tides. There is no particular drama about the turn of the tide, **but presently** a zone of wetness shows on the gray rock slopes, **and** offshore the incoming swells begin to swirl **and** break over hidden ledges. **Soon** the rocks that the high tide had concealed rise into view and glisten with the wetness left on them by the receding water.

Because she is writing about a process, most of Rachel Carson's transitional words indicate a relationship in time (*when, then, presently, soon*). But she also uses transitional words that indicate contrast (*but*), cause (*for*), and addition (*and*). As you can see, she uses these expressions to lead her readers smoothly from one idea to another.

The sentence combining exercises in this chapter are designed to give you practice in using transitional words and phrases to link your ideas. Try to use as many different ones as you can. For your convenience, here is a list of commonly used transitional words and phrases.

- Time: *then, soon, first, second, finally, meanwhile, next, at first, in the beginning*

- Contrast: *yet, but, however, instead, otherwise, on the other hand, on the contrary*

- Addition: *and, also, besides, furthermore, in addition, likewise, moreover, similarly*

- Cause–effect: *for, because, consequently, so, therefore, hence, thus, as a result*

- Example: *for example, for instance, that is, such as*

- Conclusion: *thus, hence, finally, generally, as a result, in conclusion*

PRACTICE   Add transitions to the following sentences.

1. Sometimes I am indecisive about the most trivial things. _____, this morning I spent fifteen minutes trying to decide whether to buy a cinnamon roll or a jelly doughnut.

2. California is known for its many beaches. _____, it has many excellent ski resorts.

3. Barbara and Greg have been very successful in their real estate careers. _____, they have raised five well-adjusted, happy children.

4. Only seven of our team members showed up for our weekend softball game. _____, we had to forfeit the game to the other team.

5. This afternoon I will probably jog for thirty minutes. _____, perhaps I will stay home and eat the last of my jelly doughnuts.

Sentence Combining Exercises

Combine the following sentences, using transitions as indicated in the directions.

⊚ **EXAMPLE**   Combine these sentences into two sentences. Use transitions that indicate contrast, example, and addition. Underline your transitions.

    a. Herman knows he needs to lose weight.
    b. He is unable to resist the urge to eat ice cream.
    c. Yesterday he drank a low-fat fiber shake for lunch.
    d. After work he stopped at a 31 Flavors ice cream store.
    e. He ate a large chocolate sundae.

Herman knows he needs to lose weight, <u>but</u> he is unable to resist the urge to eat ice cream. <u>For example,</u> yesterday he drank a low-fat fiber shake for lunch, <u>but</u> after work he stopped at a 31 Flavors ice cream store <u>and</u> ate a large chocolate sundae.

1. Combine the following sentences into two sentences. Use transitions that indicate addition. Underline your transitions.

    a. In the fall and winter, Rita watches pro football on television every Sunday.
    b. In the fall and winter, Rita watches college football on television every Saturday.
    c. In the spring and summer, she attends every baseball game played by her local team.
    d. She attends every tennis match hosted by her city.

    _____

    _____

    _____

    _____

2. Combine the following sentences into two sentences. Use transitions that indicate cause–effect and addition. Underline your transitions.

    a. The crocodile is an Egyptian symbol of evil and fury.
    b. The crocodile is vicious and destructive.
    c. The crocodile lives in a realm between water and earth.
    d. The crocodile is a symbol of fertility and power.

    _____

    _____

    _____

    _____

Sentence Combining Exercises

continued

3. Combine the following sentences into two sentences. Use transitions that indicate cause–effect. Underline your transitions.

   a. Horse-drawn covered wagons used to be called "Conestogas."
   b. Conestogas were originally built in the Conestoga Valley of Pennsylvania.
   c. The Conestogas supplied cigars, among other things, to the pioneers.
   d. Cigars came to be called "stogies."

   _____

   _____

   _____

   _____

4. Combine the following sentences into three sentences, using transitions that show time relationships. Underline your transitions.

   a. Brenda finished reading *Romeo and Juliet*.
   b. Brenda folded her laundry.
   c. Brenda made a list of tasks she had to complete by Monday.
   d. Brenda worked on her poem.
   e. It was very late.
   f. Brenda watched *The Late Show with David Letterman*.

   _____

   _____

   _____

   _____

continued

5. Combine the following sentences into two sentences. Use transitions that indicate cause–effect and example. Underline your transitions.

   a. Simon avoids his family.
   b. Whenever he visits his family, someone insults him.
   c. Last Christmas his mother said that he could pass for the Christmas turkey.
   d. He had gained twenty pounds.

   _____

   _____

   _____

   _____

6. Combine the following sentences into three or four sentences, using transitions that show time relationships. Underline your transitions.

   a. The holes in bread are made by bubbles of gas.
   b. Flour and water are mixed to form dough.
   c. A small amount of yeast is added.
   d. The yeast grows.
   e. The yeast gives off a gas.
   f. The gas bubbles up through the dough.
   g. The dough expands.

   _____

   _____

   _____

   _____

Sentence Combining Exercises

continued

7. Combine the following sentences into two sentences. Use transitions that indicate cause–effect and contrast. Underline your transitions.

   a. In ancient times, wedding guests threw wheat at a new bride.
   b. Wheat was a symbol of fertility and prosperity.
   c. In the first century B.C., Roman bakers began to cook the wheat into small cakes.
   d. Wedding guests did not want to give up the custom of throwing wheat.
   e. They threw the wedding cakes instead.

   _____

   _____

   _____

   _____

8. Combine the following sentences into two sentences. Join the two sentences with a transition that indicates cause–effect. Underline your transitions.

   a. Periodically the weather in Scandinavia may be too hot for the lemmings.
   b. Periodically the lemmings' food supply may change.
   c. Periodically the lemmings may feel overcrowded.
   d. Thousands of Scandinavian lemmings travel for miles.
   e. They throw themselves into the sea.
   f. They swim until they are exhausted and drown.

   _____

   _____

   _____

   _____

Sentence Combining Exercises

continued

9. Combine the following sentences into two sentences. Use transitions that indicate contrast and cause–effect. Underline your transitions.

    a. Today the paper or plastic kite is a popular child's toy.
    b. It was originally designed by the Chinese in 1200 B.C.
    c. It was designed to send coded military messages.
    d. Each kite's unique shape, color, and movements were ideal for sending coded messages.
    e. Only someone who knew the code could "read" it.

_____

_____

_____

_____

10. Combine the following sentences into three sentences. Use transitions that indicate example, cause–effect, and addition. Underline your transitions.

    a. Many superstitions have unusual origins.
    b. It is considered bad luck to walk under a ladder.
    c. A ladder leaning against a wall forms a triangle.
    d. Many ancient societies believed that a triangle was a place sacred to the gods.
    e. Walking through a triangle defiled that space.

_____

_____

_____

_____

SECTION
five

Essay and Paragraph Practice: Explaining Causes and Effects

Assignment

In Chapter Three you wrote an expository paper that used examples as support. Such an organization—one that calls for a listing of examples to support an idea—is very common in college papers and tests. Another common assignment is one that asks you to explain the **causes** or the **effects** of something. In an American history class, for example, you might be asked to explain the causes of the South's failure to win the Civil War. Or in a psychology class you might be asked to explain the long-term effects that physical abuse can have on children.

A paper that focuses on causes explains *why* a certain event might have occurred or why people do what they do. On the other hand, a paper that focuses on effects explains what has *resulted* or might result from an event, action, or behavior. In this chapter, Exercise 1C (page 220) explains the effects of chocolate on someone's mother; Exercise 2C (page 234) explains the causes of the tradition of a groom carrying a bride across the threshold; and Exercise 3C (page 246) explains the causes of some urban legends. Each of these paragraphs states the purpose of the paragraph (to explain causes or effects) in a topic sentence and then presents several specific causes or effects.

Your assignment is to write a paper that explains *either* the causes *or* the effects of a topic with which you are personally familiar. Develop your paper from one of the suggestions below or from an idea suggested by your instructor.

Prewriting to Generate Ideas

Prewriting Application: Finding Your Topic

Use prewriting techniques of freewriting, brainstorming, or clustering to decide which of the following topic ideas interests you. Write for five or ten minutes on several of these suggestions. Don't stop writing once you find one topic that might work. Try out several of them before you make a decision.

Analyzing Causes

1. Why do you or do you not admire, respect, or trust a particular person?

2. Why are you doing well or poorly in a particular course?

3. Why did your or your parents' marriage or relationship fail, or why is it a success?

4. Why was your childhood or some other period the best or worst time of your life?

5. Why did you move from one place to another?

6. Why did you buy the particular car or other item that you did?

7. Why are you attending a particular college?

8. Why did you make an important decision?

9. Why did a particular experience affect you the way it did?

10. Why will you never go to *that* restaurant, hotel, beach, or lake again?

Analyzing Effects

1. What were the effects of an important decision that you made?

2. What were the effects of your move to a new place?

3. What were the effects of your being an only child, or an oldest child, or a youngest child, or of growing up in a large family?

4. What are the effects of stress upon the way you act, feel, or think?

5. What were the effects upon you of a major change in your life—having a child? getting married? changing jobs? experiencing a divorce?

6. What have been the effects of a serious compulsion or addiction to drugs, alcohol, gambling, or overeating upon someone you know or upon his or her loved ones?

7. What have been the effects of mental, emotional, or physical abuse upon you or someone you know?

8. What have been the effects of discrimination or prejudice upon you or someone you know? (Discrimination might involve race, gender, age, sexuality, or religion.)

9. What have been the effects upon you and/or upon your family of working and/or raising a family and attending school at the same time?

10. What have been the effects upon you of some major change in your lifestyle or values?

Choosing and Narrowing the Topic

Once you have settled on several possible topics, consider these points as you make your final selection.

- Choose the more limited topic rather than the more general one.

- Choose the topic about which you could develop several causes or effects. Avoid topics that involve only one or two causes or effects.

- Choose the topic about which you have the most experience or knowledge.

- Choose the topic in which you have the most personal interest. Avoid topics about which you don't really care.

Writing a Thesis Statement or Topic Sentence

If your assignment is to write a single paragraph, you will open it with a topic sentence. If you are writing a complete essay, you will need a thesis statement at the end of your introductory paragraph. In either case, you will need a clear statement of the topic and central idea of your paper.

Prewriting Application: Working with Topic Sentences

Identify the topic sentences in Exercises 1C (page 220), 2C (page 234), and 3C (page 246). Then identify the topic and the central point in each topic sentence.

Prewriting Application: Evaluating Thesis Statements and Topic Sentences

Write "No" before each sentence that would not make an effective thesis statement or topic sentence for a paper explaining causes or effects. Write "Yes" before each sentence that *would* make an effective one. Identify each effective sentence as introducing a paper about causes or effects. Using ideas of your own, rewrite each ineffective sentence into one that might work.

_____ **1.** My father's generosity, sensitivity, and openness have made him into the most important person in my life.

_____

_____

_____ **2.** I divorced my husband on June 30 of last year.

_____

_____

_____ **3.** Although I loved living in Boulder, Colorado, several events over the past few years helped me to decide that it was time to move.

_____

_____

_____ **4.** Whenever I let myself worry too much about my job, school, or family responsibilities, everyone that I love is affected by my strange behavior.

_____

_____

_____ **5.** My life has changed in many ways since I was young.

_____

_____

_____ **6.** Many students at our local high school use marijuana, methamphetamines, and even cocaine.

_____

_____

_____ **7.** Telling my parents that I was gay was one of the best decisions that I ever made.

_____

_____

_____ **8.** Growing up as an only child helped me to become an independent, decisive, and responsible person.

_____

_____

_____ **9.** My new computer, which uses all the latest technology, came loaded with my favorite games and word processing software.

_____

_____

_____ **10.** Attending a college away from home has caused me to become a much better person in a number of ways.

_____

_____

Prewriting Application: Talking to Others

Form a group of three or four people and tell each other what topic you have chosen and whether you plan to discuss causes or effects. Use the following guidelines to discuss your papers.

1. What is the topic of the paper? Will the paper focus on causes or effects?

2. What causes or effects will be included? Can they be more specific and descriptive? Can they be explained more clearly?

3. What other causes or effects could be included? Are there any less obvious but more interesting ones?

4. Are you convinced? Have enough causes or effects been provided to illustrate the topic idea? Should any of them be explained or described more thoroughly?

5. Which cause or effect should the paper open with? Which should it close with?

Organizing Causes and Effects

Chronological and **emphatic** arrangements are perhaps the most common ways to organize several causes or effects. If you are explaining what caused you to stop smoking, a chronological arrangement would list the most remote causes first and move to the most recent causes. On the other hand, an emphatic arrangement would involve deciding which cause was the most significant one and saving it until last.

Writing the Essay

If your assignment is to write a complete essay:

- Place your **thesis statement** at the end of the introductory paragraph.

- Write a separate **body paragraph** for each cause or effect that you intend to discuss.

- Open each body paragraph with a **topic sentence** that identifies the specific cause or effect.

- Within each body paragraph, use **specific facts and details** to explain and support your ideas.

Writing the Paragraph

If your assignment is to write a single paragraph:

- Open it with a **topic sentence** that clearly identifies the topic and central idea of the paragraph.

- Use **clear transitions** to move from one cause or effect to the next.

- Use **specific facts and details** to explain and support your ideas.

Writing Application: Identifying Transitional Words, Phrases, and Sentences

Examine Exercises 1C (page 220), 2C (page 234), and 3C (page 246). Identify the transitions that introduce each new cause or effect. Then identify any other transitions that serve to connect ideas between sentences.

Rewriting and Improving the Paper

1. Revise your sentences so that they include specific and concrete details. As often as possible, use actual names of people and places. Refer to specific details whenever possible.

2. Add or revise transitions wherever doing so will help clarify your movement from one idea to another.

3. Improve your preliminary thesis statement (if you are writing an essay) or your preliminary topic sentence (if you are writing a single paragraph) so that it more accurately states the central point of your paper.

4. Examine your draft for simple sentences that can be combined to make compound, complex, or compound-complex sentences. Watch also for sentences that can be combined using participial phrases, appositives, infinitive phrases, or adjective clauses.

Rewriting Application: Responding to Paragraph Writing

Read the following paragraph. Then respond to the questions following it.

Changing Careers

Two years ago, after serving for over twenty-five years in the United States Navy, I decided that it was time to move on to new and better things, and I have never regretted that decision. One of the most pleasant effects of retiring from the military has been not having to endure any more family separations. While in the Navy, I spent most of my career aboard ship and made many six-month deployments or had to stand duty every four or five days when not on deployment. Now that I have more time to spend with my family, I have joined a family bowling league and have time to attend school events that my children are participating in. Another effect of leaving the military is that I am able to get involved with community activities because I know that I won't be moving to another city in two or three years. During one period of my career my family and I lived in San Francisco two years, Norfolk, Virginia, three years, and then San Diego. Now that I don't plan to move within two or three years, I have joined the Parent/Teachers' Association at my son's school, become an active member in the local Boy Scout troop, and become a board member of my homeowners' association. Finally, by working fewer hours than I did when I was in the Navy, I have the opportunity to go to school. I am able to use the

Montgomery G.I. Bill to supplement my income while in school and obtain a degree in Business Management. My wife and I agree that we made the right decision to leave the military when I did. The week after I retired, the ship I had been stationed on made an unexpected nine-month deployment to Somalia. I obtained a good civil service job after I retired, and my supervisor allows me to attend school in the mornings and work in the afternoons and weekends.

1. Identify the topic sentence. State its topic and central idea. Is it an effective topic sentence? Can you tell whether the paper will focus on causes or effects?

2. How many causes or effects are mentioned in this paper? Identify them.

3. Identify the transitional sentences that introduce each cause or effect. What other transitions are used between sentences in this paragraph?

4. What parts of each cause or effect could be made still more specific?

5. Consider the organization of the paragraph. Would you change the order of the causes or effects? Explain why or why not.

Rewriting Application: Responding to Essay Writing

Read the following essay. Then respond to the questions at the end of it.

A New Person

I used to be the kind of person who only thought of herself. I wanted to make a lot of money, party every weekend, and just have fun. I was probably the most self-centered person you have ever met. But in the past two years I have really changed. I have started to think about other people before I think about myself. I am happy that I am becoming a different person, but the causes of my change have been painful.

I think my change started when my boyfriend left me last year. We had been together for five years, ever since we graduated from Oceanside High School. Even though we fought a lot, I was sure that we would eventually get married and be together forever. So I was stunned and really hurt when he told me goodbye. He told me I was the most selfish person he had ever met. I was furious for a long time after that, but I kept thinking about what he had said. I began to think that maybe he was right. Maybe I was selfish.

I have also changed because of people I have met at Palomar College. When I decided to go back to school, I just wanted to get my degree and be left alone. I thought I was smarter than everyone else, so I hardly ever talked to anyone in my classes. By the end of my first semester, I was really lonely. It seemed as if everyone but me had made friends and was having fun. So I tried an experiment. I started asking people around me in class how they were doing, and if they were having trouble I offered to help. That was really a big step for me. By the end of the year, I had several new friends, and two of them are still my best friends today.

The biggest cause of my new attitude, however, came when I took a part-time job at Vista Convalescent Care. I had never worked with old people before, and I dreaded the idea of changing bedpans and cleaning up after them. But after a few weeks I really started to like the people I was taking care of, and I began to see that making them feel good made me feel good too. One little old lady in particular became my friend. Her name was Rita Gonzalez, and she had Alzheimer's. Whenever I came into her room, she was always so happy because she thought I was her daughter. Her real daughter never visited her, so I took her place, and Rita and I spent lots of afternoons together. She taught me to forget about my own problems, so when she died last month, I was heartbroken, but I was also very grateful to her.

I think I am a much better person today than I used to be, and I hope I will not forget these experiences. They have been painful, but they have taught me how to think about other people before I think about myself. I like who I am today, and I could not say that a few years ago.

1. Identify the thesis statement. State its topic and central idea. Is it an effective thesis statement? Can you tell whether the paper will focus on causes or effects?

2. Identify each topic sentence. State its topic and central idea. Does each topic sentence clearly introduce one specific cause or effect?

3. What transitional words introduce each new body paragraph?

4. Does the essay use a chronological or emphatic organization? Would you change the order of the paragraphs? Why or why not?

5. Is each cause or effect explained clearly and fully? If you would improve any, explain how you would do so.

Proofreading

When proofreading your paper, watch for the following errors:

- Sentence fragments
- Comma splices
- Fused sentences
- Misplaced modifiers
- Dangling modifiers
- Incorrect subject–verb agreement
- Incorrect pronoun case
- Incorrect pronoun–antecedent agreement or pronoun reference
- Misspelled words

Prepare a clean final draft, following the format your instructor has requested. Before you turn in your final draft, proofread it carefully and make any necessary corrections.

Chapter Four Practice Test

I. Review of Chapters One, Two, and Three

A. Underline all subjects once and complete verbs twice. Place all prepositional phrases in parentheses.

1. Neither the rhubarb cake nor the eggplant pie was a big hit at last night's party.

2. After the romantic had praised the beauty of nature, the realist decided to mow the lawn.

3. The statue of David was a work of art, but Harold would not look at it.

4. The son gathered the wax and the feathers and took them to his father.

5. The smell of fresh popcorn drifted down the hall and into the offices of the faculty.

B. Correct any fragments, fused sentences, or comma splices in the following sentences. Do nothing if the sentence is correct.

6. Persephone, asking her mother if she should eat the pomegranate.

_____

_____

7. Queequeg sharpened his harpoon soon he would need it.

_____

_____

8. The salmon, swimming swiftly upstream, did not see the bear, which flicked many of them out of the water with its huge paw.

_____

_____

9. The audience applauded loudly at the conclusion of the symphony, however, Beethoven could not hear the applause.

_____

_____

Chapter Four Practice Test

continued

10. Because the alarm clock had startled him and woken him from a deep sleep.

_____

_____

C. At the places indicated, add adjective clauses, appositives, infinitive phrases, or participial phrases to the following sentences as directed in the parentheses. Use commas where they are needed.

11. The German shepherd attacked the police officer ^ . (adjective clause)

_____

_____

12. Brittany glared at the umpire ^ as she returned to the dugout. (appositive)

_____

_____

13. ^ The cougar wandered off into the woods. (participial phrase)

_____

_____

14. Jenna trained her African gray parrot ^ whenever the doorbell would ring. (infinitive phrase)

_____

_____

15. The German shepherd ^ kept me awake all night. (participial phrase)

_____

_____

continued

D. Correct any dangling or misplaced modifiers in the following sentences. Do nothing if the sentence is correct.

16. A black rottweiler lunged at the little girl with a nasty snarl when she passed its yard.

_____

_____

17. The fire was so intense that it almost burned the entire hotel.

_____

_____

18. Pulling tiredly on their oars, the trip was nearly over.

_____

_____

19. Mr. Lincoln leaned over and petted the dog wearing his new silk hat.

_____

_____

20. Surprised by the flashing lights of the police car, Amy's new car slowly came to a stop.

_____

_____

II. Chapter Four

A. Underline the correct verb form in the parentheses.

21. Each knife, fork, and spoon on the table (has have) to be placed precisely next to

each plate.

22. In the past few years, gymnastics (seems seem) to have become very popular.

23. Here (is are) the pack of cards and the pair of dice that you requested.

24. The panel of judges (decide decides) which sculpture gets the prize.

25. Neither Clark's father nor the other citizens of Smallville (think thinks) much of Lex.

continued

B. Correct any subject–verb agreement errors in the following sentences. Do nothing if the sentence is correct.

26. An old dog and a cat with torn ears goes through the garbage each night.

27. Anything that anyone needs to know about the history of small jazz combos are included in this book.

28. One hundred dollars seems like a fair price for my collection of broken roof tiles.

29. Do Jules Verne or H.G. Wells have anything to say about this phenomenon?

30. A suspicious-looking stranger followed by three angry police officers have just entered the restaurant.

C. Underline the correct pronouns in the parentheses.

31. Someone left (her their) knife in the library, and I think it was Mrs. Peacock.

32. Before a runner enters a marathon, (you he or she they) should train for at least six months.

33. Scott and Zelda wanted to spend the weekend by (themselfs theirself themselves).

34. The army crossed the Alps on (its their) way to Italy.

35. Each of the applicants was determined to do (his or her their) very best on the exam.

D. Correct any pronoun errors in the following sentences. Do nothing if the sentence is correct.

36. Our children love sending valentines, which is their favorite holiday.

37. Whenever Elvis visited Ringo, he complained about today's music.

38. Clint was afraid that she would kill him if he played "Misty"; fortunately, this did not happen.

39. Everyone who visits the Mark Twain Cave is surprised when they see Jesse James's name inscribed on the cave wall.

40. Although many neighbors asked for their recipe, Ben and Jerry decided to keep their secret ice cream formula to theirselves.

continued

E. Underline the correct pronoun in the parentheses.

41. Spam Lite, the miracle weight-loss food, was delivered to Bill and (I me).

42. Dave Robicheaux fished in the bayou after Alastair and (he him) had returned from New Orleans.

43. Wendy said that the meteorologists, Mr. Cataclysmus and (she her), would soon report on the tornado.

44. I don't practice my guitar as often as (he him), so I don't play nearly as well.

45. Mrs. Hutchinson, (who whom) I saw at yesterday's lottery, seems to have disappeared.

F. Correct any pronoun errors in the following sentences. Do nothing if the sentence is correct.

46. The lion tried to pull the thorn out of it's paw.

47. Johann had more children than Ludwig, but Ludwig wrote more symphonies than him.

48. Do you want Tom and him to help you paint that fence?

49. Between Achilles and I, we met about thirty thousand Trojans that day.

50. Keiko asked Kerrin and I to visit her if we ever traveled to Japan.

Using Punctuation
and Capitalization

When we speak to people face to face, we have a number of signals, aside from the words we choose, to let them know how we feel. Facial expressions—smiles, frowns, grimaces—convey our emotions and attitudes. Tone of voice can tell a listener whether we feel sad or lighthearted or sarcastic about what we are saying. Hand gestures and other body language add further messages to the communication. In fact, experts tell us that these nonverbal communications make up over eighty percent of the messages in a conversation.

When we write in order to communicate with a reader, we must make up for that eighty percent of lost, nonverbal communication by using the writing signals that we know. Some of the most important signals in writing are the punctuation marks. They signal whether we are making a statement or asking a question. They indicate the boundaries of our sentences. They determine much of the rhythm and emotion of our writing.

If you are able to use punctuation effectively, you have a powerful tool to control how your writing affects your readers. If you do not know the basic rules of punctuation, you run the risk of being misunderstood or of confusing your readers. In this chapter we will discuss the essential rules of punctuation, not just so that your writing will be correct but, more important, so that you will be able to express your ideas exactly the way you want them to be expressed.

Using Commas

The comma gives writers more trouble than any of the other punctuation marks. Before printing was developed, commas came into use to tell readers when to put in a slight pause when they were reading aloud. Now, although the placement of the comma does affect the rhythm of sentences, it also conveys many messages that are more important than when to pause. Because the comma is such an important punctuation mark and because it can be troublesome to you if you don't know how to use it correctly, we take it up first. You are already familiar with several of its uses.

Comma usage can be explained by four general rules:

1. **Use commas before coordinating conjunctions that join main clauses to form a compound sentence.**

2. **Use commas between elements in a series.**

3. **Use commas after introductory elements.**

4. **Use commas before and after interrupters.**

Commas in Compound Sentences

1. When joining two main clauses with one of the coordinating conjunctions to form a compound sentence, use a comma before the conjunction.

 EXAMPLES   I don't know her, **but** I like her already.

The tableware in the restaurant was exquisite, **and** the food was some of the best I have ever tasted.

We had to remove the huge eucalyptus tree, **or** its encroaching roots would have undermined our happy home.

2. When conjunctions join other parts of a sentence, such as two words, two phrases, or two subordinate clauses, do not put commas before the conjunctions.

EXAMPLE   Every morning that scoundrel **has** a drink <u>and</u> then thoroughly **beats** his poor dog.

No comma is needed before *and* because it does not join two main clauses. Instead, it joins the verbs *has* and *beats*.

EXAMPLE   I decided to visit France because I had never had a chance to see that country <u>and</u> because my travel agent was able to offer me a special discount on the trip.

No comma is needed before *and* because it joins two subordinate clauses, not two main clauses.

 PRACTICE   Add commas to the following sentences where necessary.

1. Homer bought the Spam‚and Hortense cooked it for him.

2. Hortense served the Spam over vermicelli but Homer refused to eat it.

3. Homer cooked some hushpuppies but did not give any to Hortense.

4. Hortense refused to speak to Homer for she loved hushpuppies.

5. Homer decided to eat the hominy so Hortense ate the Spam and rice.

Commas with Elements in a Series

1. When listing three or more elements (words, phrases, clauses) in a series, separate them by commas. When the last two elements are joined by a coordinating conjunction, a comma before the conjunction is optional.

 EXAMPLES

(words)   The gazpacho was **cold, spicy, and fresh.**

(phrases)   In the mountains, he had been **thrown by his horse, bitten by a snake, and chased by a bear.**

(clauses)   To rescue the koala, **the firefighters brought a ladder, the police brought a rope, and the mayor brought a speech.**

2. When using two or more adjectives to modify the same noun, separate them with commas if you can put *and* between the adjectives without changing the meaning or if you can easily reverse the order of the adjectives.

 EXAMPLES

She eagerly stepped into the **comforting, cool** water.

A **stubborn, obnoxious** boll weevil is ruining my cotton patch.

Note that you could easily use *and* between the above adjectives. (The water is *comforting* and *cool;* the boll weevil is *stubborn* and *obnoxious.*) You could also reverse the adjectives (the *cool, comforting water* or the *obnoxious, stubborn* boll weevil).

3. On the other hand, if the adjectives cannot be joined by *and* or are not easily reversed, no comma is necessary.

 EXAMPLE

A bureaucrat wearing a **black leather jacket** and a smirk strode into the auditorium.

Notice how awkward the sentence would sound if you placed *and* between the adjectives (*a black and leather jacket*) or if you reversed them (*a leather black jacket*).

PRACTICE

Insert commas between main clauses joined by a coordinating conjunction and between items in a series.

1. The bill was only $10.50 so Vera paid it in cash.

2. Quentin looked at the sky and dreamed about applesauce sweet potato pie and creamed corn.

3. Martin finished the ninety-five items grabbed a hammer and nailed them to the church door.

4. We spotted trout in the clear cold river.

5. Elmer was exhausted for the neighbor's dog had barked all night long.

6. The dirty unkempt man stumbled into camp and the first thing he wanted was a Popsicle.

7. Rupert was proud of his pocket protector and never allowed it to get stained.

8. Ms. Caudillo could have gone to the play or she could have gone to the concert.

9. LaVere bought some flowers visited her sick friend caught the trolley and went to work.

10. Daniel looked at the soft inviting pile of pine needles and decided he would take a long refreshing nap.

Commas with Introductory Elements

When you begin a sentence with certain introductory words, phrases, or clauses, place a comma after the introductory element.

1. Use a comma after the following introductory words and transitional expressions.

Introductory Words		Transitional Expressions
next	similarly	on the other hand
first	nevertheless	in a similar manner
second	therefore	in other words
third	indeed	for example
moreover	yes	for instance
however	no	in fact
		in addition
		as a result

 EXAMPLES

First, we will strike at the heart of the matter and then pursue other clichés.

For example, let's all stand up and be counted.

2. Use a comma after introductory prepositional phrases of five or more words. However, you may need to use a comma after shorter introductory prepositional phrases if not doing so would cause confusion.

 EXAMPLES

After a long and thrilling nap, Buster went looking for a cat to chase.

After dinner we all went for a walk around the lake.

In spring, time seems to catch up with small furry animals.

Without the comma, this last sentence might look as if it begins *In springtime.*

3. Use a comma after all introductory infinitive and participial phrases.

 EXAMPLES

Blackened with soot, the little boy toddled out of the smoldering house.

Begging for her forgiveness, Homer assured Hortense that they would never run short of Spam again.

To break in your new car properly, drive at varying speeds for the first one thousand miles.

4. Use a comma after introductory adverb subordinate clauses.

EXAMPLES   **Because Umberto played the tuba so well,** he was awarded a music scholarship.

As soon as he arrived on shore, Columbus claimed the land for Spain.

Although it was raining furiously, Freida ran six miles anyway.

PRACTICE   Insert commas after introductory elements.

1. First, I will tell you about my relative who fought at the Alamo.

2. In a cave high on a mountain in Tennessee Homer was setting up his still.

3. Scanning the world Keats knew he had never seen anything like Chapman's Homer.

4. When we got to the top we wrote a message to those who would follow us.

5. Yes I have always wanted to have a wisdom tooth pulled without any anesthetic.

6. Approaching the crash site Matt Scudder slowed to a stop.

7. As the artist looked up at the ceiling he hoped the Pope would like it.

8. After spending a sleepless night Dr. Scarpetta knew who the main suspect was.

9. In a final ironic twist Abner's job in prison was making matches.

10. To find the Holy Grail Perceval spent years wandering throughout Europe and Great Britain.

Commas with Interrupters

Sometimes certain words, phrases, or clauses will interrupt the flow of thought in a sentence to add emphasis or additional information. These interrupters are enclosed by commas.

   1. Use commas to set off parenthetical expressions. Common parenthetical expressions include *however, indeed, consequently, as a result, moreover, of course, for example, for instance, that is, in fact, after all, I think,* and *therefore.*

 EXAMPLES
   The answer**, after all,** lay right under his left big toe.

   That big blue bird by the feeder is**, I think,** one of those unruly Steller's jays.

   She is**, moreover,** a notorious misspeller of the word *deceitful.*

   NOTE: Whenever a parenthetical expression introduces a second main clause after a semicolon, the semicolon takes the place of the comma in front of it.

 EXAMPLE
   Yes, you may eat your snails in front of me**; after all,** we are old friends.

 PRACTICE
Use commas to set off any parenthetical elements in the following sentences.

   1. The red Mustang, after all, did signal before turning left.

   2. Charlie Moon on the other hand knew exactly where the old woman was going.

   3. Homer wanted to impress Hortense; therefore he saved enough flour sacks to make her a dress.

   4. Peter Decker however was late getting to the synagogue.

   5. Ms. Mendoza disliked flying on airplanes; in fact she even turned down a free flight to Hawaii.

   2. Use commas to set off nonrestrictive elements. Nonrestrictive elements are modifying words, phrases, or clauses that are not necessary to identify the words they modify. They include adjective subordinate clauses, appositives, and participial phrases.

Adjective Clauses

(See pages 80–82 if you need to review adjective clauses.) If the information in an adjective clause <u>is not necessary to identify the word it modifies</u>, it is called a **nonrestrictive clause**, and it is enclosed in commas.

 EXAMPLE   Ms. Erindira Sanchez, **who is president of that company,** began twenty years ago as a secretary.

Because the name of the person is used, the adjective clause is not necessary to identify which woman began twenty years ago as a secretary, so the commas are needed.

  However, if her name is not used, the adjective clause is a **restrictive** one <u>because the woman is not already identified</u>. In this case, the commas are not necessary.

 EXAMPLE   The woman **who is president of that company** began twenty years ago as a secretary.

The following are additional examples of nonrestrictive clauses.

 EXAMPLE   My oldest brother, **who is a park ranger,** showed me his collection of arrowheads.

Because a person can have only one oldest brother, the brother is already identified, and the adjective clause is <u>not needed to identify him</u>, making it nonrestrictive.

 EXAMPLE   His home town, **which is somewhere in northeastern Indiana,** wants him to return for its centennial celebration.

A person can have only one home town, so the adjective clause is nonrestrictive.

 PRACTICE   In the following sentences, set off all nonrestrictive clauses with commas.

1. La Paloma‚ which is an old theater near my house‚ is my favorite place to

   see films.

2. *The Simpsons* which was created by Matt Groening presents a cynical view

   of the American family.

3. My oldest friend who served with me in Vietnam has been visiting me in

   San Diego.

4. The burglar who stole our Spam was caught in Hawaii.

5. The *Titanic* which was supposed to be one of the safest ships ever built

sank on its maiden voyage.

Participial Phrases

(See pages 146–147 if you need to review participial phrases.) Participial phrases that <u>do not contain information necessary to identify the words they modify</u> are nonrestrictive and are therefore set off by commas. Restrictive participial phrases do not require commas.

 EXAMPLE   (nonrestrictive)   The President, **seeking to be reelected**, traveled throughout the country making speeches and kissing babies.

Because we have only one president, the participial phrase *seeking to be reelected* is nonrestrictive. It is not necessary to identify who is meant by *President.*

 EXAMPLE   (restrictive)   The woman **sitting by the door** is a famous surgeon.

Sitting by the door is a restrictive participial phrase because it is necessary to identify which woman is the famous surgeon.

 EXAMPLE   Foxworth, **discouraged by years of failure**, decided to buy a pet chimpanzee.

Discouraged by years of failure is a nonrestrictive past participial phrase. It is not necessary to identify Foxworth.

 PRACTICE   In the following sentences, set off nonrestrictive participial phrases with commas.

1. Paul Groves, worrying about his friend's mental state, offered to build a

deck for him.

2. The woman leading the marathon is from Finland.

3. Inspector Morse embarrassed by his first name refused to reveal it.

4. Polonius trying to look important told the director that he was an actor.

5. Masayo determined not to insult her hosts told them that the food tasted

wonderful.

Appositives

(See page 158 if you need to review appositives.) Appositives usually contain information <u>not necessary to identify the words they modify</u> and are therefore nonrestrictive. Set them off with commas.

 EXAMPLES

Natalie's mother, **a lawyer in Boston,** will be coming to visit her soon.

Kleenex, **a household necessity,** was invented as a substitute for bandages during World War I because of a cotton shortage.

Parker took his stamp collection to Mr. Poindexter, **a noted stamp expert.**

 PRACTICE

In the following sentences, set off all appositives with commas.

1. The Tickled Trout a nearby seafood restaurant attracts many customers.

2. Persephone stared at the pomegranate the only fruit in sight.

3. Gary an avid hiker did not mind being called a tree hugger.

4. *The Sopranos* a series about Italian families is my favorite television program.

5. The Australian shepherd an intelligent dog was introduced into Australia to herd sheep.

---

3. <u>Use commas to separate most explanatory words from direct quotations.</u>

 EXAMPLES

Mr. Jones asked, "Where are you going?"

"I will arrive before dinner is over," **he remarked.**

"Tonight's dinner," **he said,** "will be delayed."

NOTE: Do not use commas to separate explanatory words from a partial direct quotation.

EXAMPLE

He described the clouds as "ominous, dark, and threatening."

4. <u>Use commas to set off words of direct addresses.</u> If a writer addresses someone directly in a sentence, the word or words that stand for that person or persons are set off by commas. If the word or words in direct address begin the sentence, they are followed by a comma.

EXAMPLES

And now, **my good friends,** I think it is time to end this conversation.

Mr. Chairman, I rise to a point of order.

I would like to present my proposal, **my esteemed colleagues.**

5. Use commas to set off dates and addresses. If your sentence contains two, three, or more elements of the date or address, use commas to set off these elements. The following sentences contain two or more elements.

 EXAMPLES

We visited Disneyland on **Monday, June 5,** in order to avoid the weekend rush.

We visited Disneyland on **Monday, June 5, 1998,** in order to avoid the weekend rush.

Celia has lived at **3225 Oliver Street, San Diego,** for five years.

Celia has lived at **3225 Oliver Street, San Diego, California,** for five years.

Celia has lived at **3225 Oliver Street, San Diego, California 92023,** for five years.

NOTE: The zip code is not separated from the state by a comma.

The following sentences contain only one element.

 EXAMPLES

We visited Disneyland on **Monday** in order to avoid the weekend rush.

Celia has lived at **3225 Oliver Street** for five years.

 PRACTICE

In the following sentences, use commas to set off explanatory words for direct quotations, words in direct address, and dates and addresses that have two or more elements.

1. Hester, have you lived at 4590 A Street, Salem, Massachusetts, for the past two years?

2. The package that was mailed on Friday September 13 1875 from Transylvania Ohio never made it to Carlsbad California.

3. Homer asked "Which pasture contains the best cow pies?"

4. The multi-colored togas arrived at The Debauchery 415 Cicero Street Rome Arkansas on the day before Saturnalia began.

5. Please close the door to the basement Chelsea.

PRACTICE   Use commas to set off parenthetical expressions, nonrestrictive elements, explanatory words for direct quotations, words in direct address, and dates and addresses that have two or more elements.

1. Placido‚for instance‚is rarely seen without a coffee cup.

2. A misanthrope who is a person who dislikes other people is usually not well liked.

3. *The Tell-Tale Tart* a novel by Dulcinea Baker will soon be a movie.

4. Ahab how do you like my wide-wale corduroy pants?

5. Paul Revere's famous ride took place on April 18 1775 although he did not really ride alone and never made it to his intended destination.

6. The missing coprolite was found on August 10 1954 in Rome Georgia.

7. Dave Robicheaux sadly considered his po'boy sandwich dropped during the vicious gunfight.

8. "The spiders have arrived" said Harker "and I'm ready."

9. Sherrie in fact sent me a postcard from the St. John Coltrane African Orthodox Church in San Francisco.

10. Francis please tell Mr. Ed who will not stop talking that we are tired of his silly horse jokes.

Rules for the Use of the Comma

1. <u>Use a comma before a coordinating conjunction that joins two main clauses.</u>

2. <u>Use commas to separate elements in a series.</u>

   a. Elements in a series may be words, phrases, or clauses.

   b. Two or more adjectives that modify the same noun may need to be separated with commas.

3. <u>Use a comma after an introductory element.</u> Introductory elements include:

   a. Introductory words

   b. Transitional expressions

   c. Prepositional phrases

   d. Verbal phrases

   e. Adverb clauses

4. <u>Use commas to separate interrupters from the rest of the sentence.</u> Interrupters include:

   a. Parenthetical expressions

   b. Nonrestrictive clauses

   c. Nonrestrictive participial phrases

   d. Appositives

   e. Explanatory words for direct quotations

   f. Words in direct address

   g. Dates and addresses with two or more elements

Exercise 1A

Add commas to the following sentences where necessary.

1. Satumo's father has high blood pressure,and his mother has asthma.

2. Arachna had long thin arms and legs but never considered herself unattractive.

3. She was however embarrassed about her red hourglass birthmark.

4. Angelo an Italian opera fan sang an aria for us in the car.

5. Seymour looked at me and said "I did not hear the sirens last night."

6. My dermatologist who is a funny woman sent me a copy of the movie *Funny Face* for my birthday.

7. Inside the wet crumpled piece of paper Carlton found a warning not to make any more three-point shots.

8. Shirley Temple dancing happily across the stage had a smile on her face.

9. Insulted by the editor's rejection Emily a perspicacious young poet somehow knew that in the future her poems would be recognized.

10. Icarus you must gather a pound of feathers today.

11. After he took a deep breath Gordon took a sip of milk and started on his third cherry pie.

12. On March 5 2001 the attack began but the sunny warm weather favored the enemy.

13. Sofia was wise beyond her years; however she was unable to program the VCR.

14. No the Lost Dutchman's mine was not discovered near Bumblebee Arizona in 1955.

15. Price Club which is a large wholesale warehouse recently merged with Costco.

Exercise 1B

Add commas to the following sentences where necessary.

1. Over the last fifty years, many people have noticed that Mickey Mouse has only four fingers.

2. He has in fact only three fingers and one thumb on each hand.

3. Donald Duck Goofy and Minnie Mouse also have only four fingers each.

4. If you ever visit Disneyland in Anaheim California or Disney World in Orlando Florida look at the hands of the costumed characters.

5. Even Chip and Dale who are two cartoon chipmunks have only four fingers on each hand.

6. When cartoonists and animators are asked about this phenomenon they say that there is a good reason for it.

7. It is more convenient to draw four fingers than five and it also saves time.

8. In cartoons before the seventies each frame was painstakingly drawn by hand.

9. A team of cartoonists would perform this tedious tiring work for weeks on end.

10. Because the hand is difficult to keep in proportion to the rest of the body it is the most difficult part of the anatomy to draw.

11. Many artists have particular difficulty drawing individual fingers so Mickey was drawn with one finger missing.

12. Today's computerized animation which revolutionized the cartoon industry could replace the missing digit but no one is willing to change well-known cartoon characters.

13. Therefore most of the characters in cartoons by Disney Warner Brothers and other production companies still have only four fingers.

14. Since more realistic animated characters usually have five fingers Snow White and Cinderella were spared this amputation.

continued

15. No one knows for sure which of Mickey's fingers was severed for convenience but we hope

it was not a major one.

Exercise 1C

In the following paragraph, add commas wherever they are needed.

1. When I recently transferred to Ridge Falls State University from Beach City Community College, I found the differences between the two schools disturbing, interesting, and exciting. **2.** Beach City College is of course the smaller of the two and I enjoyed the more intimate atmosphere. **3.** The classes were usually small the professors were accessible and I was able to make friends with the other students easily. **4.** In fact many of my friends from high school were also attending Beach City. **5.** My car a 1985 Ford Escort easily made the commute from my home. **6.** During my time at Beach City College I was able to keep the part-time job I had had during high school and I could save money because I was living at home. **7.** Beach City College provided me a comfortable transition from high school to college and on May 25 1997 I graduated with enough credits to transfer as a junior to a four-year college. **8.** On my first day of classes at Ridge Falls State I was almost overwhelmed by its size but I decided to persevere and not quit. **9.** In contrast to Beach City Community College the school has an enrollment of over thirty-two thousand so I felt very small and unimportant. **10.** While I was registering adding classes buying books or going to lunch in one of the cafeterias I had to stand in long lines. **11.** In addition all of the classes that I am now enrolled in are larger and one of them my Introduction to Psychology class has three hundred students in it. **12.** Moreover the professors seem more remote less friendly and less accessible to the students than those at Beach City. **13.** The cost of tuition housing food and just about everything else is of course higher at the university so I have not been able to save the kind of money that I had saved at Beach City College. **14.** However once I got over the shock of new things I found many advantages to being at Ridge Falls State. **15.** Because it is much larger than the community college I have met people from such places as Afghanistan Thailand Nigeria China and Saudi Arabia. **16.** In addition I have found that some of my professors are world-renowned scholars. **17.** Also the university is such a big place that I have access to more concerts lectures films and plays than were offered at Beach City Community College. **18.** I am glad to say I have comfortably settled in my room at Scholar's Hall Ridge Falls South Dakota and am enjoying my new life away from home.

Other Punctuation Marks

Punctuation would be simple if we could just include a page of punctuation marks at the end of a piece of writing and invite readers to sprinkle them about anywhere they choose. But if you want to be an effective writer, it helps a great deal to know how to use not only those troublesome commas but also all of the other marks of punctuation. In this section, we will take up end punctuation and the other punctuation marks.

The placement of punctuation marks can affect the meaning of a sentence profoundly. Here are a few examples.

In this sentence, the dog recognizes its owner.

EXAMPLE A clever dog knows **its** master.

In this one, the dog is in charge.

EXAMPLE A clever dog knows **it's** master.

In this sentence, we find a deliberately rude butler.

EXAMPLE The butler stood by the door and called the **guests** names as they entered.

In this sentence, he is more mannerly.

EXAMPLE The butler stood by the door and called the **guests'** names as they entered.

And in this sentence, we find a person who doesn't trust his friends.

EXAMPLE Everyone **I know** has secret ambitions.

Add two commas, and you change the meaning.

EXAMPLE Everyone, **I know,** has secret ambitions.

As you can see, punctuation marks are potent tools.

End Punctuation

The Period

1. The period is used at the end of a sentence that makes a statement or gives a command.

EXAMPLES This rule is probably the easiest of all.

Circle the subject in the above sentence.

2. The period is used with most abbreviations.

 EXAMPLES   Mr., Mrs., Dr., A.D., Ph.D., U.S., St., Rd., Blvd., Sgt., Lt.

The Question Mark

1. The question mark is used at the end of sentences that ask questions.

 EXAMPLES   Where have all the flowers gone?

Is the water hot yet?

2. A question mark is not used at the end of an indirect question.

 EXAMPLES   (direct question)   Why is Emile going to the dance?

(indirect question)   I wonder why Emile is going to the dance.

The Exclamation Point

1. The exclamation point is used after words, phrases, and short sentences that show strong emotion.

 EXAMPLES   Rats!

Not on your life!

Watch it, Buster!

Ouch! That hurt!

2. The exclamation point is not often used in college writing. For the most part, the words themselves should express the excitement.

 EXAMPLE   Chased by a ravenous pack of ocelots, Cedric raced through the forest to his condo, bolted up his stairs, swiftly locked the door, and threw himself, quivering and exhausted, onto his beanbag chair.

 PRACTICE   Use periods, question marks, and exclamation points in the following sentences.

1. Robinson wondered whether he would ever leave the island.

2. Who is on first

3. Stop, I can't breathe

4. Homer wondered if he would have enough Spam for Christmas

5. Does Roscoe want to visit the Liberace museum

6. What is the weather like outside

7. Never again

8. Rosemary studied for her Ph D at Yale

9. Are his anapests as clever as usual

10. Jack asked Carlton if it was time to leave

Internal Punctuation

The Semicolon

1. A semicolon is used to join two main clauses that are not joined by a coordinating conjunction. Sometimes a transitional word or phrase follows the semicolon.

 EXAMPLES

Thirteen people saw the incident; each one described it differently.

All tragedies end in death; on the other hand, all comedies end in marriage.

2. A semicolon can be used to join elements in a series when the elements require further internal punctuation.

 EXAMPLE

Before making his decision, Elrod consulted his banker, who abused him; his lawyer, who ignored him; his minister, who consoled him; and his mother, who scolded him.

3. Do not use a semicolon to separate two phrases or two subordinate clauses.

 EXAMPLE

(incorrect)   I will pay you for the work when you return the tape deck that was stolen from our car; and when you repair the dented left fender.

The Colon

1. A colon is used to join two main clauses when the second clause is an example, an explanation, or a restatement of the first clause.

 EXAMPLES

The past fifty years had been a time of turmoil: war, drought, and famine had plagued the small country.

The garden was a delight to all insects: aphids abounded in it, ladybugs exulted in it, and praying mantises cavorted in it.

2. A colon is used when a complete sentence introduces an example, a series, a list, or a direct quotation. Often a colon will come after the words *follows* or *following*.

 EXAMPLES

The paper explored the comic elements of three Melville novels: *Moby Dick, Mardi,* and *Pierre.*

The list of complaints included the following items: leaky faucets, peeling wallpaper, and a nauseous green love seat.

3. A colon is generally not used after a verb.

EXAMPLES

| (incorrect) | At the store I bought: bread, eggs, and bacon. |
| (correct) | At the store I bought bread, eggs, and bacon. |

 PRACTICE

In the following sentences, add semicolons and colons where necessary.

1. You crack three eggs into the pan; then you stir them slowly.

2. Homer bought the following items bag balm, cow chip hardener, and an okra peeler.

3. Billy thought he had hidden all of the rope however, Claggart found a piece long enough.

4. Nora had never seen Paris, Hoboken, Sioux Falls, or Rome.

5. Dee wanted some keepsakes for her house therefore, she asked her mother to give her a quilt.

Quotation Marks

1. Quotation marks are used to enclose direct quotations and dialogue.

EXAMPLES

"When a stupid man is doing something he is ashamed of, he always declares that it is his duty."
                                                    —George Bernard Shaw

Woody Allen said, "If my film makes one more person miserable, I've done my job."

2. Quotation marks are not used with indirect quotations.

 EXAMPLES

| (direct quotation) | Fernando said, "I will be at the airfield before the dawn." |
| (indirect quotation) | Fernando said that he would be at the airfield before the dawn. |

3. Place periods and commas inside quotation marks.

EXAMPLES   Flannery O'Connor wrote the short story "A Good Man Is Hard to Find."

"Always forgive your enemies—nothing annoys them so much," quipped Oscar Wilde.

4. Place colons and semicolons outside quotation marks.

EXAMPLES   Priscilla was disgusted by the story "The Great Toad Massacre": it was grossly unfair to toads and contained too much gratuitous violence.

Abner felt everyone should read the essay "The Shocking State of Okra Cookery"; he had even had several copies made just in case he found someone who was interested.

5. Place the question mark inside the quotation marks if the quotation is a question. Place the question mark outside the quotation marks if the quotation is not a question but the whole sentence is.

EXAMPLES   The poem asks, "What are patterns for?"

Did Mark Twain say, "Never put off until tomorrow what you can do the day after tomorrow"?

6. Place the exclamation point inside the quotation marks if the quotation is an exclamation. Place it outside the quotation marks if the quotation is not an exclamation but the whole sentence is.

EXAMPLES   "An earwig in my ointment!" the disgusted pharmacist proclaimed.

Please stop saying "It's time to leave"!

PRACTICE   Add semicolons, colons, and quotation marks to the following sentences.

1. Dante said, "I like this place, but I would like to leave now"; however, Virgil told him that no one was allowed to leave.

2. In spring the rains come then the small animals emerge.

3. Whose last words were My kingdom for a horse?

4. My favorite Mae West quotation is When I'm good, I'm very good, but when I'm bad, I'm better.

5. Miles picked up his horn and said, Let's begin this gig.

6. Where is the ring? asked Gandalf.

7. Was it Mark Twain who said, I believe that our Heavenly Father invented man because he was disappointed in the monkey?

8. When he got to the top of the hill and watched the stone roll back to the bottom, Sisyphus shouted, Not again!

9. Queequeg never hesitated he just picked up the harpoon and threw it.

10. Oscar Wilde once said, Consistency is the last refuge of the unimaginative.

The Apostrophe

1. <u>Apostrophes are used to form contractions.</u> The apostrophe replaces the omitted letter or letters.

I am	I'm	did not	didn't
you are	you're	is not	isn't
it is	it's	were not	weren't
they are	they're	will not	won't
does not	doesn't	cannot	can't

2. <u>Apostrophes are used to form the possessives of nouns and indefinite pronouns.</u>

   a. Add 's to form the possessive of all singular nouns and all indefinite pronouns.

    EXAMPLES

   (singular nouns)   The **girl's** hair was shiny.

   Charles's car is rolling down the hill.

   (indefinite pronouns)   **Everyone's** watch was affected by the giant magnet.

   (compound words)   Mr. Giuliano left on Monday to attend his **son-in-law's** graduation.

   (joint possession)   **Vladimir and Natasha's** wedding was long and elaborate.

   b. Add only an apostrophe to form the possessive of plural nouns that end in *s*. However, add 's to form the possessive of plural nouns that do not end in *s*.

    EXAMPLES

   (plural nouns that end in *s*)   The **Joneses'** cabin had been visited by an untidy bear.

   We could hear the three **friends'** conversation all the way down the hall.

(plural nouns that do not end in *s*)   During the storm the parents were concerned about their **children's** safety.

c. Expressions referring to time or money often require an apostrophe.

EXAMPLES   Please give me one **dollar's** worth.

Two **weeks'** vacation is simply not enough.

3. Do not use apostrophes with the possessive forms of personal pronouns.

Incorrect	*Correct*
her's	hers
our's	ours
their's	theirs

NOTE: *It's* means "it is." The possessive form of *it* is *its*.

PRACTICE   Add apostrophes (or *'s*) to the following sentences where necessary.

1. Everyone was looking for Alice's rabbit; he wouldn't come when we called him.

2. Mr. Jones friends placed an inappropriate sticker on his cars bumper.

3. Did you enjoy Emma Thompsons part in that movie?

4. When I quit, I was given a months salary.

5. Marias brother wouldnt admit that he had read his sisters diary.

6. Its a shame that the meteor shower wont be visible from here.

7. As he looked at his cars fender, he knew that it couldve been worse.

8. His brother-in-laws judge gave him two weeks reprieve.

9. Staring over the rim of Sylvias soup bowl was a cockroach.

10. The childrens pet Gila monster ran away to the desert.

◉ PRACTICE

Write sentences of your own according to the instructions.

1. Write a complete sentence in which you use the possessive form of *women*.

   The women's basketball team is now playing in

   the semifinals.

2. Write a complete sentence in which you use the possessive form of *Louis*.

   _____

   _____

3. Write a complete sentence in which you use the possessive form of *father-in-law*.

   _____

   _____

4. Write a complete sentence in which you use the possessive form of *mice*.

   _____

   _____

5. Write a complete sentence in which you use the possessive form of *Ms. Lewis* and the contraction for *did not*.

   _____

   _____

Section Two Review

1. Use a **period** at the end of sentences that make statements or commands.

2. Use a **period** to indicate most abbreviations.

3. Use a **question mark** at the end of sentences that ask questions.

4. Do not use a **question mark** at the end of an indirect question.

5. Use an **exclamation point** after exclamatory words, phrases, and short sentences.

6. Use the **exclamation point** sparingly in college writing.

7. Use a **semicolon** to join two main clauses that are not joined by a coordinating conjunction.

8. Use a **semicolon** to separate elements in a series when the elements require further internal punctuation.

9. Do not use a **semicolon** to separate two phrases or two subordinate clauses.

10. Use a **colon** to join two main clauses when the second main clause is an example, an explanation, or a restatement.

11. Use a **colon** to introduce an example, a series, a list, or a direct quotation.

12. Do not use a **colon** to introduce a series of items that follows a verb.

13. Use **quotation marks** to enclose direct quotations and dialogue.

14. Do not use **quotation marks** with indirect quotations.

15. Place periods and commas inside **quotation marks.**

16. Place colons and semicolons outside **quotation marks.**

17. If a quotation is a question, place the question mark <u>inside</u> the **quotation marks.** If the quotation is not a question, but the whole sentence is, place the question mark <u>outside</u> the quotation marks.

18. If the quotation is an exclamation, place the exclamation point <u>inside</u> the **quotation marks.** If the quotation is not an exclamation, but the whole sentence is, place the exclamation point <u>outside</u> the quotation marks.

19. Use **apostrophes** to form contractions.

20. Use **apostrophes** to form the possessives of nouns and indefinite pronouns.

Exercise 2A

Add periods, question marks, exclamation points, semicolons, colons, quotation marks, and apostrophes (or 's) to the following sentences as necessary.

1. The firefighter shouted, "Watch out!"

2. Bonnie wondered why Clyde was spending so much time in the bank

3. Wont it be cloudy tomorrow asked Icarus

4. To make his new home complete, Homer needed the following items a lava lamp, a cow chip rack, a velvet portrait of Roy Orbison, and his John Deere beer mug

5. Barry Bonds refused to shake his teammates hand

6. One of Ben Jonsons lines about Shakespeare is He was not of an Age but for all time

7. Brent asked Bruce, Shall we eat Thai or Indian food today

8. The news was very good therefore, we ordered pizza

9. Did Thoreau write, As if you could kill time without injuring eternity

10. Before she ended her lecture, Theresa Wright, Ph D , couldnt help mentioning the secret code

11. The ski patrol came as fast as its skimobile would go then the paramedic examined Rebeccas leg

12. Homers son wanted to carry on the cow-chip throwing tradition however, cows were becoming scarce

13. Shouldnt we ask Susans permission before we use her loose cannon

14. The cavalry captain raised his sword and bellowed, Charge

15. Lawrence Putnam, M D , went to Afghanistan with the following items goggles, water purifying tablets, a Swiss Army knife, and a dozen boxes of chocolate

Exercise 2B

Add periods, question marks, exclamation points, semicolons, colons, quotation marks, apostrophes (or *'s*), and commas to the following sentences where necessary.

1. The lobsters were bound for Rudy's Fish House, 591 Triton Street, Kansas City, Kansas.

2. Attention yelled the Marine drill instructor to the new recruits

3. Are the British really coming or was Paul just joking

4. The students did not respond to Fergals knock knock jokes however they woke up when he started imitating Queen Elizabeth

5. Mark Twain said Im opposed to millionaires but it would be dangerous to offer me the position

6. There ain't no way to find out why a snorer cant hear himself snore said Tom Sawyer

7. Louis car became stuck in the snow luckily, the yeti rescued him

8. Did Aaron really ask to borrow your plaid cummerbund for the presidents concert

9. Rory asked Can Darby come to visit

10. Drop that cotton candy right now hollered the police officer

11. The groups agent said Youll need the following to succeed in this business tattoos on both forearms a scar on one cheek tight leather pants ear plugs and little sensitivity to music

12. Macbeth wondered if somebodys dagger was there in front of him

13. Wheres my bow asked Eros

14. The childrens lemonade stand was not doing very well until my friends baseball team stopped by.

15. As their ship docked in its new home port the sailors looked forward to some time off unfortunately Captain Bligh wouldnt allow them to leave the ship

Exercise 2C

In the following paragraph, correct any errors in the use of periods, exclamation points, question marks, semicolons, colons, quotation marks, or apostrophes.

1. King Lear, the central character in Shakespeare's *The Tragedy of King Lear*, and Willy Loman, the protagonist in Arthur Miller's *Death of a Salesman*, are similar characters in some ways. **2.** For instance, both character's mistakenly believe that their favorite child no longer loves them, therefore, they respond with anger and resentment. **3.** Lears three daughters are: Goneril, Regan, and Cordelia. **4.** Goneril and Regan insincerely flatter Lear, Cordelia refuses to do so. **5.** When Lear asks her what she will say to show her love, she replies: Nothing, my lord as a result, Lear disinherits her. **6.** Willy Loman also think's he has lost the love of his son Biff. **7.** In one scene he addresses Biff this way You vengeful, spiteful mutt! **8.** Then, just a few lines later, he realizes that Biff actually love's him. **9.** Lear and Loman are also similar: in that both seem to be losing their minds. **10.** From the very start of King Lear, there is evidence that Lears' thoughts are not rational. **11.** Even his closest counselor tells Lear he is acting foolishly, however, the king will not listen. **12.** By the middle of the play: Lear seems completely mad! **13.** Similarly, Willy Loman is having trouble distinguishing between: reality and fantasy. **14.** Willy constantly drifts into scene's from his past; or talks to his dead brother. **15.** Finally, both main characters are abandoned by children they thought were loyal to them. **16.** Lear is stripped of all his dignity by Goneril and Regan therefore, he ends up wandering through a raging storm with the court fool. **17.** Willy Loman is abandoned by his son Happy; who leaves him in the bathroom of a restaurant. **18.** When a woman remind's Happy about Willy, Happy makes this unsettling statement No, that's not my father. He's just a guy. **19.** In many ways these two plays are quite different, however, the two main characters' have some remarkable similarities.

Titles, Capitalization, and Numbers

The rules regarding titles, capitalization, and numbers are not, perhaps, as critical to clear writing as the ones for the punctuation marks discussed in the previous two sections. In fact, you can forget to capitalize at all without losing the meaning of what you are writing. So why should you learn to apply these rules correctly? The answer is simple. You should know how to apply them for the same reason you should know whether it is appropriate to slap a person on the back or to kiss him on both cheeks when you are first introduced. **How people write** says as much about them as **how they act**. Your ability to apply the rules presented in this section, as well as in other sections, identifies you as an educated person.

Titles

1. Underline or place in italics the titles of works that are published separately, such as books, magazines, newspapers, and plays.

   - Books: <u>Huckleberry Finn</u>, <u>Webster's Dictionary</u>

   - Plays: <u>Hamlet</u>, <u>Death of a Salesman</u>

   - Pamphlets: <u>How to Paint Your House</u>, <u>Worms for Profit</u>

   - Long musical works: Beethoven's <u>Egmont Overture</u>, Miles Davis's <u>Kind of Blue</u>

   - Long poems: <u>Paradise Lost</u>, <u>Beowulf</u>

   - Newspapers and magazines: <u>The New York Times</u>, <u>Newsweek</u>

   - Films: <u>Forrest Gump</u>, <u>Titanic</u>

   - Television and radio programs: <u>Dawson's Creek</u>, <u>Morning Edition</u>

   - Works of art: Rembrandt's <u>The Night Watch</u>, <u>Venus de Milo</u>

 EXAMPLES   Hortencia has subscriptions to <u>Newsweek</u> and <u>The New Yorker</u>.

   The Los Angeles Chamber Orchestra played Bach's <u>Brandenburg Concerto Number Five</u>.

2. Use quotation marks to enclose the titles of works that are parts of other works, such as articles, songs, poems, and short stories.

   - Songs: "Honeysuckle Rose," "Yesterday"

   - Poems: "Stopping by Woods on a Snowy Evening," "The Waste Land"

- Articles in periodicals: "Texas Air's New Flak Attack," "Of Planets and the Presidency"
- Short stories: "Paul's Case," "Barn Burning"
- Essays: "A Modest Proposal," "Once More to the Lake"
- Episodes of radio and television programs: "Tolstoy: From Rags to Riches," "Lord Mountbatten: The Last Viceroy"
- Subdivisions of books: "The Pulpit" (Chapter Eight of *Moby Dick*)

 EXAMPLES   The professor played a recording of Dylan Thomas reading his poem "After the Funeral."

Many writing textbooks include Jonathan Swift's essay "A Modest Proposal."

PRACTICE   In the following sentences, correct any errors in the use of titles.

1. At the beach I sat next to a woman who was reading Toni Morrison's novel Paradise.

2. In Nathaniel Hawthorne's short story Young Goodman Brown, the main character loses his faith in the goodness of people.

3. On the table in the coroner's office was a stack of Time and Wonderful Endings magazines.

4. Brent has memorized W. S. Merwin's poem The Last One.

5. The movie The Wizard of Oz mixes both black-and-white and color photography.

Capitalization

1. Capitalize the personal pronoun *I*.

 EXAMPLE   In fact, I am not sure I like the way you said that.

2. Capitalize the first letter of every sentence.

 EXAMPLE   The road through the desert was endlessly straight and boring.

3. <u>Capitalize the first letter of each word in a title except for *a, an,* and *the,* coordinating conjunctions, and prepositions.</u>

   NOTE: The first letter of the first word and the first letter of the last word of a title are always capitalized.

   - Titles of books: <u>Moby Dick</u>, <u>Encyclopaedia Britannica</u>

   - Titles of newspapers and magazines: <u>People</u>, <u>Cosmopolitan</u>, <u>Los Angeles Times</u>

   - Titles of stories, poems, plays, and films: "The Lady with the Dog," "The Road Not Taken," <u>Othello</u>, <u>Gone with the Wind</u>

4. <u>Capitalize the first letter of all proper nouns and adjectives derived from proper nouns.</u>

   - Names and titles of people: Coretta Scott King, Mr. Birch, Mayor Golding, President Roosevelt, Cousin Alice, Aunt Bea

   - Names of specific places: Yosemite National Park, Albuquerque, New Mexico, London, England, Saudi Arabia, Rockefeller Center, London Bridge, Elm Street, Venus, the Rio Grande, the Rocky Mountains, the Midwest

   NOTE: Do not capitalize the first letter of words that refer to a direction (such as "north," "south," "east," or "west"). Do capitalize these words when they refer to a specific region.

 EXAMPLES

Texas and Arizona are in the **Southwest.**

The police officer told us to drive **east** along the gravel road and turn **north** at the big pine tree.

   - Names of national, ethnic, or racial groups: Indian, Native American, Spanish, Irish, Italian, African American

   - Names of groups or organizations: Baptists, Mormons, Democrats, Republicans, American Indian Movement, Boy Scouts of America, Indianapolis Colts, U.S. Post Office

   - Names of companies: Ford Motor Company, Montgomery Ward, Coca Cola Bottling Company

   - Names of the days of the week and months of the year but not the seasons: Thursday, August, spring

   - Names of holidays and historical events: Memorial Day, the Fourth of July, the French Revolution, the Chicago Fire

   - Names of <u>specific</u> gods and religious writings: God, Mohammed, Talmud, Bible

5. The names of academic subjects are not capitalized unless they refer to an <u>ethnic or national origin or are the names of specific courses.</u> Examples include mathematics, political science, English, History 105.

PRACTICE   Correct any errors in the use of titles or capitalization.

1. In february, the San Diego Symphony will present a series of concerts of Mozart's works.

2. a morning for flamingos, a novel by james lee burke, takes place primarily in the south.

3. newsweek magazine had a picture of new york on the cover this week.

4. uncle javier was humming the song my way when he heard that frank sinatra had died.

5. several prominent citizens of sioux falls, south dakota, are veterans of operation desert storm.

6. during the christmas holidays, one can see beautiful decorations in santa fe and albuquerque.

7. in california, the native american tribes are having a legal battle with the state government over gambling.

8. every actor wants a chance to play the leading role in william shakespeare's play hamlet.

9. charlie showed marisa his collection of t.v. guide magazines.

10. the thrift store run by the episcopal church on state street has decided to move three blocks north this summer.

Numbers

The following rules about numbers apply to general writing rather than to technical or scientific writing.

1. Spell out numbers that require no more than two words. Use numerals for numbers that require more than two words.

EXAMPLES   Last year it rained on only **eighty-four** days.

In 1986 it rained on more than **120** days.

2. Always spell out a number at the beginning of a sentence.

EXAMPLE   **Six hundred ninety** miles in one day is a long way to drive.

3. In general, use numerals in the following situations:

- Dates: August 9, 1973   30 A.D.

- Sections of books and plays: Chapter 5, page 22
      Act 1, scene 3, lines 30–41

- Addresses: 1756 Grand Avenue
      Hemostat, Idaho 60047

- Decimals, percents, and fractions: 75.8   30%, 30 percent   1/5

- Exact amounts of money: $7.95 $1,300,000

- Scores and statistics: Padres 8 Dodgers 5   a ratio of 6 to 1

- Time of day: 3:05   8:15

NOTE: Round amounts of money that can be expressed in a few words can be written out: *twenty cents, fifty dollars, one hundred dollars.* Also, when the word *o'clock* is used with the time of day, the time of day can be written out: *seven o'clock.*

4. When numbers are compared, are joined by conjunctions, or occur in a series, either consistently use numerals or consistently spell them out. Although either method is acceptable, using numerals is often clearer—and certainly easier.

EXAMPLE   For the company picnic we need **twenty-five** pounds of fried chicken, **fifteen** pounds of potato salad, **one hundred twenty-five** cans of soda, **eighty-five** paper plates, **two hundred thirty** napkins, and **eighty-five** sets of plastic utensils.

OR

For the company picnic we need **25** pounds of fried chicken, **15** pounds of potato salad, **125** cans of soda, **85** paper plates, **230** napkins, and **85** sets of plastic utensils.

PRACTICE   Correct any errors in the use of numbers in the following sentences.

Twenty thousand

1. ~~20,000~~ fans attended the Metallica concert at the stadium, and ~~20~~ *twenty* of them

   were ejected for various offenses.

2. Jessica fed her goldfish at six o'clock and then again at eight fifty-five.

3. For the retirement party, Charlie brought 15 pastries, Woz brought 1 Clark

   Bar, Barbara brought one hundred fifteen pounds of fresh tuna, and

   Carlton brought 3 chocolate cheese cakes.

4. After August sixth, nineteen forty-five, the world seemed a more dangerous

   place.

5. Only three hundred people showed up to watch the Padres beat the Cubs

   by a score of 8 to 2.

Section Three Review

1. Underline or place in italics the **titles** of works that are published separately, such as books, plays, and films.

2. Use quotation marks to enclose the **titles** of works that are parts of other works, such as songs, poems, and short stories.

3. **Capitalize** the personal pronoun *I*.

4. **Capitalize** the first letter of every sentence.

5. **Capitalize** the first letter of each word in a title except *a, an, the,* coordinating conjunctions, and prepositions.

6. **Capitalize** all proper nouns and adjectives derived from proper nouns.

7. **Do not capitalize** names of academic subjects unless they refer to an ethnic or national origin or are the names of specific courses.

8. Spell out **numbers** that require no more than two words. Use numerals for numbers that require more than two words.

9. Always spell out a **number** at the beginning of a sentence.

10. In general, use **numerals** for dates, sections of books and plays, addresses, decimals, percents, fractions, exact amounts of money, scores, statistics, and time of day.

11. When **numbers** are compared, are joined by conjunctions, or occur in a series, either consistently use numerals or consistently spell them out.

The following sentences contain errors in the use of titles, capitalization, and numbers. Correct any errors you find.

1. The movie *fatal attraction* caused much discussion about how men treat women and women treat men.

2. shirley jackson's short story the lottery was shown as an episode on the television series the twilight zone.

3. general wellington directed the british troops against napoleon at the battle of waterloo.

4. At 8 o'clock last sunday morning, 10 people had breakfast together at sunrise deli.

5. When sylvia mispronounced mr. haas's name 3 times, he said that she had made a freudian slip.

6. On his vacation to russia, john kept trying to talk to people about catholic marxist philosophy.

7. On his way to rome on march fifteenth, forty-four b.c., brutus bought a cheap dagger for the equivalent of five dollars and ninety-five cents.

8. After he typed the memorandum on his apple computer, the secretary ordered three reams of copy paper, 250 file folders, four boxes of pencils, and 150 filters for the coffee machine.

9. The msg computer company donated two thousand three hundred forty dollars to homer and hortense college for computer programs to study the effect of a spam diet on discontented students.

10. On my favorite CD, entitled chopin's nocturnes, arthur rubenstein plays the piano.

11. When the tonight show was over, jay sat and read his favorite magazine, beckett baseball monthly.

12. In my essay entitled the effects of road rage, I included a quotation from car and driver magazine.

Exercise 3A

continued

13. bruce smiled as he told the class the significance of willy loman's two heavy valises in the play death of a salesman.

14. Every day at the chicago art institute, over 150 people ask guards about the secret meaning of the pitchfork in grant wood's painting american gothic.

15. After he wrote the essay how spam changed my life and improved my marriage, homer mailed copies of it to the 3 people whom he had met in his health 101 class.

Exercise 3B

Compose sentences of your own according to the instructions.

1. Write a sentence that includes the author and title of a book.

   During his vacation, Rafael read Jane Smiley's novel

   A Thousand Acres.

2. Write a sentence that describes a song you like and the musician who wrote it or performs it.

3. Tell what movie you last saw in a theater and how much you paid to see it.

4. Write a sentence that tells what school you attend and what classes you are taking.

5. Write a sentence that tells the number of people in your family, the number of years you have gone to school, the number of classes you are taking, and the approximate number of students at your school.

6. Write a sentence that mentions a magazine you have read lately. If possible, include the title of an article.

7. In a sentence, describe your favorite television program.

Exercise 3B

continued

8. Tell where you would go on your ideal vacation. Be specific about the name of the place and its geographic location.

_____

_____

9. Write a sentence that includes your age and address. (Feel free to lie about either one.)

_____

_____

10. Write a sentence that names a musician or musical group that you like and a tape or compact disc that you like.

_____

_____

11. Write a sentence that includes the name of a local newspaper, its approximate circulation, and the average number of pages during the week.

_____

_____

12. Write a sentence that includes a work of art that you know about and the name of the artist. If you need to, make up the name of a work of art and its artist.

_____

_____

13. Write a sentence that includes the score of the last baseball, football, or basketball game you were aware of. If you are not a sports fan, make up a score.

_____

_____

Exercise 3B

continued

14. Write a sentence that tells what time you get up on Mondays, what time your first class starts, what time you have lunch, and what time you usually have dinner.

_____

_____

Exercise 3C

In the following paragraph, correct any errors in the use of capitalization, numbers, or titles.

1. Computer technology has transformed the M̶ovie I̶ndustry, creating visual effects that are often stunning in their realism, but the story lines of these new movies are not much different from those of 4̶0̶ *forty* years ago. **2.** Consider, for example, "Jurassic Park" of the 1990s and "Mysterious Island" of the 1950s. **3.** Both movies involve a group of about 5 people who are trapped on an Island inhabited by huge, dangerous animals that do not exist anywhere else. **4.** The animals in Jurassic Park, of course, are Dinosaurs; in Mysterious Island they are a gigantic bee, crab, and bird. **5.** As the magazine article <u>Monsters And Madness</u> points out, the plots in both movies are about the same. **6.** Two other movies that are not so different from each other are Mimic of nineteen ninety-seven and Them of the late nineteen fifties. **7.** Mimic involves cockroaches that have been genetically altered by a Scientist working in the Eastern part of <u>New York</u>. **8.** They live in old subway tunnels of new york city and have mutated until they are able to mimic the size and appearance of Humans. **9.** 100s of them are feasting on captured humans and are threatening to establish new colonies in the Spring, but luckily they are destroyed by fire and explosives. **10.** According to a review in newsweek, the plot of "Them" from the 1950s is very similar. **11.** In it ants have been mutated by radiation from Atomic testing. **12.** The giant Queen Ant and a consort of over 25 males have flown into the sewer tunnels under "Los Angeles" and have started a colony that threatens Civilization. **13.** They are destroyed the same way the cockroaches in <u>Mimic</u> are, with fire and explosives. **14.** Finally, the movie Independence Day, which came out on the fourth of july a few years ago, is similar in many ways to the 1950s Invaders From Mars. **15.** As the los angeles times newspaper points out in an article entitled save us from the aliens, both movies involve Aliens from Outer Space intent upon taking over the Planet. **16.** In addition, the 2 movies feature similar bug-headed enemies with no apparent sympathy or concern for Humanity. **17.** And in both movies representatives of the <u>Military</u> are called upon to save the day. **18.** Obviously, computer technology has made the movies of today exciting, but plots themselves have not changed much in the past 40 years.

Sentence Practice: Sentence Variety

Writing is challenging. As we have pointed out a number of times already, writing is a process that requires constant and countless choices. Much head scratching and crossing out go on between the beginning and the end of composing a paragraph. Each sentence can be framed in numerous ways, each version changing—subtly or dramatically—the relationships among the ideas.

Sometimes a short sentence is best. Look at the one that begins this paragraph and the one that begins the paragraph above. At other times you will need longer sentences to get just the right meaning and feeling. Sentence combining exercises give you an opportunity to practice how to express ideas in various ways by encouraging you to move words, phrases, and clauses around to achieve different effects.

When you construct a sentence, you should be aware not only of how it expresses your ideas but also of how it affects the other sentences in the paragraph. Consider the following paragraph as an example. It is the opening paragraph of Rachel Carson's book *The Edge of the Sea*.

> The edge of the sea is a strange and beautiful place. All through the long history of the earth it has been an area of unrest where waves have broken heavily against the land, where the tides have pressed forward over the continents, receded, and then returned. For no two successive days is the shoreline precisely the same. Not only do the tides advance and retreat in their eternal rhythms, but the level of the sea itself is never at rest. It rises or falls as the glaciers melt or grow, as the floor of the deep ocean basins shifts under its increasing load of sediments, or as the earth's crust along the continental margins warps up or down in adjustment to strain and tension. Today a little more land may belong to the sea, tomorrow a little less. Always the edge of the sea remains an elusive and indefinable boundary.

As you can see, Rachel Carson opens her paragraph with a short, simple sentence. Then she writes a sentence that is much longer and more complicated because it begins to explain the general ideas in the first one. It even seems to capture the rhythm of the sea against the land. She follows that one with another short, simple sentence. As the paragraph continues, she varies the length and complexity of her sentences according to what she needs to say. Notice how she ends the paragraph with another simple statement that matches her opening sentence.

Sentence Combining Exercises

In the following sentence combining exercises, you will practice writing sentences so that some are short and concise and others are lengthier and more complex.

 EXAMPLE   Combine the following sentences into either two or three sentences. Experiment with which sounds best.

    a. There was a feud.
    b. It began simply enough.
    c. The Smiths' youngest son refused to marry the Millers' favorite daughter.
    d. Mrs. Miller fed Grandfather Smith some potato salad.
    e. The potato salad was tainted.
    f. They were at the annual Presidents' Day picnic.
    g. Nothing was the same after that.

> *The feud began simply enough. When the Smiths' youngest son refused to marry the Millers' favorite daughter, Mrs. Miller fed Grandfather Smith some tainted potato salad at the annual Presidents' Day picnic. Nothing was the same after that.*

1. Combine the following sentences into three sentences.

    a. There was a choice.
    b. It was not difficult to make.
    c. Jake was not the one who had robbed the stage.
    d. Jake knew that the townspeople were convinced he was guilty.
    e. The townspeople planned to lynch him if they caught him.
    f. Jake had to steal a horse.
    g. Jake had to leave town now.

continued

2. Combine the following sentences into three sentences.

    a. The male stickleback fish must be quite shy.
    b. He usually has a silver-colored belly.
    c. He is brown to green everywhere else.
    d. During mating season, his belly turns bright red.
    e. Perhaps he is trying to attract a mate.
    f. Perhaps he is blushing.

_____

_____

_____

_____

3. Combine the following sentences into two sentences.

    a. Mr. Darian told Harrison the bad news.
    b. The roof was leaky.
    c. The hot water heater wasn't working.
    d. Its heating element was broken.
    e. Mr. Darian said that between them they would have to raise money.
    f. The money was to fix the roof.
    g. The money was to get a new water heater.

_____

_____

_____

_____

continued

4. Combine the following sentences into two or three sentences.

    a. Some dictators are called benevolent.
    b. They do good things for the people.
    c. Napoleon Bonaparte was considered benevolent.
    d. Under Napoleon, industry expanded.
    e. Universities flourished.
    f. The civil law system was improved.
    g. The judicial system was reorganized.
    h. The Bank of France was established.
    i. Most dictators, however, are not benevolent.

_____

_____

_____

_____

5. Combine the following sentences into three sentences.

    a. The crow is despised by some people.
    b. The crow is respected by other people.
    c. The crow has a larger brain than most other birds.
    d. The crow can quickly learn that a "scarecrow" is nothing to fear.
    e. Hunters have discovered something about the crow.
    f. Crows can distinguish between a farmer and a hunter.
    g. The farmer is going about his business.
    h. The hunter has a rifle and plans to shoot the crow.

_____

_____

_____

_____

Sentence Combining Exercises

continued

6. Combine the following sentences into two or three sentences.

    a. One of the legends about the discovery of coffee involves an Arab goatherd.
    b. His name was Kaldi.
    c. It was about 850 A.D.
    d. He was puzzled by the strange behavior of his goats.
    e. He sampled some berries.
    f. His goats had been feeding on the berries.
    g. He felt a strong sense of exhilaration.
    h. He announced his discovery to the world.

_____

_____

_____

_____

7. Combine the following sentences into three sentences.

    a. In 1946 the United States conducted several atomic bomb tests.
    b. The tests took place on the Bikini atoll in the Marshall Islands.
    c. At the same time, the French introduced a new bathing suit.
    d. The bathing suit was skimpy.
    e. The bathing suit suggested an uninhibited state of nature.
    f. The bathing suit seemed to have the impact of an atomic bomb.
    g. It was quickly named the "bikini."

_____

_____

_____

_____

Sentence Combining Exercises

continued

8. Combine the following sentences into three sentences.

    a. The house was almost silent.
    b. A couple sat at a table.
    c. The table was in the kitchen.
    d. They were talking softly.
    e. They were talking about their children.
    f. The children were sleeping.
    g. The children were in their rooms upstairs.
    h. A clock was on a wall.
    i. The wall was filled with brightly colored crayon drawings.
    j. The clock had looked down on almost twenty years of family meals.
    k. The clock ticked quietly.

_____

_____

_____

_____

9. Combine the following sentences into three sentences.

    a. The first piece of Tupperware was a bathroom tumbler.
    b. It was made of polyethylene.
    c. It was made by Earl Tupper.
    d. Earl Tupper was a Du Pont chemist.
    e. He made it in 1945.
    f. The tumblers were popular.
    g. Next he made bowls.
    h. The bowls were in a variety of sizes.
    i. They had a revolutionary new seal.
    j. Flexing of the bowl's tight-fitting lid caused air to be expelled.
    k. The expelling of the air formed a vacuum.
    l. The vacuum caused outside air pressure to reinforce the seal.

_____

_____

_____

_____

Sentence Combining Exercises

continued

10. Combine the following sentences into three or four sentences.

a. Today's "hot dog" really is named after a dog.
b. The popular sausage was first developed in the 1850s.
c. It was developed in Frankfurt, Germany.
d. Some people called it a "frankfurter," after the city.
e. Others called it a "dachshund sausage."
f. It had a dachshund-like shape.
g. In 1906 a New York cartoonist was drawing a vendor.
h. The vendor was selling "hot dachshund sausages."
i. The vendor was at a baseball game.
j. The cartoonist abbreviated the term to "hot dog."
k. The name stuck.

_____

_____

_____

_____

Essay and Paragraph Practice: Comparing and Contrasting

Assignment

Comparing or contrasting two topics is an activity that you participate in nearly every day. When you recognize that two people have much in common, you have observed similarities between them. When you decide to take one route rather than another, you have noticed differences between the two routes. Even something as simple as buying one toothpaste rather than another involves some sort of comparison and contrast. In fact, recognizing similarities and differences affects every part of our lives. How could you know if you were looking at a tree or a bush if you were not able to see their differences as well as their similarities?

Much college writing involves comparing or contrasting two topics. You may be asked to compare (show similarities between) the results of two lab experiments in a biology class or to contrast (show differences between) the religious beliefs of two cultures in an anthropology class. In addition, in many classes you may be asked to write papers or reports or to take essay exams in which you show both the similarities and the differences between two related topics.

Exercises 1C, 2C, and 3C in this chapter are comparison/contrast paragraphs. Exercise 1C contrasts Ridge City State University with Beach City Community College; Exercise 2C compares King Lear in *The Tragedy of King Lear* to Willy Loman in *Death of a Salesman*; and Exercise 3C compares several movies of the 1990s to those of the 1950s. Note that each of these paragraphs opens with a topic sentence that makes a statement about similarities or differences.

Your assignment is to write an essay or a paragraph (whichever your instructor assigns) that compares and/or contrasts two related topics. Develop your paper from the ideas that follow.

Prewriting to Generate Ideas

Prewriting Application: Finding Your Topic

As you read the following topics, remember that the one that looks the easiest may not result in the best paper for you. Use the techniques of freewriting, brainstorming, and/or clustering to develop your reactions to several of these ideas before you choose one of them. Look for the topic idea that interests you the most, the one to which you have an emotional or personal reaction.

1. Compare and/or contrast your city or neighborhood with one you used to live in.

2. Compare and/or contrast a place as it is today with the way it was when you were a child.

3. Compare and/or contrast what you expected college to be like before you enrolled in your first class with what you found it to be like later on.

4. If you are returning to school after several years' absence, compare and/or contrast your last school experience with your current one.

5. Compare and/or contrast the characteristics of someone you know with a stereotype. For example, if you know an athlete or a police officer, compare and/or contrast that person's actual personality with the stereotype people have of athletes or police officers.

6. Compare and/or contrast your latest vacation or trip with your vision of the ideal vacation or trip.

7. Compare and/or contrast two sports, two athletes, or two teams.

8. Compare and/or contrast the person you are today with the person you were several years ago.

9. Compare and/or contrast any two places, persons, or events that you remember well.

10. If you have a background in two cultures, compare and/or contrast a few specific characteristics of both cultures.

Choosing and Narrowing the Topic

Once you have settled on several possible topics, consider these points as you make your final selection.

- Choose the more limited topic rather than the more general one.

- Choose the topic about which you could discuss several, not just one or two, similarities or differences.

- Choose the topic about which you have the most experience or knowledge.

- Choose the topic in which you have the most personal interest. Avoid topics about which you do not really care.

Writing a Thesis Statement or Topic Sentence

If your assignment is to write a single paragraph, you will open it with a topic sentence. If you are writing a complete essay, you will need a thesis statement at the end of your introductory paragraph. In either case, you will need a clear statement of the topic and central idea of your paper.

Prewriting Application: Working with Topic Sentences

Identify the topic sentences in Exercises 1C (page 285), 2C (page 297), and 3C (page 310). Then identify the topic and the central point in each topic sentence. Finally, state whether the topic sentence is introducing a paragraph that will examine similarities or differences.

Prewriting Application: Evaluating Thesis Statements and Topic Sentences

Write "No" before each sentence that would not make an effective thesis statement or topic sentence for a comparison or contrast paper. Write "Yes" before each sentence that *would* make an effective one. Determine whether each effective sentence is introducing a comparison paper or a contrast paper. Using ideas of your own, rewrite each ineffective sentence into one that might work.

_____ **1.** I had not seen my hometown of Monroe, South Dakota, for over fifteen years, so when I visited it last summer I was amazed at how little it had changed.

_____

_____

_____ **2.** My father and mother love to watch the Kentucky Derby.

_____

_____

_____ **3.** Many holidays that are common to both Mexico and the United States are celebrated in very different ways.

_____

_____

_____ **4.** Our society is much worse in this day and age than it used to be.

_____

_____

_____ **5.** This year's San Diego Padres is a better team than last year's in several key areas.

_____

_____

_____ **6.** *Roxanne,* a 1980s movie starring Steve Martin, contains many similarities to the play *Cyrano de Bergerac.*

_____

_____

_____ **7.** About the only thing that snowboarders and skiers have in common is that they share the same mountain.

_____

_____

_____ **8.** While walking down the Las Vegas Strip last year, I was amazed at how bright and colorful everything was, even at two o'clock in the morning.

_____

_____

_____ **9.** Although both the San Diego Zoo and the Wild Animal Park feature exotic animals, the two places are not at all similar.

_____

_____

_____ **10.** Many things have happened to me in the past few years to make me a more tolerant person.

_____

_____

Prewriting Application: Talking to Others

Form a group of three or four people and discuss the topics you have chosen. Your goal here is to help each other clarify the differences or similarities that you are writing about. Explain your points as clearly as you can. As you listen to the others in your group, use the following questions to help them clarify their ideas.

1. Is the paper focusing on similarities or on differences?

2. Exactly what similarities or differences will be examined in the paper? Can you list them?

3. Which similarities or differences need to be explained more clearly or fully?

4. Which points are the most significant or most interesting? Why?

5. Which similarity or difference should the paper open with? Which should it close with?

Organizing Similarities and Differences

Point-by-Point Order

One of the most effective ways to present your ideas when you compare or contrast two topics is called a **point-by-point** organization. Using this method, you cover one similarity or difference at a time. For example, if you were contrasting snowboarders and skiers, one of the differences might be the general age level of each group. The first part of your paper would then contrast the ages of most snowboarders with the ages of most skiers. Another difference might be the clothing worn by the two groups. So you would next contrast the clothing of snowboarders with the clothing of skiers. You might then contrast the physical activity itself, explaining what snowboarders do on the snow that is different from what skiers do. Whatever points you cover, you take them one at a time, point by point. An outline of this method for a single paragraph would look like this:

Point by Point—Single Paragraph

Topic Sentence:	About the only thing that snowboarders and skiers have in common is that they share the same mountain.

I. Ages

    A.   Snowboarders

    B.   Skiers

II. Clothing

    A.   Snowboarders

    B.   Skiers

III. Physical Activity

    A.   Snowboarders

    B.   Skiers

Concluding Sentence

Point by Point—Essay

If you are writing a complete essay, the point-by-point pattern changes only in that you devote a separate paragraph to each point. Develop each paragraph with details and examples to illustrate the differences or similarities you are discussing

Introductory Paragraph

Introductory sentences

ending with a

thesis statement

Thesis Statement: About the only thing that snowboarders and skiers have in common is that they share the same mountain.

1st Body Paragraph

I. *Topic sentence* about the difference in ages

    A.   Snowboarders

                Examples

    B.   Skiers

                Examples

2nd Body Paragraph

II. *Topic sentence* about the difference in clothing

    A.   Snowboarders

                Examples

    B.   Skiers

                Examples

3rd Body Paragraph

III. *Topic sentence* about the difference in technique

    A.   Snowboarders

                Examples

    B.   Skiers

                Examples

Concluding Paragraph

> Concluding sentences
>
> bringing the essay
>
> to a close

Subject-by-Subject Order

Another method of organization presents the topics **subject by subject.** Using this method, you cover each point of one topic first and then each point of the second topic. Be careful with this organization. Because the points are presented separately rather than together, your paper might end up reading like two separate descriptions rather than like a comparison or contrast of the two topics. To make the comparison or contrast clear, cover the same points in the same order, like this:

Subject by Subject—Single Paragraph

> *Topic Sentence:*   About the only thing that snowboarders and skiers have in common is that they share the same mountain.
>
> I. Snowboarders
>
>   A.   Ages
>
>   B.   Clothing
>
>   C.   Technique
>
> II. Skiers
>
>   A.   Ages
>
>   B.   Clothing
>
>   C.   Technique
>
> *Concluding Sentence*

Subject by Subject—Essay

The following example illustrates a paper with two body paragraphs—one for each subject. Depending on the complexity of your topic or assigned length of your paper, you may need to write more than one body paragraph per subject.

Introductory Paragraph

> Introductory sentences
>
> ending with a
>
> **thesis statement**
>
> *Thesis Statement:* About the only thing that snowboarders and skiers have in common is that they share the same mountain.

1st Body Paragraph

I. *Topic sentence* about characteristics of snowboarders

   A.   Ages

              Examples

   B.   Clothing

              Examples

   C.   Technique

              Examples

2nd Body Paragraph

II. *Topic sentence* about characteristics of skiers

   A.   Ages

              Examples

   B.   Clothing

              Examples

   C.   Technique

              Examples

Concluding Paragraph

Concluding sentences

bringing the essay

to a close

Prewriting Application: Organization of the Comparison/Contrast Paragraph

Examine Exercise 1C (page 285), Exercise 2C (page 297), and Exercise 3C (page 310). Outline the paragraph in each exercise to determine its point-by-point or subject-by-subject organization.

Writing the Paper

Now write the rough draft of your paper. Pay particular attention to transitions as you write. If you are using a point-by-point organization, use a clear transition to introduce each point of comparison or contrast. For subject-by-subject organizations, write a clear transition as you move from the first subject of your paper to the second. In addition, as you write the second half of a subject-by-subject paper, use transitional words and phrases that refer to the first half of the paper in order to emphasize the similarities or differences.

Writing Application: Identifying Transitional Words, Phrases, and Sentences

Examine Exercises 1C (page 285), 2C (page 297), and 3C (page 310).

1. Identify the organizational pattern of each as point-by-point or subject-by-subject.

2. Identify transitions that introduce each point of comparison or contrast in a point-by-point paper or that move from one subject to another in a subject-by-subject paper.

3. In the subject-by-subject paper, identify transitions in the second half of the paper that emphasize the comparison or contrast by referring to the subject of the first half.

4. Identify any other transitions that serve to connect ideas between sentences.

Rewriting and Improving the Paper

1. Revise your sentences so they include specific and concrete details. As much as possible, use actual names of people and places, and refer to specific details whenever possible.

2. Add or revise transitions wherever doing so would help clarify movement from one idea to another.

3. Improve your preliminary thesis statement (if you are writing an essay) or your preliminary topic sentence (if you are writing a single paragraph) so that it more accurately states the central point of your paper.

4. Examine your draft for sentence variety. If many of your sentences tend to be of the same length, try varying their length and their structure by combining sentences using the techniques you have studied in the Sentence Practice sections of this text.

Rewriting Application: Responding to Paragraph Writing

Read the following paragraph. Then respond to the questions following it.

Romeo and Juliet—Then and Now

The 1968 movie version of William Shakespeare's play *Romeo and Juliet* contrasts with the updated version of 1996 in a number of ways. First, the 1968 director had the characters battle each other with swords. That is the way they fought back then, but today's youth couldn't really relate to that kind of situation. In the 1996 version the director wanted to show a weapon that the audience had seen on TV shows and in other movies. Swords were replaced with shiny, artistic-looking handguns. Another contrast between the '68 version and the '96 one is the style of costumes. The '68 designers kept the clothing as it would have looked during Shakespeare's time, making the male actors wear puffy-sleeved shirts, tights, and little beanie hats. The women had to endure much worse attire, such as long, heavy dresses. The designers in the updated version knew that today's youth wouldn't sit through a movie about guys wearing tights or women wearing clothes that hid everything. Instead, they had the men wear shirts that were colorful, comfortable, and modern. They also wore basic black and dark blue pants. I felt I could take the characters more seriously in normal clothes than in the old English attire. Although both versions did keep the original words of the play, I am glad that the new version changed the music of the earlier one. For instance, the boring love song "A Time for Us" was replaced by a touching, romantic tune called "Kissing You." The new music helped me follow the plot a little better. When I watched the old version, there wasn't very much background music at all. I really had to follow what was going on by watching the actors, and even then the movie was hard to follow. In conclusion, I think the director of the '96 version did a wonderful job making *Romeo and Juliet* into a movie that appeals to the young people of today.

1. Identify the topic sentence. State its topic and central idea. Is it an effective topic sentence? Can you tell whether the paper will focus on similarities or differences?

2. Is this a point-by-point or subject-by-subject organization? How many points of contrast are covered in this paper? Identify them.

3. Identify the transitional sentences that introduce each major section of the paragraph. What other transitions are used between sentences?

4. Consider the organization of the paragraph. Would you change the order of the contrasts? Explain why or why not.

5. Consider the sentence variety. What sentences would you combine to improve the paragraph?

Rewriting Application: Responding to Essay Writing

Read the following essay. Then respond to the questions at the end of it.

Guamuchil

I was born in Guamuchil, Mexico, which is a small town near the Gulf of California. It is about six hundred miles south of the border in the state of Sinaloa. I have wonderful memories of growing up there, and I have wanted to visit it for many years. Therefore, I was really excited my husband and I decided to return to my hometown in 1994. Unfortunately, I found many changes there.

The very first difference I saw was the bridge that we crossed to enter the city from north to south. It used to be an attractive green bridge that crossed a wide flowing river. It had brightly painted rails that protected sidewalks on each side of it. In contrast to what I had described to my husband, the bridge now looked old and rundown. The paint on the rails was peeling off, and in some places the rails were crushed into the sidewalk because they had been hit by cars and never fixed. Even the river that I used to see every time I went across the bridge was almost gone. A very small stream was all that we could see.

Another thing that I had told my husband was that, even though the city was small, it had good streets and was well kept. I had even mentioned that many new stores with large, clean parking lots were being built when I had left. Unfortunately, the streets and stores now were very different. From the entrance of the city to the middle of it, we kept finding streets where the pavement was cracked and broken. In some streets as well as in parking lots, there were many big holes. And the stores were even worse. They looked run-down, and many of them were out of business. I was very unhappy at the sight.

Finally, when I lived in Guamuchil, it was a lively place, but now all that had changed. When I was young, I knew that we were not the richest town in the state, but the houses, shops, and cars remained well painted at all times, so the overall appearance of the city was presentable. However, when I visited it in 1994, everybody seemed to have lost hope for a better future, and they did not have the will or perhaps the money to fix the things they owned or to maintain a lively city instead of an old, run-down town.

I have not been back to Guamuchil since 1994, but I think I will visit it again soon. I know it will not be the way it was when I was young, but it is still my hometown, and I will never forget that.

1. Identify the thesis statement. State its topic and central idea. Is it an effective thesis statement? Can you tell whether the paper will focus on similarities or differences?

2. Identify each topic sentence. State its topic and central idea. Does each topic sentence clearly introduce one specific similarity or difference?

3. What transitional words introduce each new body paragraph?

4. Does the essay use a point-by-point or a subject-by-subject organization? Would you change the order of the paragraphs? Why or why not?

5. Is each similarity or difference explained clearly and fully? If you would improve any, explain how you would do so.

Proofreading

When proofreading your paper, watch for the following errors:

Sentence fragments, comma splices, and fused sentences

Misplaced modifiers and dangling modifiers

Errors in subject–verb agreement

Errors in pronoun case, pronoun–antecedent agreement, and pronoun reference

Errors in comma use

Errors in the use of periods, question marks, exclamation points, colons, semicolons, and quotation marks

Errors in capitalization, titles, and numbers

Misspelled words

Prepare a clean final draft, following the format your instructor has requested.

Chapter Five Practice Test

I. Review of Chapters Two, Three, and Four

A. Correct any fragments, fused sentences, or comma splices in the following sentences. Do nothing if the sentence is correct.

1. A dissatisfied customer standing in line behind twenty-five other angry people.

_____

_____

2. The game was beginning, however, Barry Bonds was busy at the tattoo parlor.

_____

_____

3. As Merlin was speaking to Arthur.

_____

_____

4. Leaving the harbor, Aeneas looked for Dido she was standing on the cliff.

_____

_____

5. Homer stared impatiently at the red light, he did not want to be late for his meeting with his nutrition counselor.

_____

_____

B. Correct any dangling or misplaced modifiers in the following sentences. Do nothing if the sentence is correct.

6. After eating the entire gallon of ice cream, Homer's depression was worse than ever.

_____

_____

continued

7. To see the shuttle liftoff, a telescope was purchased.

_____

_____

8. The girl who was riding the horse with red tennis shoes waved at her brother.

_____

_____

9. It was already 6:05, so Wyatt was only able to grab one pistol.

_____

_____

10. Staring at the two paths, the one less traveled seemed to be the best choice.

_____

_____

C. Correct any subject–verb agreement errors in the following sentences. Do nothing if the sentence is correct.

11. Each of the skiers in Salt Lake City want to win a gold medal.

12. Do the captain or the other pirates know where the treasure map is?

13. The crew have been looking for the map all week.

14. There is an aardvark and a Tasmanian devil waiting to see the veterinarian.

15. Twenty years of fighting and wandering were a long time for Odysseus to be away

from Penelope.

D. Correct any pronoun use errors in the following sentences. Do nothing if the sentence is correct.

16. Someone on one of the upper floors was playing a song by the Rolling Stones on his

saxophone.

17. Malcolm dropped the radio onto the glass-topped table, but it was not harmed.

continued

18. The police officer asked Igor and I to step out of the car.

19. I wondered if it was her who asked for asparagus with her Spam.

20. My brother was surprised when I told him that you are supposed to pull to the side of the road when you hear a siren.

II. Chapter Five

A. Add commas to the following sentences where necessary. Do nothing if the sentence is correct.

21. The hot bright sun was high in the sky but Icarus did not notice.

22. After living in Denver Colorado for two years Omar decided to return to Deadwood South Dakota.

23. Barbara did you decide to use the Flannery O'Connor story or do you prefer the Eudora Welty one?

24. During the last week in May Harey bought some baskets some artificial grass seven packets of dye two dozen chocolate bunnies and three hundred marshmallow eggs.

25. When the smoke finally cleared the sailors knew that December 7 1941 would some-day be infamous.

26. Before the beginning of the play Tennessee found some glass figurines and placed them on the stage.

27. Bill brought his favorite dish a Spam and catfish pie to the potluck dinner; however most people refused to even taste it.

28. Torta Koolagord who was on a diet was surprised at her father's present five pounds of chocolate.

29. Nora said "A tarantula appeared from under the rock and scared the coyote away."

30. Oprah wanted to feature the author's book on her show but he rudely refused.

continued

B. Add periods, exclamation points, question marks, quotation marks, semicolons, colons, and apostrophes (or 's) where necessary. Do not add or delete any commas.

31. Diana wondered if her arrows were sharp enough

32. Humpty asked, Do you think you can put me back together

33. These supplies are absolutely necessary four cans of Spam, a pound of cayenne pepper, eight cloves of garlic, two pounds of onions, and a case of Alka Seltzer

34. Three girls by the Thames screamed, Look, the bridge is falling down

35. All of his friends planned to take the whale-watching tour however, Pinocchio didnt want to go with them

36. The dam had a small hole in it the little Dutch boy put his finger in it

37. Ahab, we really should leave that whale alone, advised Starbuck

38. Willys sons were neither as successful nor as well-liked as Charleys son

39. Dante asked, Are you sure you know how to get out of here

40. Polyphemus kept shouting for help fortunately, no one came to his assistance

C. In the following sentences correct any errors in the use of titles, capitalization, and numbers. Do not add or delete any commas. Do nothing if the sentence is correct.

41. Last night I read joseph conrad's short story the secret sharer 2 times.

42. william shakespeare, who was born in england in fifteen sixty-four, wrote the play entitled as you like it.

43. More than 500 people were standing in line to see the movie harry potter and the sorcerer's stone.

44. 785 people asked for their money back after attending the concert by the chula vista philharmonic kazoo band last friday.

45. Peter Sprague, who performs on the compact disc blurring the edges, is a member of the san diego jazz society.

continued

46. Every friday night, Homer's heart yearns for hershey chocolate bars and orville redenbacher's popcorn.

47. By the end of the revolutionary war, only his mother still loved benedict arnold.

48. After Henry finished preparing for his math test, he started to write his english paper on wallace stevens's poem the emperor of ice cream.

49. After 3 weeks of teaching, professor tait knew the names of all the juniors in her class.

50. By one forty-five in the afternoon, we had purchased 5 antique napkin holders, twenty-two straw hats, and 113 wooden clothespins.

Choosing the Right Words and Spelling Them Correctly

English is a diverse language. It has borrowed words from hundreds of different sources. *Moccasin*, for instance, is Native American in origin; *patio* comes from Spanish; *colonel* and *lieutenant* entered English from Norman French; and *thermonuclear* is both Greek and Latin. All of this diversity makes English a complex and interesting language, but it also makes it quite difficult sometimes.

As you know, we have three words that sound just like *to* and three words that sound just like *there*. In fact, English is full of words that sound alike or that have such similar meanings that they are often mistaken for one another. A careful writer learns to make distinctions among these words.

Failing to make correct word choices or to spell words correctly can cause a number of problems. Most importantly, you may fail to make your ideas clear, or you may confuse your reader. In addition, you may lose the confidence of your reader if your writing contains misspelled or poorly chosen words. Sometimes, you can even embarrass yourself.

For instance, here is a fellow who wants to meet either a fish or the bottom of a shoe:

EXAMPLE   When I went to college, I did not know a **sole.**

This person has writing mixed up with the building trade:

EXAMPLE   I began to take my talent for writing for **granite,** but I lacked the ability to organize my thoughts in a coherent **manor.**

And here the early American settlers enjoy a means of transportation that hadn't yet been invented:

EXAMPLE   The pioneers appeared to prefer the open **planes** to the dense forests.

Most misspellings and incorrect word choices, however, are not as humorous or embarrassing as these. Instead, they are simple errors in word choice that are usually caused by carelessness and a lack of attention to detail.

Use Your Dictionary

This chapter will cover errors in word choice and spelling caused by irregular verbs and by words that are commonly confused. It will also present several of the basic "rules" of spelling. However, if you are not sure of a particular spelling (the difference between *effect* and *affect,* for instance), consult your dictionary. A dictionary shows how to spell, pronounce, and use words. A dictionary gives you the definitions of words, shows you the principal parts of verbs, and tells you whether or not a word is appropriate for formal writing. In addition, most dictionaries contain other useful information, such as biographical and geographical data.

one

Irregular Verbs

Because verbs in the English language change their spelling in a variety of ways to express different verb tenses, spelling them correctly can sometimes be a challenge. To use verbs correctly, you need to know the basic verb forms. These forms are known as the **three principal parts of the verb**: the **present**, the **past**, and the **past participle.**

You use the present to form both the present and future tenses, the past to form the past tense, and the past participle (with *have, has, had*) to form the perfect tenses.

Most verbs, the **regular verbs**, form the past and past participle by adding *d* or *ed* to the present. For example, the three principal parts of *create* are *create* (present), *created* (past), and *created* (past participle). The three principal parts of *talk* are *talk, talked,* and *talked.*

However, about two hundred verbs form the past and past participle in different ways. These verbs are called the **irregular verbs**. They are some of the oldest and most important verbs in English, such as *eat* or *fight* or *buy*—basic human actions. Because these words are so common, you should know their principal parts. Here is a list of the principal parts of most irregular verbs.

Present	*Past*	*Past Participle*
am, are, is	was, were	been
beat	beat	beaten
become	became	become
begin	began	begun
bend	bent	bent
bet	bet	bet
bite	bit	bitten
bleed	bled	bled
blow	blew	blown
break	broke	broken
bring	brought	brought
build	built	built
burst	burst	burst
buy	bought	bought
catch	caught	caught
choose	chose	chosen
come	came	come
cost	cost	cost
cut	cut	cut
dig	dug	dug
do, does	did	done

Present	Past	Past Participle
draw	drew	drawn
drink	drank	drunk
drive	drove	driven
eat	ate	eaten
fall	fell	fallen
feed	fed	fed
feel	felt	felt
fight	fought	fought
find	found	found
fly	flew	flown
forget	forgot	forgotten or forgot
freeze	froze	frozen
get	got	got or gotten
give	gave	given
go, goes	went	gone
grow	grew	grown
hang	hung	hung
hang (to execute)	hanged	hanged
have, has	had	had
hear	heard	heard
hide	hid	hidden
hit	hit	hit
hold	held	held
hurt	hurt	hurt
keep	kept	kept
know	knew	known
lay (to place or put)	laid	laid
lead	led	led
leave	left	left
lend	lent	lent
let	let	let
lie (to recline)	lay	lain
light	lit	lit
lose	lost	lost
make	made	made
mean	meant	meant
meet	met	met
pay	paid	paid
prove	proved	proved or proven

Present	Past	Past Participle
put	put	put
quit	quit	quit
read	read	read
ride	rode	ridden
ring	rang	rung
rise	rose	risen
run	ran	run
say	said	said
see	saw	seen
sell	sold	sold
send	sent	sent
set	set	set
shake	shook	shaken
shine	shone or shined	shone or shined
shoot	shot	shot
show	showed	shown
shrink	shrank	shrunk
shut	shut	shut
sing	sang	sung
sink	sank	sunk
sit	sat	sat
sleep	slept	slept
slide	slid	slid
speak	spoke	spoken
speed	sped	sped
spend	spent	spent
spin	spun	spun
stand	stood	stood
steal	stole	stolen
stick	stuck	stuck
sting	stung	stung
strike	struck	struck
swear	swore	sworn
sweep	swept	swept
swim	swam	swum
swing	swung	swung
take	took	taken

Present	Past	Past Participle
teach	taught	taught
tear	tore	torn
tell	told	told
think	thought	thought
throw	threw	thrown
wake	woke or waked	woken or waked
wear	wore	worn
weave	wove	woven
weep	wept	wept
win	won	won
wind	wound	wound
wring	wrung	wrung
write	wrote	written

Special Problems with Irregular Verbs

Lie–Lay

1. The irregular verb *lie* means "to recline." It never takes a direct object. The principal parts of this verb are *lie, lay,* and *lain.*

 EXAMPLES

On Saturdays, I **lie** in bed until at least 11:00.

Last Saturday, I **lay** in bed until almost 1:00.

Today, I **have lain** in bed too long.

2. The verb *lay* means "to place or put." It takes a direct object. Its principal parts are *lay, laid,* and *laid.*

 EXAMPLES

As Paul enters the house, he always **lays** his keys on the table.

Yesterday Paul **laid** his keys on the television set.

After he **had laid** the flowers on the kitchen table, Mr. Best kissed his wife.

Sit–Set

1. The verb *sit* means "to be seated." It never takes a direct object. Its principal parts are *sit, sat,* and *sat.*

 EXAMPLES

At the movies, Juan usually **sits** in the back row.

Last week Juan **sat** in the middle of the theater.

2. The verb *set* means "to place or put." It takes a direct object. Its principal parts are *set, set,* and *set*.

 EXAMPLES   At night Floyd always **sets** a glass of water by his bed.

Cora **set** her books on the librarian's desk.

Rise–Raise

1. The verb *rise* means "to stand" or "to attain a greater height." It never takes a direct object. Its principal parts are *rise, rose,* and *risen*.

 EXAMPLES   I like it when the sun **rises** over the mountains on a clear day.

All of the people **rose** every time the queen entered the room.

2. The verb *raise* is a regular verb. It means "to elevate." It takes a direct object. Its principal parts are *raise, raised,* and *raised*.

 EXAMPLES   Every morning a Boy Scout **raises** the flag in front of the school.

Christopher always politely **raised** his hand whenever he had a question.

Verbs with *U* in the Past Participle

Because these verbs sound odd, some people tend to use the past form when they should be using the past participle. Here are the ones that are most often confused.

drink	drank	**drunk:**	So far I **have drunk** eight glasses of water today.
swim	swam	**swum:**	Petra **has swum** thirty-five laps today.
shrink	shrank	**shrunk:**	The grocer wondered why his profits **had shrunk.**
sing	sang	**sung:**	Often Carmine **has sung** the National Anthem before hockey games.

 PRACTICE   Underline the correct verb form in the parentheses.

1. In the daytime, Michelle's pet rat just (lays <u>lies</u>) in the corner of his cage

and sleeps.

2. After he had (drank drunk) three glasses of Spam smoothie, Homer felt a

little lightheaded.

3. Byron bragged that he had (swam swum) all the way even with a bad foot.

4. Darby (lay laid) the dead gopher by the back door.

5. Virginia walked up the spiral staircase of her lighthouse, and then she

    (set sat) down to read a novel.

6. Lee could see the surrender documents (lying laying) by Grant's right hand.

7. The suitors asked Penelope why her knitting had (shrank shrunk).

8. Adam asked her if she had also (drank drunk) the bottle of wine that was

    (sitting setting) under the tree.

9. Although Emmy had (sang sung) well on the Hominy Grits' latest album,

    she could not (rise raise) enough money to accompany them on their

    concert tour.

10. The old waiter had (laid lain) flat on his back for three hours before he

    admitted that he couldn't fall asleep.

Section One Review

1. The **three principal parts of a verb** are **present, past,** and **past participle.**

2. **Regular verbs** form the past and past participle by adding *d* or *ed* to the present.

3. **Irregular** verbs form the past and past participle in a variety of other ways. See the lists on pages 336–339.

4. Irregular verbs that often cause confusion are *lie/lay, sit/set, rise/raise,* and verbs with *u* in the past participle.

Exercise 1A

Underline the correct form of the verb in the parentheses.

1. Participating on the swim team, Naomi figures she has (swam <u>swum</u>) thousands of miles.

2. When Juanita (saw seen) the damage to her car, she started to cry.

3. When Calvin heard my story, he (busted burst) out laughing.

4. Paris knew that his selfishness had (costed cost) his city much heartache.

5. By the end of the day, books and papers (lay laid) all over the floor.

6. Grendel watched the men (setting sitting) in the mead house.

7. Quasimodo realized that, as he was talking to the woman, he had not (rang rung) the bells.

8. Everyone stood in silence as the full moon (raised rose) above the horizon.

9. Caesar crossed the Rubicon River and then realized that his favorite toga had (shrank shrunk).

10. Jimmy started to cry when his paper boat (sank sunk) to the bottom of the bathtub.

11. Mr. Valenzuela thought that he had (lain laid) his key on the desk in his office.

12. After Alma had (threw thrown) her computer into the river, she began her search for enlightenment.

13. Hester (wrang wrung) out her special dress, and then she (hanged hung) it on the clothesline.

14. Job (set sat) down and pondered the causes of just about everything.

15. After the bride and groom had (shook shaken) the hand of each guest, they were ready for the reception to be over.

In the blanks, write the correct form of the verb indicated.

1. Clete looked down and saw that a ten dollar bill ____*lay*____ by his right shoe. (lie)

2. At last night's concert a strange man _____ next to my sister and me. (sit)

3. Hercules was _____ several tasks to complete. (give)

4. He didn't know just how hot the sun could be until he had _____ so close to it. (fly)

5. Stephanie has already _____ every bottle of iced tea in the refrigerator. (drink)

6. The witch asked Hansel to look into the oven to see if the cake had _____. (rise)

7. Rip did not realize that he had _____ there sleeping for so long. (lie)

8. Mrs. Chen told the doctor that she had _____ seven glasses of water each day. (drink)

9. When Theo saw Vincent's painting, he knew his brother had _____ the night sky in a very different way. (see)

10. Although Homer had _____ to visit Hortense, he spent the first hour of his visit eating the leftovers in her refrigerator. (come)

11. Have the bells indicating the end of the service _____ yet? (ring)

12. As soon as Macbeth had _____ that morning, he knew that he had not been dreaming. (rise)

13. Antigone was angry because her brother's body had been _____ out on the battlefield for days without being buried. (lie)

14. After he had drunk some wine, the poet always bragged that he had _____ the Hellespont. (swim)

15. After drinking the potion, Alice noticed that she had _____ to the size of a rabbit. (shrink)

Exercise 1C

Check the following paragraph for correct verb forms. Underline any incorrect verb forms and write the correct forms above them.

1. I agree with the American writer Henry David Thoreau, who has ~~wrote~~ *written* that most people lead lives of "quiet desperation," always looking for happiness in the wrong places. **2.** For instance, last night I seen several television commercials that show what many Americans value. **3.** A commercial for Zima beer shown a sexy scene of a man and woman in a bar, as if a good beer would bring sex and romance. **4.** I actually have friends who have drank Zima because they think it makes them attractive. **5.** Another commercial advertised Princess Cruises. **6.** It showed the sun raising in the east as happy people laid around the pool of a huge ship. **7.** These examples may seem silly, but I have knowed many people who think a beer or a cruise or a cell phone would make them happy. **8.** Thoreau would probably have bust out laughing at these ideas. **9.** He felt that people throughout history have spended way too much time working to get things that they thought would make them happy. **10.** He seen that when people finally got these things, they were still unhappy and discontented. **11.** Not long ago the ten-year-old son of a friend of mine begged her to buy him a pair of sports shoes that costed over $120. **12.** When my friend told him that she could not afford such expensive shoes, he set down and cried. **13.** He had came to believe that he had to have the shoes to be liked. **14.** I agree with the English writer William Wordsworth, who wrote, "Getting and spending we lay waste our powers." **15.** Both Wordsworth and Thoreau knew that if we spent our time looking for happiness in things and possessions, we would miss the real happiness that is laying right in front of us, and we would always be "desperate." **16.** In my life I choose to believe that what I have bought or wore or ate is not as important as whether I have appreciated nature and my fellow human beings. **17.** Henry David Thoreau and William Wordsworth would agree with me.

Commonly Confused Words

Most word choice errors are made either because two words sound alike or look alike or because their meanings are so similar that they are mistakenly used in place of each other. Here are some of the most commonly confused sets of words.

A/an/and

A is used before words that begin with **consonant sounds**. It is an article, a type of **adjective**.

⊚ **EXAMPLES**   **a** porcupine, **a** bat, **a** sword, **a** good boy

An is used before words that begin with **vowel sounds**. It is also an article.

⊚ **EXAMPLES**   **an** apple, **an** honor, **an** unusual cloud formation

And is a **coordinating conjunction** used to join words, phrases, or clauses.

⊚ **EXAMPLE**   Homer **and** Hortense

Accept/except

Accept means "to take or receive what is offered or given." It is a **verb**.

⊚ **EXAMPLE**   Severino gladly **accepted** the reward for the money he had returned.

Except means "excluded" or "but." It is a **preposition**.

⊚ **EXAMPLE**   Flowers were in everyone's room **except** Sonia's.

Advice/advise

Advice means "an opinion about what to do or how to handle a situation." It is a **noun**.

⊚ **EXAMPLE**   The counselor gave Phillipa **advice** about how to apply for graduate school.

Advise means "to give advice" or "to counsel." It is a **verb**.

⊚ **EXAMPLE**   The judge **advised** the defense attorney to control his temper.

Affect/effect

Affect means "to influence" or "to produce a change in." It is a **verb**.

EXAMPLE   The continued destruction of the ozone layer will **affect** future weather patterns drastically.

Effect is "a result" or "something brought about by a cause." It is a **noun**.

EXAMPLE   The decorator liked the **effect** of the newly painted room.

NOTE: *Effect* can be used as a verb when it means "to bring about" or "to cause."

EXAMPLE   The reward **effected** a change in the lion's behavior.

All ready/already

All ready means "everyone or everything is prepared or ready."

EXAMPLE   After a strenuous game of softball, we were **all ready** for a cold root beer.

Already means "by or before a specific or implied time."

EXAMPLE   By the time he had climbed the first flight of stairs, Bob was **already** out of breath.

All right/"alright"

All right means "satisfactory" or "unhurt."

EXAMPLE   After she fell from her horse, Hannah smiled and said she was **all right**.

Alright is a misspelling. Do not use it.

Among/between

Among means "in the company of" or "included with." Use it when discussing <u>three or more</u> things or ideas. It is a **preposition**.

EXAMPLE   **Among** the demands of the workers was drinkable coffee.

Between means "in or through the space that separates two things." Use it only when you are discussing <u>two things or ideas</u>. It is a **preposition**.

EXAMPLE   Betty could not choose **between** Sid and Slim.

Amount/number

Use *amount* to refer to things that are usually not separated, such as milk, oil, salt, or flour.

EXAMPLE   The **amount** of sugar the recipe calls for is two cups.

Use *number* to refer to things that are usually separated or counted individually, such as people, books, cats, or apples.

EXAMPLE   The large **number** of people in the small room made the air stuffy.

Anxious/eager

Anxious means "apprehensive, uneasy, worried." It is an **adjective**.

EXAMPLE   The lawyer was **anxious** about the jury's verdict.

Eager means "keen desire or enthusiasm in pursuit of something." It is also an **adjective**.

EXAMPLE   The children were **eager** for summer vacation to begin.

Are/our

Are is a **linking verb** or a **helping verb**.

EXAMPLES   We **are** late for dinner.

We **are** leaving soon.

Our is a **possessive pronoun**.

EXAMPLE   **Our** dinner was delicious.

Brake/break

Brake is the device that stops or slows a vehicle. It may be used as a **noun** or a **verb**.

EXAMPLES   The service station attendant told Molly that her **brakes** were dangerously worn.

Arlo **braked** just in time to avoid going over the cliff.

Break can also be used as a **noun** or a **verb**. As a **verb**, it means "to cause to come apart by force."

EXAMPLE Every time Humphrey walks through a room, he **breaks** something.

As a noun, *break* means "an interruption of an action or a thing."

EXAMPLES When there was a **break** in the storm, we continued the game.

The worker fixed the **break** in the water pipe.

Choose/chose

Choose means "select." It is a **present tense verb.**

EXAMPLE Every Friday afternoon, the children **choose** a movie to watch in the evening.

Chose means "selected." It is the **past tense** of *choose.*

EXAMPLE Last Friday, the children **chose** Pocahontas.

Complement/compliment

A *complement* is "that which completes or brings to perfection." It is a **noun** or a **verb.**

EXAMPLES The bright yellow tie was a handsome **complement** to Pierre's new suit.

The bright yellow tie **complemented** Pierre's new suit.

A *compliment* is "an expression of praise, respect, or courtesy." It is a **noun** or a **verb.**

EXAMPLES Whenever Mr. Trujillo receives a **compliment** for his beautiful sculptures, he smiles and blushes.

Whenever his wife **compliments** Mr. Trujillo for his beautiful sculpture, he smiles and blushes.

Conscience/conscious

Conscience is "a knowledge or sense of right and wrong." It is a **noun.**

EXAMPLE Javier said that his **conscience** kept him from looking at Lucy's paper during the physics examination.

Conscious can mean either "aware" or "awake." It is an **adjective.**

EXAMPLE As he walked through the dark woods, Frank was **conscious** of the animals all around him.

Disinterested/uninterested

Disinterested means "neutral" or "impartial." It is an **adjective**.

 EXAMPLE   A judge must remain **disinterested** as he considers a case before him.

Uninterested means "not interested." It is an **adjective**.

 EXAMPLE   Shirley was profoundly **uninterested** in the subject of the lecture.

 PRACTICE   Underline the correct word in the parentheses.

1. The hikers were so (eager anxious) to get to the trail that they forgot to get (advice advise) about the local weather.

2. No matter what they do wrong, some people never seem to be bothered by (a an) uneasy (conscious conscience).

3. Dido could never (except accept) that Aeneas had had such a dramatic (effect affect) on her.

4. Sancho said that the food should be shared (between among) Don Quixote, Dulcinea, and him or he would have to (brake break) his oath.

5. (A An) ideal jury should be composed of twelve (uninterested disinterested) people.

6. The best (advise advice) I ever received (affected effected) my life in many ways.

7. The play had (all ready already) begun, but Claudius was (disinterested, uninterested) in the opening scene anyway.

8. Jovita's high fever made her mother (anxious, eager) even though Jovita insisted that she felt (alright all right).

9. The (number amount) of persons in the king's party seemed important to Oedipus.

10. Zachary's artistic temperament (compliments complements) Priscilla's rational practicality.

11. The Bobolinks knew that (are our) chances of winning were small if we did not give our center a (break brake).

12. General Lee would have to (chose choose) to send General Pickett's troops up the hill if he wanted to (brake break) through the Union lines.

Fewer/less

Use *fewer* to discuss items that can be counted separately, such as trees, automobiles, or pencils. It is an **adjective**.

 EXAMPLE When the cutters had finished, there were many **fewer** trees in the grove.

Use *less* to refer to amounts that are not usually separated, such as water, dirt, sand, or gasoline. It is an **adjective**.

 EXAMPLE Because of the drought, there is **less** water in the lake this year.

Lead/led

As a **noun**, *lead* is a heavy metal or a part of a pencil. As a **verb**, it is the present tense of the verb *to lead*, meaning "to guide" or "to show the way."

 EXAMPLES The diver used weights made of **lead** to keep him from floating to the surface.

Every summer Mr. Archer **leads** his scout troop on a long backpacking trip.

Led is the past or past participle form of the **verb** *to lead*.

 EXAMPLE Last summer, Mr. Archer **led** his scout troop on a backpacking trip.

Loose/lose

Loose means "not confined or restrained, free, unbound." It is an **adjective**.

 EXAMPLE Mr. Castro was chasing a cow that had gotten **loose** and was trampling his garden.

Lose means "to become unable to find" or "to mislay." It is a **verb**.

 EXAMPLE I was afraid I would **lose** my contact lenses if I went swimming with them.

Passed/past

Passed is the past or past participle form of the **verb** *to pass,* which means "to go or move forward, through, or out."

EXAMPLE   As I drove to school, I **passed** a serious traffic accident.

Past as an **adjective** means "gone by, ended, over." As a **noun,** it means "the time that has gone by." As a **preposition,** it means "beyond."

EXAMPLES   His **past** mistakes will not bar him from further indiscretions.

In the **past,** I have always been in favor of opening doors for women.

Horst waved as he drove **past** Jill's house.

Personal/personnel

Personal means "private" or "individual." It is an **adjective.**

EXAMPLE   Helen feels her political ideas are her **personal** business.

Personnel means "persons employed in any work or enterprise." It is a **noun.**

EXAMPLE   The sign on the bulletin board directed all **personnel** to report to the auditorium for a meeting.

Precede/proceed

Precede means "to go before." It is a **verb.**

EXAMPLE   The Great Depression **preceded** World War II.

Proceed means "to advance or go on." It is a **verb.**

EXAMPLE   After a short pause, Mrs. Quintan **proceeded** with her inventory.

Principal/principle

As an **adjective,** *principal* means "first in rank or importance." As a **noun,** it usually means "the head of a school."

EXAMPLES   Kevin's **principal** concern was the safety of his children.

At the assembly the **principal** discussed drug abuse with the students and teachers.

A *principle* is a "fundamental truth, law, or doctrine." It is a **noun.**

EXAMPLE   One of my **principles** is that you never get something for nothing.

Quit/quite/quiet

Quit means "to stop doing something." It is a **verb.**

EXAMPLE   George **quit** smoking a year ago.

Quite means "completely" or "really." It is an **adverb.**

EXAMPLE   It was **quite** hot during the whole month of August.

Quiet means "silent." It is usually used as an **adjective,** but it can be used as a **noun.**

EXAMPLES   The **quiet** student in the third row rarely said a word.

In the **quiet** of the evening, Hank strummed his guitar.

Than/then

Use *than* to make comparisons. It is a **conjunction.**

EXAMPLE   It is cloudier today **than** it was yesterday.

Then means "at that time" or "soon afterwards" or "next." It is an **adverb.**

EXAMPLE   Audrey mowed the backyard, and **then** she drank a large iced tea.

Their/there/they're

Their is a **possessive pronoun** meaning "belonging to them."

EXAMPLE   All of the people in the room suddenly started clinking the ice in **their** drinks.

There is an **adverb** meaning "in that place."

EXAMPLE   "Let's park the car **there,**" proclaimed Fern.

They're is a contraction for *they are.*

EXAMPLE   "**They're** back," said the little girl ominously.

Threw/through

Threw is the past tense form of the **verb** *to throw.*

EXAMPLE   Hector **threw** the spear with godlike accuracy.

Through is a **preposition** meaning "in one side and out the other side of."

EXAMPLE   The ship sailed **through** the Bermuda Triangle without peril.

To/too/two

To is a **preposition** meaning "in the direction of."

EXAMPLE   Jeremy went **to** his rustic cabin by the babbling brook for a poetic weekend.

Too is an **adverb** meaning "also" or "more than enough."

EXAMPLES   Cecily was at the spree **too**.

The senator found that the burden of public adulation was **too** heavy.

Two is the number after *one*.

EXAMPLE   Bill has **two** daughters and one cat and too many televisions, so he wants to go to Jeremy's rustic cabin too.

We're/were/where

We're is a contraction for *we are*.

EXAMPLE   **We're** almost there.

Were is a **linking verb** or a **helping verb** in the past tense.

EXAMPLES   We **were** late for dinner.

Our hosts **were** eating dessert when we arrived.

Where indicates **place**.

EXAMPLES   **Where** is the key to the cellar?

He showed them **where** he had buried the money.

Your/you're

Your is a **possessive pronoun** meaning "belonging to you."

EXAMPLE   "**Your** insights have contributed greatly to my sense of well-being," said the toady.

You're is a contraction for *you are*.

EXAMPLE   "**You're** just saying that because **you're** so nice," replied the other toady.

PRACTICE   Underline the correct words in the parentheses.

1. The (<u>number</u> amount) of players on the team is decreasing because of (to <u>too</u> two) many injuries, so the managers announced that (there <u>they're</u> their) probably going to cancel the next game.

2. There have been (fewer less) houses built in our area this year (than then) there were last year.

3. (You're Your) decision to ask the (principal principle) to resign is a good one.

4. After you have gone (passed past) the *Queen Mary,* turn left and drive (through threw) Long Beach.

5. As the tour guide (lead led) the visitors deep into Mammoth Cave, she warned them to stay on the marked path because they could easily (loose lose) (there their they're) way.

6. The mariners told Odysseus (their there they're) (personal personnel) reasons for wanting to go back to Ithaca.

7. The gentle questioning by Socrates (lead led) many people to new (principals principles) by which they could live their lives.

8. (To Too Two) hours is not (to too two) long (to too two) study for an exam.

9. The (number amount) of mariners on the ship was much (fewer less) (then than) when they had set out.

10. Determined not to (loose lose) his temper, Mr. Potatohead (proceeded preceded) to explain his position.

11. It was (quiet quit quite) early when I woke up, so I was (quiet quit quite) as I made the coffee.

12. The Lotus Eaters (where we're were) glad to show the mariners (where we're were) they could find (an and a) abundance of the plants.

Section Two Review

Be careful when you use the following words:

a/an/and

accept/except

advice/advise

affect/effect

all ready/already

all right/"alright"

among/between

amount/number

anxious/eager

are/our

brake/break

choose/chose

complement/compliment

conscience/conscious

disinterested/uninterested

fewer/less

lead/led

loose/lose

passed/past

personal/personnel

precede/proceed

principal/principle

quit/quite/quiet

than/then

their/there/they're

threw/through

to/too/two

we're/were/where

your/you're

Underline the correct word in the parentheses.

1. The prospects for victory are much greater now (then <u>than</u>) they were just five minutes ago.

2. Do you think that (less fewer) people (break brake) the speed limit now that police are using radar?

3. The graduates were (eager anxious) to receive (there their they're) diplomas.

4. Natty Bumpo (preceded proceeded) to divide the deer meat (among between) his three friends.

5. Mrs. Mallard had (quite quit quiet) a difficult time (accepting excepting) the fact that her husband was still alive.

6. When Dr. Frankenstein was (through threw), he wondered what (effect affect) the new brain would have on his experiment.

7. Hamlet did not want to have Ophelia's despair on his (conscious conscience).

8. Karl wanted to talk about the last game of the World Series, but his date was completely (disinterested uninterested) in baseball.

9. The small (number amount) of mourners at his sister's funeral angered Laertes.

10. (You're Your) catcher's mitt looks (alright all right), even though it is thirty years old.

11. When we got to the bookstore, the famous author had (all ready already) left.

12. Claude knew his (compliments complements) would not please Mrs. Turpin.

13. Ulysses was afraid that if he stayed away (to too two) long, he would (lose loose) his wife and home.

14. Jack Aubrey's men went to (their there they're) battle stations when they saw the ship that they (were where we're) approaching.

15. Dr. Maturin was caring for (to too two) of the sailors who were (to too two) wounded (to too two) go on deck.

Exercise 2B

Correct any word choice errors in the following sentences.

1. Mr. Fernandez felt honored as he ~~excepted~~ *accepted* his award for heroism.

2. Are neighbors have all ready decided to move to Fresno.

3. Aeneas knew that his conscious was going too bother him long after he left Carthage.

4. It is alright with me if your going to see *Lord of the Rings* for an eighth time.

5. The best advise Harold's father ever gave him was to chose his friends carefully.

6. Lewis and Clark thanked the native people who had lead them threw the mountains.

7. As time past, Pip worried that he might loose his head over Estella.

8. The McDonalds anxiously looked forward to there upcoming trip to the Bahamas.

9. Tantalus was hungrier and thirstier then he had ever been.

10. Theresa complemented her son for the amount of A's he had received.

11. General Grant and President Lincoln where disinterested in Lee's supply of Confederate money.

12. The principle of Ishmael's school gave him time off too go to sea.

13. You're Spam recipe will make a tasty dessert for are company's personal.

14. The three witches agreed between themselves that before things settled down in Scotland, a few hearts would brake.

15. Mario's conscious began to bother him when he realized the affect his lie would have on his friends.

Exercise 2C

Edit the following paragraph for word use. Underline any incorrect words, and write the correct words above them.

1. Many students and administrators at Beach City College want to prevent skinheads and

neo-Nazis from presenting ~~they're~~ *their* disgusting views, but the reasons they give are not strong

enough to violate the ~~principal~~ *principle* of free speech. **2.** Many administrators say that it is quit danger-

ous to let these people on campus. **3.** There advise is to bar them from speaking. **4.** However,

when members of the student council discussed the matter between themselves, they past a reso-

lution in support of free speech. **5.** According to them, if the administrators are afraid the audi-

ence will brake the law by attacking the speakers, than they should hire security personal for the

speech. **6.** Another reason administrators are not anxious to have these speakers on campus is

that most students are disinterested in there racist views. **7.** I, for one, am happy that most stu-

dents will chose to ignore these speakers, but my conscious tells me that we still have to let them

speak. **8.** Less than ten people may show up to listen, but we must not loose sight of the fact that

are Constitution supports all free speech, not just popular speech. **9.** Finally, a large amount of

students have objected to these speakers because racist ideas have lead to violence and even war

in the passed. **10.** I have to admit that these racist ideas make me feel ill, but we need to except

the principal that we can't listen just too the people with whom we agree. **11.** Threw my studies

in political science, I have learned that the best way to fight the affect of dangerous ideas is to

respond with worthy ideas. **12.** When the founders of are country where writing the Constitu-

tion, they did not say that only certain groups had the right of free speech. **13.** To protect are

own free speech, we have to protect the speech of all people, even speech that is quiet abhorrent

to us and are beliefs.

SECTION
three

Spelling Rules

Spelling words correctly should be simple. After all, if you can say a word, it would just seem to make sense that you should be able to spell it. Why, then, is accurate spelling such a problem for some people? Well, as anyone who has ever written anything in English knows, one of the problems is that the same sound is spelled different ways in different situations. For instance, the long *e* sound may be spelled *ea,* as in *mean; ee,* as in *seem; ei,* as in *receive; ie,* as in *niece;* or *e-consonant-e,* as in *precede.* On the other hand, many words in English use similar spellings but have totally different pronunciations, as in *rough, bough, though, through,* and *cough.* As if these problems weren't enough, there are times when consonants are doubled (*rob* becomes *robbed*), times when consonants are not doubled (*robe* becomes *robed*), times when a final *e* is dropped (*move* becomes *moving*), and times when the final *e* is not dropped (*move* becomes *movement*). Unfortunately, these are just a few of the variations that occur in the spelling of English words—so perhaps it is understandable that accurate spelling poses a problem for many people.

In this section, you will study various rules of spelling that will help you through specific spelling situations. However, before we examine the specific rules of spelling, consider these points to improve your spelling in any writing activity.

Techniques to Improve Your Spelling

1. <u>Buy and use a dictionary.</u> Small, inexpensive paperback dictionaries are available in nearly every bookstore or supermarket. Keep one next to you as you write and get used to using it.

2. <u>Pay attention to your own reactions as you write.</u> If you are not confident of the spelling of a word, assume you have probably misspelled it and use your dictionary to check it.

3. <u>Don't rely too much on spelling checkers.</u> Although spelling checkers are excellent tools that you should use, don't assume they will solve all of your spelling problems, because they won't. They are particularly useless when you confuse the kinds of words covered in the previous section, such as *their, there,* and *they're.*

4. <u>Pronounce words carefully and accurately.</u> Some misspellings are the result of poor pronunciation. Examine the following misspelled words. Pronounce and spell them correctly. Extend the list with examples of other words you have heard mispronounced.

	Incorrect	*Correct*	*Incorrect*	*Correct*
	athelete	_____	perfer	_____
	discription	_____	perscription	_____
	enviroment	_____	probally	_____
	heigth	_____	realator	_____
	libary	_____	suprise	_____
	nucular	_____	unusal	_____
	paticular	_____	usally	_____

5. <u>Use memory tricks.</u> You can memorize the spelling of many words by using some memory techniques.

 EXAMPLES

There is **a rat** in *separate.*

The first **ll**'s are parallel in *parallel.*

Dessert *has two ss's because everyone wants two desserts.*

6. <u>Read more often.</u> The most effective way to become a better speller (and, for that matter, a better writer and thinker) is to read on a regular basis. If you do not read novels, perhaps now is the time to start. Ask your instructor to recommend some good books, newspapers, and magazines.

7. <u>Learn the rules of spelling.</u> The following explanations should help you improve your spelling. However, note that each of these "rules" contains numerous exceptions. You must use a dictionary if you have any doubt about the spelling of a word.

Using *ie* or *ei*

You have probably heard this bit of simple verse:

> Use *i* before *e*
> Except after *c*
> Or when sounded like *ay*
> As in *neighbor* or *weigh.*

Although there are exceptions to this rule, it works in most cases.

EXAMPLES	IE	EI (after C)	EI (sounded like Ay)
	grief	deceive	sleigh
	niece	ceiling	eight
	belief	receipt	weigh
	achieve	perceive	neighbor

Exceptions:

EXAMPLES

ancient	conscience	foreign	neither	science	stein
caffeine	deity	height	protein	seize	their
codeine	either	leisure	proficient	society	weird

PRACTICE   Supply the correct *ie/ei* spellings in the following sentences.

1. A silver sh*ie*ld fell to the floor and landed on the b*ei*ge carpet.

2. For Christmas, Homer rec__ved a case of Spam from his best fr__nd.

3. Michelangelo looked at the c__ling and wondered how much paint would

   be suffic__nt.

4. Robert stopped his sl__gh by some snowy woods and breathed a qu__t

   sigh of rel__f.

5. N__ther Henrietta nor Homer knew how they would ever ach__ve th__r

   goal of growing a Spam-flavored artichoke.

Keeping or Changing a Final -y

When you add letters to a word ending in -*y*, change the *y* to *i* if it is preceded by a consonant. If it is preceded by a vowel, do not change the -*y*. A major exception: If you are adding -*ing*, never change the y.

EXAMPLES

Preceded by a Consonant				*Preceded by Vowel*			
study	+ ed	=	studied	delay	+ ed	=	delayed
pretty	+ est	=	prettiest	buy	+ er	=	buyer
happy	+ ness	=	happiness	employ	+ ment	=	employment

Exceptions:

study	+	ing	=	studying	say	+	d	=	said
worry	+	ing	=	worrying	pay	+	d	=	paid

⊚ **PRACTICE**   Add the suffix in parentheses to each of the following words.

1. study   (ed)   _studied_

          (es)   _studies_

          (ing)   _studying_

2. angry   (est)   ———

          (er)   ———

          (ly)   ———

3. portray   (ed)   ———

          (s)   ———

          (ing)   ———

          (al)   ———

4. busy   (ness)   ———

          (er)   ———

          (est)   ———

5. employ   (er)   ———

          (ed)   ———

          (able)   ———

Keeping or Dropping a Silent Final -*e*

When a word ends in a silent -*e*, drop the -*e* when you add an ending that begins with a vowel. Keep the -*e* when you add an ending that begins with a consonant.

 EXAMPLES

		Before a Vowel					*Before a Consonant*	
move	+ ing	=	moving		hope	+ less	=	hopeless
advise	+ able	=	advisable		move	+ ment	=	movement
pure	+ ity	=	purity		safe	+ ly	=	safely

Exceptions:

EXAMPLES

courage	+ ous	=	courageous		judge	+ ment	=	judgment
change	+ able	=	changeable		argue	+ ment	=	argument
notice	+ able	=	noticeable		true	+ ly	=	truly

PRACTICE   Add the ending shown to each word, keeping or dropping the final -*e* when necessary.

1. require   +   ment   =   *requirement*

2. require   +   ing   =   _____

3. inspire   +   ing   =   _____

4. love   +   able   =   _____

5. love   +   ly   =   _____

6. manage   +   ing   =   _____

7. manage   +   ment   =   _____

8. complete   +   ly   =   _____

9. judge   +   ment   =   _____

10. notice   +   able   =   _____

Doubling the Final Consonant

In a single-syllable word that ends in one consonant preceded by one vowel (as in *drop*), double the final consonant when you add an ending that starts with a vowel. If a word has two or more syllables, the same rule applies *only if the emphasis is on the final syllable.*

 EXAMPLES

One Syllable				*Two or More Syllables* *(emphasis on final syllable)*			
drop + ing = dropping				expel + ing = expelling			
slap + ed = slapped				occur + ence = occurrence			
thin + est = thinnest				begin + er = beginner			

PRACTICE   Add the indicated endings to the following words. Double the final consonants where necessary.

1. brag   +   ing   =   *bragging*

2. wild   +   est   =   _____

3. refer   +   ed   =   _____

4. proceed +   ing   =   _____

5. dim   +   er   =   _____

6. clean   +   er   =   _____

7. commit   +   ed   =   _____

8. forget   +   able =   _____

9. happen   +   ing   =   _____

10. compel +   ed   =   _____

Using Prefixes

A **prefix** is one or more syllables added at the start of a word to change its meaning. **Do not change any letters of the root word when you add a prefix to it.** (The **root** is the part of the word that carries its central idea.)

 EXAMPLES

prefix	**+**	*root*	**=**	*new word*
im	+	possible	=	impossible
mis	+	spell	=	misspell
il	+	legal	=	illegal
un	+	necessary	=	unnecessary

PRACTICE Circle the correct spellings.

1. dissappoint   (disappoint)

2. unatural   unnatural

3. dissatisfied   disatisfied

4. illegible   ilegible

5. mistrial   misstrial

6. imoral   immoral

7. mispell   misspell

8. ireversible   irreversible

9. ilicit   illicit

10. unethical   unnethical

Forming Plurals

1. Add *-s* to make most nouns plural. Add *-es* if the noun ends in *ch, sh, ss,* or *x.*

(ⓢ) **EXAMPLES**

Add -s		*Add -es*	
street	streets	church	churches
dog	dogs	bush	bushes
problem	problems	hiss	hisses
issue	issues	box	boxes

2. If the noun ends in *o,* add *-s* if the *o* is preceded by a vowel. Add *-es* if it is preceded by a consonant.

(ⓢ) **EXAMPLES**

Add -s					*Add -es*				
stereo	+	s	=	stereos	hero	+	es	=	heroes
radio	+	s	=	radios	potato	+	es	=	potatoes

Exceptions: *pianos, sopranos, solos, autos, memos*

3. Some nouns that end in *-f* or *-fe* form the plural by changing the ending to *-ve* before the *s.*

(ⓢ) **EXAMPLES**

half	+	s	=	hal**ves**
wife	+	s	=	wi**ves**
leaf	+	s	=	lea**ves**

4. Some words form plurals by changing spelling.

(ⓢ) **EXAMPLES**

woman	=	women
goose	=	geese
foot	=	feet
child	=	children

5. Many words borrowed from other languages also form plurals by changing spelling.

(ⓢ) **EXAMPLES**

alumnus	=	alumni
alumna	=	alumnae
analysis	=	analyses
basis	=	bases
medium	=	media
crisis	=	crises
criterion	=	criteria

memorandum   =   memoranda

phenomenon   =   phenomena

PRACTICE   Write the plural forms of the following words.

1. tax   *taxes*

2. monkey   _____

3. echo   _____

4. knife   _____

5. match   _____

6. month   _____

7. kiss   _____

8. stereo   _____

9. candy   _____

10. phenomenon   _____

Commonly Misspelled Words

Many words that are commonly misspelled do not relate to any particular spelling rule. In such cases, you need to be willing to use a dictionary to check the correct spelling.

PRACTICE   Correct each of the misspelled words below. Use a dictionary when you are unsure of the correct spelling.

1. accross   *across*   4. behavor   _____

2. alot   _____   5. brillient   _____

3. athelete   _____   6. buisness   _____

7. carefuly   _____

8. carreer   _____

9. competion   _____

10. definate   _____

11. desparate   _____

12. develope   _____

13. diffrent   _____

14. dinning   _____

15. discribe   _____

16. dosen't   _____

17. embarass   _____

18. enviroment   _____

19. exagerate   _____

20. Febuary   _____

21. fasinate   _____

22. goverment   _____

23. grammer   _____

24. heigth   _____

25. imediate   _____

26. intrest   _____

27. knowlege   _____

28. mathmatics   _____

29. neccessary   _____

30. ocassion   _____

31. oppinion   _____

32. oportunity   _____

33. orginal   _____

34. particlar   _____

35. potatoe   _____

36. preform   _____

37. prehaps   _____

38. probally   _____

39. ridiclous   _____

40. seperate   _____

41. simular   _____

42. sincerly   _____

43. studing   _____

44. suprise   _____

45. temperture   _____

46. Thrusday   _____

47. unusal   _____

48. writting   _____

Section Three Review

1. Using *ie* or *ei*:

> Use *i* before *e*
>
> Except after *c*
>
> Or when sounded like *ay*
>
> As in *neighbor* or *weigh*.

2. Keeping or Changing a Final *-y*:

   - Change the *-y* to *-i* when the *y* follows a consonant.
   - Do not change the *-y* to *-i* if the *y* follows a vowel.
   - Do not change the *-y-* to *-i* if you are adding *-ing*.

3. Keeping or Dropping a Silent Final *-e:*

   - In general, drop the final *-e* before an ending that begins with a vowel.
   - In general, keep the final *-e* before an ending that begins with a consonant.

4. Doubling the Final Consonant:

   - In a one-syllable word, double the final consonant only if a single vowel precedes the final consonant.
   - In a word of more than one syllable, apply the above rule only if the last syllable is accented.

5. Using Prefixes:

   - A prefix is one or more syllables added at the start of a word to change its meaning. Do not change any letters of the root word when you add a prefix to it.

6. Forming Plurals

   - Add *-s* to make most nouns plural. Add *-es* if the noun ends in *ch, sh, ss,* or *x*.
   - If a noun ends in *o*, add *-s* if the *o* is preceded by a vowel. Add *-es* if the *o* is preceded by a consonant.
   - Some nouns that end in *-f* or *-fe* form the plural by changing the ending to *-ve* before the *s*.
   - Some words, especially words borrowed from other languages, form plurals by changing spelling.

7. Using Your Dictionary:

   - Whenever you're in doubt about the spelling of a word, consult your dictionary.

Exercise 3A

Correct any spelling errors in the following sentences by crossing out the incorrectly spelled word and writing the correct spelling above it.

1. Jerry's ~~neice~~ *niece* was sure that too much ~~studing~~ *studying* would ruin her social life.

2. Idaho is famous for its potatoes, but Seymour was disastisfied with the weather there.

3. Serena could not beleive that she had mispelled such an easy word.

4. The movment to ban all mustaches has caused many arguements in our household.

5. Two weeks after Jenna had enlistted in the Marine Corps, she finally admitted that she had

    made a serious mistake.

6. Eight tiny reindeer pulled the sliegh high over the tops of the chimnies.

7. The last time Ernie tryed to lose wieght, he ended up in the hospital.

8. Condors are rarly seen in the wild, and it is ilegal to hunt them.

9. The most noticable difference between Angelica and her brother is that her heroes are all

    astronauts.

10. Minerva's knowlege was limited when it came to astrophysics, but her intrest was great.

11. The extinction of the dinosaurs probally occured as the result of a meteor strike.

12. An extremly early frost caused the leafs to fall from most of the trees in early September.

13. Hector was dissappointed by his team's preformance, but he bought season tickets for the

    next year anyway.

14. Do you truely believe that there is a goverment conspiracy to hide the truth of John F.

    Kennedy's assasination?

15. Sharon's excitment was obvious when she presented her most valueable possession to us.

Exercise 3B

Correct any spelling errors in the following sentences by crossing out the incorrectly spelled word and writing the correct spelling above it. If a sentence is correct, do nothing to it.

1. When the police arrived Maxwell ~~discribed~~ *described* the person who had stolen his two ~~radioes~~ *radios*.

2. Brent's consceince began to bother him when he realized that he should have left the last doughnut for Steve.

3. Hester was disappointed to hear that her favorite athelete had recently commited two serious crimes.

4. The customer angrily demanded that he be given his money back even though he had lost his receipt.

5. Bruce had always been a dutyful son, but latly his behavor had become quite questionable.

6. Both countrys decided it was uneccessary to go to war over such a trivial matter.

7. When the opposing attornies started a fistfight, the judge declared a misstrial.

8. High above the crowd, the couragous circus preformer walked accross a thin tightrope.

9. Harold had always wanted to collect butterflys, but he definately did not like the idea of killing them.

10. Alot of times misstakes are ireversible unless you correct them at once.

11. When the senator publically announced that he was quiting, everyone in the audeince gaspped.

12. Tex had been ropeing cattle since she was a little girl, so she was eager to enter the upcomming rodeo.

13. Lawrence stared at the ceiling, unable to believe how fierce the grief was that he felt ever since his neighbor had committed that weird, heinous act.

14. In Andrea's opion, warm tempertures and clear skys are usally preferable to cold wind and snow.

15. Herman was controling the model airplane while his father was giveing him encouragment.

Exercise 3C

Correct any spelling errors in the following sentences by crossing out the incorrectly spelled word and writing the correct spelling above it. If a sentence is correct, do nothing to it.

1. People who refuse to eat in places like McDonald's or Taco Bell are ~~definately~~ *definitely* ~~makeing~~ *making* a big mistake. **2.** One reason that I perfer fast-food resterants is that they provide tasty, hot meals without requireing me to spend too much money. **3.** At McDonald's I can order a Big Mac, a large order of frys, and a Deit Coke for under $4. **4.** And the McDonald's in my nieghborhood is now offerring Big Macs for under a dollar, making a meal there even more afforddable than ever. **5.** As a full-time student who has never been very good at manageing his money (much less at studing for tests), I am commited to spending as little as I can on food, so McDonald's is proually the best place for me to eat. **6.** Another reason I like fast food is that alot of these places offer a vareity of choices. **7.** It isn't like the old days when a person was unnable to get anything except a burger and fries (although I am not above admitting that I do love a good burger and fries). **8.** Today, depending on the occassion, I can order salads, diffrent kinds of finger food, chicken, fish, stuffed baked potatos, and even Chinese food. **9.** Just last Febuary, Jack-in-the-Box started offerring a "variety pack": three miniature chimichangas, three egg rolls, and three peices of spicy chicken—all for less than five dollers. **10.** Finally, I like fast-food restarants because they are so conveneint. **11.** I have to be at the buisness where I work twenty minuts after my last class ends, so I don't have much time to eat. **12.** Luckily, I can swing into the local Carl's Jr., grab a fast-food dinner, and have it completly eaten by the time I drive the ten miles to work. **13.** Because I have had the chance to eat dinner, I arrive at my job feeling refreshed and ready to go. **14.** I know that many people think fast food is unutritious and unnhealthy, but my own expereince tells me that they are mistakken. **15.** I am never disatisfied when I eat at a fast-food place.

Sentence Practice:
Effective and Meaningful Sentences

These final sentence combining exercises are presented without specific directions. There will be a number of possible combinations for each group. Experiment to discover the most effective way to combine the sentences, supplying transitional words where necessary. You may also want to change the order in which the ideas are presented.

Sentence Combining Exercises

 EXAMPLE

    a. The first marathon was run in 1896.
    b. It was run at the Olympic Games in Athens, Greece.
    c. The marathon was founded to honor the Greek soldier Pheidippides.
    d. He is supposed to have run from the town of Marathon to Athens in 409 B.C.
    e. The distance is 22 miles, 1470 yards.
    f. He ran to bring the news of the victory of the Greeks over the Persians.
    g. In 1924 the distance was standardized to 26 miles, 385 yards.

> *The first marathon was run at the Olympic Games in Athens, Greece, in 1896. The marathon was founded to honor the Greek soldier Pheidippides, who, in 409 B.C., is supposed to have run from the town of Marathon to Athens, a distance of 22 miles, 1470 yards, to bring the news of the victory of the Greeks over the Persians. In 1924 the distance was standardized to 26 miles, 385 yards.*

1. Combine the following sentences.

    a. Wall Street takes its name from a wall.
    b. The wall is in lower Manhattan.
    c. The Dutch erected the wall.
    d. The wall was erected in the seventeenth century.
    e. The wall was erected as a defense against Indians.

_____

_____

_____

_____

_____

Sentence Combining Exercises

continued

2. Combine the following sentences.

    a. Some people feel boxing should be outlawed.
    b. Boxing is a violent sport.
    c. Two people try to knock each other unconscious.
    d. One boxer hits the other boxer in the face.
    e. The brain of the boxer who is hit slams against the inside of his skull.
    f. He has a concussion.
    g. He is knocked out.

_____

_____

_____

_____

_____

3. Combine the following sentences.

    a. Many people think that scalping enemies was a practice started by Indians.
    b. In fact, early colonists instituted "scalping."
    c. It was a profitable way to control the "Indian problem."
    d. In the Bay Colony in 1703, a scalp brought twelve pounds sterling.
    e. By 1722 one scalp brought one hundred pounds.
    f. Benjamin Franklin supported the practice.
    g. He urged the Pennsylvania legislature to approve a bounty on Indian scalps.

_____

_____

_____

_____

_____

Sentence Combining Exercises

continued

4. Combine the following sentences.

   a. There is a custom of hanging holly in the house at Christmas.
   b. Old Germanic races of Europe used to hang evergreen plants indoors in winter.
   c. The plants were a refuge for the spirits of the forest.
   d. Holly was considered a symbol of survival by pre-Christian Romans.
   e. The Romans used it as a decoration during their Saturnalia festival at the end of December.
   f. Christians began to celebrate Christmas at the end of December.
   g. Many of the old customs like hanging holly were preserved.

   _____

   _____

   _____

   _____

   _____

5. Combine the following sentences.

   a. The Battle of Hastings took place in 1066.
   b. It is said to be the most important event in the history of the English language.
   c. The Norman French defeated the English.
   d. It is known as the Norman Conquest.
   e. The Normans spoke French.
   f. French became the dominant language in England for a while.

   _____

   _____

   _____

   _____

   _____

Sentence Combining Exercises

continued

6. Combine the following sentences.

    a. The English commoners tended the animals in the fields.
    b. The words for animals before we eat them are *cow, pig, deer,* and *lamb.*
    c. These are original English words.
    d. The Norman French nobility ate the meat of the animals the English tended in the fields.
    e. The words for animals when we eat them are *steak, pork, venison,* and *mutton.*
    f. These words came from French.

    _____

    _____

    _____

    _____

    _____

7. Combine the following sentences.

    a. The Normans conquered the English in battle.
    b. Many military terms in English are borrowed from French.
    c. *Lieutenant, sergeant, colonel, peace, war, soldier, army,* and *navy* come from French.
    d. The Normans became the rulers.
    e. Many titles of rule were imposed by the French.
    f. *Crown, prince, princess, realm, royal, palace,* and *nation* are terms that come from French.
    g. The Normans brought a number of political and legal terms into English.
    h. *Parliament* comes from French.
    i. *Judge, jury, verdict, innocent, defendant,* and *sentence* are from French.

    _____

    _____

    _____

    _____

    _____

Sentence Combining Exercises

continued

8. Combine the following sentences.

   a. An optometrist tested 275 major league baseball players.
   b. He found that having cross-dominant eyesight can help a person hit a baseball better.
   c. Cross-dominant eyesight refers to seeing better with the left eye if a person is right-handed and vice versa.
   d. Only about 20 percent of the general population has cross-dominant eyesight.
   e. Over 50 percent of the baseball players that he examined have it.

   _____

   _____

   _____

   _____

   _____

9. Combine the following sentences.

   a. The name of the "pup tent" supposedly originated during the Civil War.
   b. General Sherman's backwoodsmen were being inspected by General Grant.
   c. The backwoodsmen objected to too much discipline.
   d. Grant walked by their tents.
   e. The soldiers got down on all fours.
   f. They barked and howled like hound dogs.
   g. The little tents used by soldiers began to be called "pup tents."

   _____

   _____

   _____

   _____

   _____

Sentence Combining Exercises

continued

10. Combine the following sentences.

     a. George Hancock was a Chicago Board of Trade reporter.
     b. He is credited with devising the official forerunner of softball.
     c. It was Thanksgiving Day, 1887.
     d. He wanted to liven things up.
     e. He was at the Farragut Boat Club.
     f. He started a game.
     g. He used a battered boxing glove as a ball.
     h. He used a broomstick as a bat.
     i. His game has been called Indoor–Outdoor.
     j. It has been called Kitten Ball.
     k. It has been called Playground Ball.
     l. It has been called Diamond Ball.
    m. It has been called Mush Ball.
     n. It was 1932.
     o. It received its present name of softball.

_____

_____

_____

_____

_____

Essay and Paragraph Practice: Expressing an Opinion

Assignment

You have now written narrative and descriptive papers (in Chapters One and Two) and several expository papers (in Chapters Three, Four, and Five). Your final writing assignment will be to state and support an **opinion.** As in earlier chapters, Exercises 1C, 2C, and 3C in this chapter have been designed as paragraph models of this assignment. Exercise 1C argues that Thoreau is correct in his belief that people look for happiness in the wrong places; Exercise 2C expresses the opinion that the principle of free speech protects even racist speakers; and Exercise 3C claims that people who refuse to eat in fast food restaurants are making a mistake.

Note that each of these paragraphs includes a topic sentence that expresses an opinion supported by details and examples drawn from the writer's personal knowledge or experience. For instance, the paragraph in Exercise 1C presents examples to support Thoreau's opinion that people look for happiness in the wrong places. These examples suggest that many people think that the clothes they wear, the beer they drink, or even the shampoo they use can affect how happy they are. Your assignment is to write a paper in which you express an opinion that you support with examples and details drawn from your own experiences or observations.

Prewriting to Generate Ideas

Prewriting Application: Finding Your Topic

Use prewriting techniques to develop your thoughts about one of the following topics or a topic suggested by your instructor. Before you choose a topic, prewrite to develop a list of possible reasons and examples that you can use to support your opinion. Don't choose a topic if you do not have examples with which you can support it.

1. Choose a proverb and show why it is or is not good advice. Consider these:

   Don't count your chickens before they hatch.

   The early bird gets the worm.

   Look before you leap.

If at first you don't succeed, try, try again.

If you can't beat 'em, join 'em.

Money can't buy happiness.

2. Support an opinion about the condition of your neighborhood, your college campus, your home, or some other place with which you are familiar.

3. Some people compete in nearly everything they do, whether it be participating in sports, working on the job, or studying in college classes. Other people find competition distracting and even offensive. Write a paragraph in which you support your opinion about competition.

4. Do you eat in fast-food restaurants? Write a paragraph in which you support your opinion about eating in such places.

5. Should parents spank children? Write a paper in which you support your opinion for or against such discipline.

6. Should high school students work at part-time jobs while going to school? Write a paper in which you support an opinion for or against their doing so.

7. Do you know couples who live together without marrying? Write a paper in which you support an opinion for or against such an arrangement.

8. Is peer pressure really a very serious problem for people today? Write a paper in which you support an opinion about the seriousness of peer pressure.

9. Is racism, sexism, homophobia, or religious intolerance still a common problem in our society? Write a paper in which you support your opinion one way or the other.

10. Do general education requirements benefit college students? Write a paper in which you support your opinion about such classes.

Choosing and Narrowing the Topic

Once you have settled on several possible topics, consider these points as you make your final selection.

- Choose the more limited topic rather than the more general one.

- Choose the topic about which you could discuss several, not just one or two, reasons in support of your opinion.

- Choose the topic about which you have the most experience or knowledge.

- Choose the topic in which you have the most personal interest. Avoid topics about which you don't really care.

Writing a Thesis Statement or Topic Sentence

If your assignment is to write a single paragraph, you will open it with a topic sentence. If you are writing a complete essay, you will need a thesis statement at the end of your introductory paragraph. In either case, you will need a clear statement of the topic and central idea of your paper.

Prewriting Application: Working with Topic Sentences

Identify the topic sentences in Exercises 1C (page 345), 2C (page 360), and 3C (page 374). What are the topic and the central point in each topic sentence?

Prewriting Application: Evaluating Thesis Statements and Topic Sentences

Write "No" before each sentence that would not make an effective thesis statement or topic sentence *for this assignment.* Write "Yes" before each sentence that would make an effective one. Using ideas of your own, rewrite each ineffective sentence into one that might work.

_____ **1.** The intersection of Whitewood and Los Alamos is one of the most dangerous traffic spots in our city.

_____

_____

_____ **2.** Sometimes the old proverb "If at first you don't succeed, try, try again" is the worst advice that one can give a person.

_____

_____

_____ **3.** Racism has existed in our country for many years.

_____

_____

_____ **4.** My father and mother are not married and never have been.

_____

_____

_____ **5.** Not everyone needs to be married to have a strong relationship
and a happy family.

_____

_____

_____ **6.** Almost every young teenager could benefit from participating in
competitive sports.

_____

_____

_____ **7.** Many high schools students today work at part-time jobs.

_____

_____

_____ **8.** Body piercing can be a heathy, safe expression of one's
individuality.

_____

_____

_____ **9.** There are several good reasons why a person should never drink
any carbonated soft drinks.

_____

_____

_____ **10.** Most people's family values are going straight downhill.

_____

_____

Prewriting Application: Talking to Others

Form a group of three or four people and discuss the topics you have chosen. Your goal here is to help each other clarify your opinions and to determine if you have enough evidence to support it. Explain why you hold your opinion and what specific reasons and examples you will use to support it. As you listen to the others in your group, use the following questions to help them clarify their ideas.

1. Can the opinion be reasonably supported in a brief paper? Is its topic too general or broad?

2. What specific examples will the writer provide as support? Are they convincing?

3. What is the weakest reason or example? Why? Should it be made stronger or completely replaced?

4. Which reasons or examples are the strongest? Why?

5. Which reason or example should the paper open with? Which should it close with?

Organizing Opinion Papers

An **emphatic** organization, one that saves the strongest supporting material until last, is perhaps most common in opinion papers. If you have a list of three, four, or five good reasons in support of your opinion, consider arranging them so that you build up to the strongest, most convincing one.

Writing the Essay

If your assignment is to write a complete essay:

- Place your **thesis statement** (which should clearly state your opinion) at the end of the introductory paragraph.

- Write a separate **body paragraph** for each reason that supports your opinion.

- Open each body paragraph with a **topic sentence** that identifies the one reason the paragraph will discuss.

- Within each body paragraph, use specific **facts, examples,** and **details** to explain and support your reason.

Writing the Paragraph

If your assignment is to write a single paragraph:

- Open it with a **topic sentence** that clearly identifies your opinion.

- Use **clear transitions** to move from one reason in support of your opinion to the next.

- Use specific **facts, examples,** and **details** to explain and support your reasons.

Writing Application: Identifying Transitional Words, Phrases, and Sentences

Examine Exercises 1C (page 345), 2C (page 360), and 3C (page 374). Identify the transitionals that introduce each new reason offered in support of the opinion. Then identify any other transitions that serve to connect ideas between sentences.

Rewriting and Improving the Paper

1. Revise your examples so they are specific and concrete. As much as possible, use actual names of people and places.

2. Add or revise transitions wherever doing so would help clarify movement from one idea to another.

3. Improve your preliminary thesis statement (if you are writing an essay) or your preliminary topic sentence (if you are writing a single paragraph) so that it more accurately states the central point of your paper.

4. Examine your draft for sentence variety. If many of your sentences tend to be of the same length, try varying their length and their structure by combining sentences using the techniques you have studied in the Sentence Practice sections of this text.

Rewriting Application: Responding to Paragraph Writing

Read the following paragraph. Then respond to the questions following it.

School Sports

Many of my relatives believe that playing sports in high school and college is a waste of time and energy, but I disagree. I believe that school sports can help a person stay out of trouble and can lead to bigger and better things. I know, for instance, that sports can help young people who are heading for trouble with the law. I have a close friend who grew up in a very hostile environment. His parents abused him, and he belonged to gangs ever since he was very young. He had been in and out of juvenile court several times when he discovered something special about himself. He discovered that he is a good athlete. He began to excel at baseball and football. He developed a love for both sports. After playing football at Escondido High School, he earned a full scholarship to the University of Nevada. Playing sports can also help people emotionally. For example, sports have helped me learn to control my anger. I am a very emotional person, and when I get angry I just want to hit someone—hard. Whenever I feel like that, I get out on the football field and get physical. By the end of a hard practice, I'm ready to go back and live my life. Football helps me when I'm stressed out or depressed, too. I can always count on my teammates to bring me back up when I'm down. Furthermore, playing sports encourages students to stay in school and motivates them to do well. I'm the kind of person who hates school, but through sports I have learned that the road to success includes an education. There have been many times when I have wanted to drop out of school, but always holding me back is my love for the game of football. I know that football is not always going to be there for me, but school sports have changed my life and have affected the lives of many others as well.

1. Identify the topic sentence. State its topic and central idea. Does it express a definite opinion?

2. How many supporting points are presented in this paper? Identify them.

3. Identify the transitional sentences that introduce each major supporting point. What other transitions are used between sentences?

4. Consider the organization of the paragraph. Would you change the order of the supporting material? Explain why or why not.

5. Consider the sentence variety. What sentences would you combine to improve the paragraph?

Rewriting Application: Responding to Essay Writing

Read the following essay. Then respond to the questions at the end of it.

City Life

Because my father was in the navy, our family moved many times when I was growing up. As a result, I have lived in many different sizes of cities and towns all across the United States, from a tiny farm town outside Sioux Falls, South Dakota, to San Diego, California, one of the largest cities in the United States. After all these moves, I have developed my own opinions about where I want to spend my life. I know that small-town life has its attractions for some people, but as far as I'm concerned large cities offer the kind of life I like to live.

One of the reasons I like living in large cities is that there is always so much to do. I can see plays and movies, attend cultural and sporting events, go shopping, or take walks in the park. For example, within a one-week period last month, I went with my parents to see <u>Phantom of the Opera,</u> I attended a Padres' baseball game with some friends, I spent a day at the Del Mar Fair, and I went shopping at Horton Plaza Mall. I am sure I could not have had that kind of week in a small town. This weekend I plan to visit the San Diego Wild Animal Park, where condors have been saved from extinction and are now being released into the wild.

I also like large cities because I get the chance to meet people from so many different cultural and ethnic backgrounds. For instance, in one of my first college classes, I met a person from South Vietnam who has become one of my good friends. He and his family have been in the United States for ten years, and they have all sorts of terrifying stories to tell about how they fled their country to start a new life. I also have many Hispanic and African-American friends, a natural result of growing up in an area that has a large mix of people.

Finally, I enjoy large cities for a very practical reason. Because there are so many different kinds of companies and industries where I live, I can be relatively sure that I will always be able to find a job somewhere. My goal is to become a software designer, and a large city is exactly the kind of place where I will find many job opportunities. San Diego is the home of many high-tech companies, like Qualcomm, Peregrine, and Oracle.

> Whether I end up working for one of these companies or starting my own software business, a large city like San Diego is the place to be.
>
> I suppose life in large cities is not for everybody, but it sure is for me. I cannot imagine spending my day watching the cows or listening to crows in some tiny rural town. Maybe someday I will want the peace and quiet of a place like that, but not today.

1. Identify the thesis statement. State its topic and central idea. Is it an effective thesis statement? Does it state a definite opinion?

2. Identify each topic sentence. State its topic and central idea. Does each topic sentence clearly state a reason in support of the thesis?

3. What transitional words introduce each new body paragraph?

4. Consider the organization of the body paragraphs. Would you change their order in any way? Why or why not?

5. Is each reason supported with specific facts, examples, and details? Identify where such specific support is used. Where would you improve the support?

Proofreading

When proofreading your paper, watch for the following errors:

Sentence fragments, comma splices, and fused sentences

Misplaced modifiers and dangling modifiers

Errors in subject–verb agreement

Errors in pronoun case, pronoun–antecedent agreement, or pronoun reference

Errors in comma use

Errors in the use of periods, question marks, exclamation points, colons, semicolons, and quotation marks

Errors in capitalization, titles, and numbers

Errors in the use of irregular verbs or in word choice

Misspelled words

Now prepare a clean final draft, following the format your instructor has asked for.

Chapter Six Practice Test

I. Review of Chapters Three, Four, and Five

A. Correct any misplaced or dangling modifiers. Do nothing if the sentence is correct.

1. Walking slowly through the park, it was a beautiful day.

   _____

   _____

2. Ms. Wray almost fainted when Mr. Kong asked her to dance.

   _____

   _____

3. James gave the kitten to his good friend that he had treated for ticks.

   _____

   _____

4. Rolling over the dirt road, a Honda Civic approached my horse with two flat tires and slowly came to a stop.

   _____

   _____

5. Smiling at his accomplishment, his science project was finally finished.

   _____

   _____

B. Correct any subject–verb agreement or pronoun use errors in the following sentences. Do nothing if the sentence is correct.

6. The mumps are an illness often discussed by the staff of the clinic.

7. Turbo was going to give the key to his new car to Sofia, but it had disappeared.

8. Each man, woman, and child in the stadium have a chance to win $1000.

9. Homer wrote the Spam factory and requested free samples for Hortense and himself.

10. Anyone who rides a horse must be sure that you let it know who is in charge.

continued

C. Add commas to the following sentences where necessary.

11. Under the old elm tree in Luther's backyard a 1976 Ford Pinto is rusting away and a discarded mattress is slowly disintegrating.

12. When Suzie arrived she saw that people had left brownies nachos cupcakes pretzels and peanuts on the counter in the office.

13. Mr. Dungeness walked sideways all the way to 523 Jones Street Seawater Maine; unfortunately the tartar sauce had arrived at the same address in Clamdevon New York last week.

14. Jenna's pet bird a friendly African gray parrot calls her name whenever she walks by.

D. Add periods, question marks, exclamation points, quotation marks, semicolons, colons, and apostrophes (or 's) where necessary and correct any mistakes in the use of capitalization, titles, and numbers. Do not add or delete any commas.

15. Linda said that she would be late as a result, she would not be able to pick up any of these items for the picnic the volleyball, the volleyball net, the frisbee, the barbecue, or the charcoal

16. Dont you want to visit my Fathers farm asked Dylan.

17. Was it Woody Allen who said, Eighty percent of success is showing up

18. According to the london times newspapers, three hundred fifteen people couldnt find their car keys this morning

19. In an article entitled padres bash dodgers, brent read that the final score was padres fifteen, dodgers three

20. Aurora enjoyed her english class last spring, but her brothers psychology class sounded interesting too.

Chapter Six Practice Test

continued
II. Chapter Six

A. In the blanks, write in the correct forms of the verbs indicated.

21. When he opened the office door, Jack saw a box of Clark Bars _____ on Steve's desk. (lie)

22. Hermes had _____ almost the entire race before anyone noticed the wings on his feet. (run)

23. Homer asked Hortense if she had _____ the scales to weigh the cow chips. (bring)

24. The guests had _____ nearly all of the champagne by the time the bride and groom showed up. (drink)

25. Thomas doubted that anyone had ever really _____ across the English Channel. (swim)

B. Correct any verb form errors in the following sentences. Do nothing if the sentence is correct.

26. The first baseman was telling the pitcher how badly Roseanne had sang the National Anthem.

27. After Othello saw the handkerchief, he wanted to lay down and take a nap.

28. No one paid any attention to the huge gray elephant setting in the middle of the living room.

29. As she lay in her bed, Emily thought she heard the buzz of a fly.

30. As Omar walked across the parking lot, the quart of milk he was carrying fell to the ground and bursted.

C. Underline the correct word in the parentheses.

31. Although Bill had (lead led) the entire race, in the end Cyrano won by a nose.

32. The (principal principle) reason to leave at three in the morning is to beat the traffic.

continued

33. Natasha had no idea what (effect affect) the CD by Eminem would have on her mother.

34. During his talk, Sam gave the listeners (advice advise) about how to develop a good heart.

35. Once they had eaten, the three friends decided to divide the bill evenly (among between) themselves.

D. Correct any incorrect word choices in the following sentences. Do nothing if the sentence is correct.

36. Bill's sporty new jacket perfectly complimented his neatly pressed slacks.

37. After young Woz returned the Clark Bar to the candy counter, his conscious was clear.

38. The amount of people who attended the concert surprised even its organizers.

39. Archibald was already to recite his poem, but the audience had already left the church.

40. Flatcars carrying more tanks then we had ever seen rolled across the railroad tracks in Flagstaff, Arizona.

E. Underline the correctly spelled words in the parentheses.

41. No matter how (thier their) father dressed, the sisters were always (embarassed embarrassed).

42. The lead vocalist could not stop (worring worrying) about what looked like (tomatos tomatoes) in the hands of some members of the audience.

43. The team was (disappointed dissappointed) when the (atheletic athletic) director cancelled the game.

44. It had never (occurred occured) to the banker that the safe would be (completely completly) empty.

45. The biggest (suprise surprise) was the (requirement requirment) that we all wear formal dress.

continued

F. Correct any spelling errors in the following sentences by crossing out the incorrectly spelled word and writing the correct spelling above it.

46. My nieghbor's kitchen has a lovly view of the lake.

47. The goverment forms contained an amazing number of mispellings.

48. The minister's discription of heaven made the theif even more determined to change his ways.

49. Homer was refering to bread, not money, when he admitted he had stolen some dough.

50. Chelsea knew her answer was probally wrong, but in her excitment she didn't really care.

I. Chapter One

A. Underline all subjects once and all verbs twice.

1. Have you noticed all the mosquitoes around here?

2. Flies and mosquitoes filled the air above the stagnant pond.

3. Kate Chopin wrote in the nineteenth century, yet she was not recognized as a great artist until the twentieth century.

4. Cecil tried not to blush when some of the students praised his poem.

5. At the end of the line were two children, each holding an entrance ticket.

B. In the space provided, indicate whether the underlined word is a noun (N), pronoun (Pro), verb (V), adjective (Adj), adverb (Adv), preposition (Prep), or conjunction (Conj).

_____ **6.** Humpty was <u>slowly</u> rocking back and forth on the wall.

_____ **7.** From his <u>secret</u> hiding place, Frank saw the last pods loaded onto the trucks.

_____ **8.** Henry wanted to think, <u>so</u> he moved to Walden Pond.

_____ **9.** Marlowe <u>will</u> play drums in the riverboat jazz band.

_____ **10.** Emile was sure that <u>someone</u> had been stealing his mail.

C. In the following sentences, place all prepositional phrases in parentheses.

11. Some of the people sneered at Elvis's haircut.

12. A large moth flew into the house and up the stairs.

13. Driving down Highway 51, Bobby Zimmerman felt like a rolling stone.

14. John was seldom without his glasses, even when he was alone with Yoko.

15. In spite of his promise to stay awake, Homer began to snore during the soprano's passionate solo.

continued
II. Chapter Two

A. Correct all fragments, comma splices, and fused sentences. If the sentence is correct, do nothing to it.

16. Michael Jordan, coming out of retirement.

_____

_____

17. Roxanne opened her eyes and noticed his nose, then she began to giggle.

_____

_____

18. Wondering where he was going, Faith watched as her husband walked into the forest.

_____

_____

19. The old sailor watched the albatross he decided to shoot it.

_____

_____

20. Dimmesdale bought some new T-shirts his chest had begun to itch.

_____

_____

21. While Nero was playing his fiddle.

_____

_____

22. Fortunato was not a mason, however, he knew what a brick wall looked like.

_____

_____

continued

23. Adam woke up his ribs were bandaged.

_____

_____

24. Just do it.

_____

_____

25. Staring at the ceiling as the Pope suggested some changes.

_____

_____

B. Compose simple, compound, complex, and compound-complex sentences according to the instructions.

26. Write a simple sentence that contains at least one prepositional phrase.

_____

_____

27. Write a compound sentence. Use a coordinating conjunction and appropriate punctuation to join the clauses.

_____

_____

28. Write a compound sentence. Use a transitional word or phrase and appropriate punctuation to join the clauses.

_____

_____

continued

29. Write a complex sentence. Use *when* as the subordinator.

_____

_____

30. Write a compound-complex sentence. Use the subordinator *because* as well as a transitional word with appropriate punctuation.

_____

_____

III. Chapter Three

A. Correct any misplaced or dangling modifiers in the following sentences. If the sentence is correct, do nothing to it.

31. Thinking of all of the boys who wanted to date her, Penelope's hands began unraveling her shawl.

_____

_____

32. A huge brown bear approached the boy with angry yellow eyes and then turned away.

_____

_____

33. Awakening in the morning, a run on the beach seemed like a good idea.

_____

_____

34. Mr. Sprat's wife only preferred lean meat.

_____

_____

continued

35. Singing loudly and off key, even the dog ran out of the room.

_____

_____

36. Two fierce tigers stared at the tourists that were on loan from the San Diego Zoo.

_____

_____

37. Maria asked Placido quietly to sing the song.

_____

_____

38. Breathing a sigh of relief, the lost camper finally heard a familiar voice.

_____

_____

39. A Siamese cat licked the little girl that had only three legs when she began to pet it with a tongue like sandpaper.

_____

_____

40. Starving after a long hike, the eyes of the soldiers spotted the watermelon field.

_____

_____

B. Add phrases or clauses to the following sentences according to the instructions. Be sure to punctuate carefully.

41. Add a verbal phrase. Use the verb *hope*.

Pete bought two lottery tickets.

_____

_____

continued

42. Add an adjective clause.

The thief lurked near the priceless painting.

_____

_____

43. Add a present participial phrase to the beginning of this sentence. Use the verb *reach*.

The warriors prepared for battle.

_____

_____

44. Add an appositive phrase after one of the nouns in this sentence.

The minister would not tell the parishioners about the black veil.

_____

_____

45. Add an infinitive verbal phrase to this sentence. Use the verb *hang*.

After searching all day, Rosario found the perfect picture.

_____

_____

IV. Chapter Four

A. Correct any subject–verb agreement errors in the following sentences by crossing out the incorrect verb form and writing in the correct form above it. If the sentence is correct, do nothing to it.

46. Each suit of clothes for the ceremonies have been carefully selected.

47. A herd of buffalo often cross this stream in the evening.

48. Does his coworkers or employer ever complain about his attitude?

49. A mother cat with her kittens have made a home under my bed.

continued

50. Somebody from one of the tour groups have left a backpack on the bus.

51. Forty pounds of Spam were all that Hortense could get into the back seat.

52. Rice or baked potatoes serve as a good side dish for many meals.

53. Anyone who has heard one of Yo Yo Ma's concerts know that he plays wonderfully.

54. Here is several stamps for your collection.

55. Each of the representatives from the three clubs want to make a speech tonight.

B. Correct any pronoun use errors in the following sentences by crossing out the incorrect pronoun and writing in the correct one above it. In some cases you may have to rewrite part of the sentence. If the sentence is correct, do nothing to it.

56. When a fan walks into Baltimore's new baseball park, you are amazed by how green the grass is.

57. The Captain told Ensign Pulver and myself to water the palm tree.

58. Art put his paper in his briefcase, but later he couldn't find it.

59. Maria and Henry had both danced for many years; nevertheless, Henry was not nearly as graceful as her.

60. The lightning bolt struck a tree, which then burst into flames; this terrified John.

61. During December the church opened their doors for the homeless at night.

62. The new members of the math club wanted to solve the problem by themself.

63. Hillary looked back and saw that the winners of the marathon would be Barbara and her.

64. The coach told us to run ten laps and then turn out our lights by 8:00, which I really didn't want to do.

65. At the dog show one of the owners kept stepping out of their assigned position.

continued
V. Chapter Five

A. Add commas to the following sentences where necessary. If the sentence is correct, do nothing to it.

66. No I do not want catsup on my filet mignon nor do I want Tabasco sauce.

67. The waiter served the soup lit the candles picked up the salad plates and tried to remain dignified as he spilled the wine into the diner's lap.

68. On November 8 2001 Andrea walked out of her office and headed for the beach.

69. A dose of Beano for example is suggested as part of your pre-dinner preparations.

70. After writing a series of short choppy sentences Ernest decided to try to write some longer ones.

71. The boys who left the bag burning on the porch ran around the corner and began to giggle.

72. The orangutan one of the most intelligent apes is a friendly gregarious animal.

73. Because he was in a hurry Bond flew the Concord to Paris France last night.

74. Arlene stood before the volunteers and announced "We need help cooking food cleaning walls washing clothes and babysitting the children."

75. Mother Teresa of course was a holy woman but even she was not perfect.

B. Add periods, exclamation points, question marks, semicolons, colons, quotation marks, or apostrophes (or 's) where necessary in the following sentences. If the sentence is correct, do nothing to it. Do not add or delete any commas.

76. Does the class think the instructors behavior is acceptable

77. Jason said, Run up the mainsail we can still be there by nightfall

78. Maxwells list included the following items a telephone in his shoe, a pen with invisible ink, and a secret agent trench coat.

79. Hasnt the sky fallen yet asked Henny Penny in a disappointed voice

80. Elvis asked Priscillas brother why he had stepped on his blue suede shoes

continued

C. Correct any errors in the use of capitalization, titles, or numbers in the following sentences. If the sentence is correct, do nothing to it.

81. william faulkner's novel light in august is set in the south.

82. Angel's high school is 10 miles south of bram stoker street.

83. ms. hohman brought in 25 copies of cosmopolitan for her class called introduction to women's issues.

84. Many people in our literature class were disgusted by jonathan swift's essay a modest proposal.

85. Dinner at the star of the sea restaurant cost us over one hundred twenty-five dollars.

VI. Chapter Six

A. In the following sentences correct any errors in the use of irregular verbs by crossing out the incorrect forms and writing in the correct ones above. If the sentence is correct, do nothing to it.

86. The raven setting on the desk kept saying the same thing over and over.

87. The ducks had swam most of the way to shore when they seen the black duckling.

88. A long fat rattlesnake laid on the warm rock and shutted its eyes.

89. By the end of the party, no one had ate any of the game hen stuffed with Spam that Homer and Hortense had brung.

90. The moon had already rose when Stan's nails begun to grow.

B. In the following sentences, correct any spelling errors caused by using the wrong word. Cross out any incorrect words and write the correct words above. If the sentence is correct, do nothing to it.

91. Elmer's principle problem was that Bugs was to clever for him.

92. If your sure you do not want the package, you should refuse to except it.

93. Each year less people visit the Queen Mary then the year before.

continued

94. Last year two floral elephants lead the Rose Parade as it preceded down Colorado Boulevard.

95. Muriel did not want to loose her job, so she began to reduce the amount of breaks that she took.

C. Correct any spelling errors in the following sentences by crossing out the incorrect spellings and writing the correct spellings above them.

96. Torvald was begining to see something diffrent about Nora's attitude.

97. Iago claimed that Desdemona had decieved him about the thiefs who had stolen the handkerchief.

98. Breaking into an ancient tomb is ilegal, but Lara Croft did not truely think she had a choice.

99. The butler thought the guests would probally find no noticable difference in the statues.

100. When Bobby felt the temperture rise an unusal amount, he knew a hard rain was going to fall.

Answers to Practices

Chapter One

Page 3:

2. Huck, Jim, Cairo, fog
3. Pandora, box, hand
4. Humpty, men, wall, problem
5. Frazier, sophistication, love, Lydia

Page 4:

2. Persephone, pomegranate, top, bush
3. Homer, plate, Spam, table
4. ship, iceberg, band, tune
5. Lewis, Clark, woman, mountains
6. Alice, amazement, cat, grin
7. Love, tolerance, characteristics, racism, prejudice
8. Dr. Frankenstein, neighbors, success, experiment
9. Carol Burnett, wit, humor, intelligence, empathy, humans
10. poet, situations, city, nature, insight

Pages 5–6:

2. nouns: guard, border, officer
   pronouns: her, us
3. nouns: investigator, scene, crime
   pronouns: himself, he
4. nouns: players, team, victory, jerseys, opponents
   pronouns: Some, our, their, their
5. nouns: P.T. Barnum, suckers
   pronouns: you, what
6. nouns: dancer, rattlesnake, shoulders
   pronouns: it, his
7. nouns: quarks, quasars
   pronouns: Who, anything
8. nouns: piggy, market
   pronouns: Each, us, which
9. nouns: collection, books, Herman Melville, Nathaniel Hawthorne
   pronouns: My, anything
10. nouns: bell, tour, home, John Donne, copy, poems
    pronouns: everyone, whom, his

Page 6:

Answers will vary. Here are some possible ones.

2. <u>Homer</u> will share <u>his</u> <u>Spam</u> with <u>his</u> <u>sister</u>.
3. <u>He</u> told <u>me</u> about <u>his</u> <u>fight</u> at the <u>restaurant</u>.
4. <u>Emily</u> liked the <u>brownies</u> that <u>I</u> bought at the <u>fair</u>.
5. After <u>John</u> washed <u>his</u> <u>car</u>, <u>he</u> asked <u>his</u> <u>girlfriend</u> to go to the <u>movies</u> with <u>him</u>.

Page 7:

2. sank
3. dyed
4. eats
5. talked

Page 8:

2. is
3. seemed
4. felt
5. am

Page 9:

2. verb: wanted
   tense: past
3. verb: will visit
   tense: future
4. verb: destroyed
   tense: past
5. verb: practices
   tense: present

Page 11:

2. MV
3. HV
4. HV
5. MV
6. MV

7. HV
8. HV
9. MV
10. HV

Pages 11–12:

A.

2. HV: have
   MV: caused
3. HV: was
   MV: selling

4. HV: Has
   MV: crossed
5. HV: could have
   MV: stayed

B. Answers will vary. Here are some possible ones.

7. The chief <u>fried</u> the snails and <u>served</u> them to his mother.
8. Janus <u>can</u> <u>look</u> both ways at the same time.

9. <u>Has</u> Shakespeare <u>written</u> the tragedy that I <u>paid</u> him for?
10. Lady Godiva <u>should</u> not <u>have</u> <u>ridden</u> her horse when she <u>was</u> not <u>wearing</u> any clothes.

Page 13:

2. HV: could
   MV: believe
   Verbal: Standing
3. HV: had
   MV: prepared
   Verbal: To please

4. HV: was
   MV: looking
   Verbal: giving
5. MV: ignored
   Verbal: picking

Page 13:

2. HV: have been
   MV: talking
   Verbal: to monopolize
3. HV: Does
   MV: want
   Verbal: to marry
4. MV: has
5. HV: were
   MV: yelling, waving
   Verbal: circling
6. HV: was
   MV: wondering
   Verbal: picking
   Verbal: to play

7. HV: should have
   MV: been
8. HV: was
   MV: jumping
9. HV: have been
   MV: trying
   Verbal: to find
10. HV: Have
    MV: asked
    Verbal: to bring

Page 14:

2. S: prison
   MV: sits
3. S: prisoners
   HV: would
   MV: drown

4. S: men
   HV: were
   MV: shot
5. S: Alcatraz
   HV: was
   MV: closed

Page 15:

2. S: okra
HV: was
MV: served

3. S: Pearl
HV: could be
MV: seen

4. S: reward
MV: was

5. S: men
MV: faced

Page 16:

2. S: owl, pussycat
MV: were

3. S: Superman, Batman
MV: grabbed, headed

4. S: Wolverine
MV: wanted
S: they
HV: had
MV: invited

5. S: boat
MV: departed
S: Ishmael, Starbuck
MV: came

Page 17:

2. S: Thelonious
MV: was

3. S: Lee
HV: could have
MV: won

4. S: beings
MV: are

5. S: You (understood)
MV: Raise

Pages 17–18:

2. subject: Sonny
verb: could have treated

3. subject: Neil Armstrong
verb: might have hesitated

4. subject: hearing
verb: had begun

5. subject: delegate
verb: Does want

6. subject: Godzilla
verb: was looking

7. subject: You (understood)
verb: tell

8. subject: Gregor
verb: had become
subject: he
verb: refused

9. subject: problems
verb: were

10. subject: Little Mermaid
verbs: looked, winked

Pages 18–19:

Answers will vary. Here are some possible ones.

    S   *MV*
2. The doctor left the building
    MV
and called a taxi.

    S *HV* *MV*
3. His car was running well last night.

   HV *S* *MV*
4. Did she find the missing briefcase?

    MV
5. Leave the restaurant now.

    MV   *S*
6. There were three great bands at the concert.

    S   *S*
7. The man from Peru and his son
  MV
flew to Los Angeles.

    S   *HV* *MV*   *S*
8. Stanley might visit Rome after he
  MV
sees his sister.

    S *HV* *MV*   *S*
9. Homer has finished his Spam, and he
 HV *MV*
has washed the dishes.

    S *MV*   *S* *MV*
10. John left the party because he needed

to study for a test.

Page 26:

2. *Hot* and *crispy* modify *fries*.

3. *Usually* modifies *has*, and *tuna* modifies *sandwich*.

4. *Tedious* modifies *movie*, and *mercifully* modifies *short*.

5. *Tiny* modifies *animals*, and *continually* modifies *ran*.

Page 27:

A.

2. We attended an unusual concert last Saturday.

3. Our two turtledoves keep fighting with that stupid partridge in the pear tree.

4. My rusty old Honda might give out if it does not see a competent mechanic soon.

5. Kate Chopin wrote many wonderful stories, but most people of her time would not read them.

B. Answers will vary. Here are some possible ones.

7. An *angry* aardvark wandered into our *front* yard and looked for ants.

8. The *eccentric* writer preferred to use a *battered* typewriter for his novels.

9. The *Thanksgiving* turkey on the table was surrounded by *steamed* vegetables.

10. Officials tried to blame the mess on the *many* birds that lived near the *dirty* pond.

Page 29:

A.

2. The fireman often told the story of that incredibly horrible day.

3. The black widow sometimes gleefully destroys her mate.

4. As Ichabod Crane rode swiftly down the lane, he was already beginning to worry about the headless horseman.

5. Dido was excruciatingly sad as she stood on the rather sheer cliff.

B. Answers will vary. Here are some possible ones.

7. Bill *sometimes* craves a bebop concert.

8. The audience saw the band and applauded *loudly*.

9. Homer looked *sadly* into the abyss and stared at the splendid sunset.

10. The boat leaned *precariously* as the wind from the north filled its sails.

Pages 35–36:

A.

2. subject: Homer
   verb: loved
   subject: he
   verb: had
   conjunctions: but, or
3. subject: Yeni
   verb: was
   subject: vacation
   verb: was
   conjunctions: for

4. subject: Scully
   verb: was interested
   subject: she
   verb: did care
   conjunction: nor
5. subject: Michelle
   verb: had worked
   subject: she
   verb: received
   conjunctions: and, so

B.

7. but, yet
8. and
9. for
10. so

Page 37:

2. near, of
3. during, to
4. from, with
5. behind, at

Pages 38–39:

A.

2. Prep   Obj
   (from a popular drinking song)
3. Prep Obj
   (of Fort McHenry)
   Prep Obj
   (in 1814)
4. Prep   Obj
   (by the sight)
   Prep   Obj
   (of the American flag)
   Prep   Obj
   (over the fort)
5. Prep   Obj
   (During the attack)
   Prep   Obj
   (of "The Star-Spangled Banner")
   Prep Obj
   (on the back)
   Prep   Obj
   (of an envelope)

6. Prep Obj
   (with a tune)
   Prep   Obj
   (in many taverns)
7. Prep Obj
   (in Heaven)
   Prep   Obj
   (by John Stafford Smith)
   Prep Obj
   (in 1780)
8. Prep Obj Obj Obj   Obj
   (about wine, song, love, and revelry)
9. Prep   Obj
   (at official ceremonies)
   Prep   Obj
   (for many years)
10. Prep   Obj
    (In spite of its popularity)
    Prep   Obj
    (until March 3, 1931)

Page 48:

1. The farmer waited in front of the bank.
2. The **old** farmer waited in front of the bank.
3. The old farmer **in overalls** waited in front of the bank.
4. The old farmer in **faded** overalls waited in front of the bank.
5. The old farmer in faded overalls waited **patiently** in front of the bank.

Chapter Two

Pages 77–78:

2. MC
3. MC
4. N
5. SC
6. MC

7. SC
8. MC
9. SC
10. N

Page 78:

2. PP
3. PP
4. PP
5. SC
6. SC

7. PP
8. PP
9. SC
10. PP

Pages 78–79:

2. The yacht returned to the harbor (when) the sun began to set.

3. After the battle in the lake, Beowulf returned to the hall.

4. Puck gave the potion to Titania, (who) was sleeping.

5. (If) the apple feels soft, Chelsea won't eat it.

6. A reformed slave trader wrote "Amazing Grace," (which) is played at police officers' funerals.

7. The bagpipers played "Amazing Grace" (because) Chief Martinez had requested it.

8. Sergio tried to help the man (whose) shoe was caught in the escalator.

9. Darby rested (after) she had guarded the house all night.

10. Stonewall looked at the mountain (where) the Yankees were loading their cannons.

Page 80:

2. (Whenever) Homer sees a shelf of Spam cans, his mouth waters.

3. The sprinklers would not work (because) the water had been shut off.

4. (Even though) his license had expired, Bill insisted upon driving.

5. Everyone stood and stared (as) the unicorn stepped on stage.

Page 80:

Answers will vary. Here are some possible ones.

2. <u>After he saw his friends from Tennessee,</u> Mr. Jackson posed for the twenty-dollar bill.

3. Georgia liked her place in New Mexico <u>even though it was overrun with cockroaches.</u>

4. Homer asked for a bag for his leftover black-eyed peas <u>when he had finished his dinner.</u>

5. <u>After Homer and Hortense finished their catfish,</u> they threw the hushpuppies under the table to their dogs.

Page 81:

2. A saxophone player (whom) we all like was the first act.

3. A drummer (who) lives next door to us played with her.

4. The Billie Holiday Special, (which) is my favorite, is a bagel in the shape of a gardenia.

5. A Dalmatian (that) everyone calls Thelonious greets people at the door.

Page 82:

Answers will vary. Here are some possible ones.

2. About 9:00 every evening musicians <u>who live in the area</u> gather by the coffee bar.

3. The muscians wear colorful clothes <u>that never seem to match.</u>

4. The cats <u>that live in the back room</u> are called Coltrane and Miles.

5. Everyone <u>who frequents Holesome Gatherings</u> enjoys the music and food.

Pages 82–83:

2. Thelonious likes "'Round Midnight" because it is a song by Thelonious Monk. (Adv)

3. The piano player likes to sit below the poster of Duke Ellington that is hanging on the back wall. (Adj)

4. When the temperature drops, Coltrane and Miles lie by the fire. (Adv)

5. The man who owns the shop once played bass with Dizzy Gillespie. (Adj)

Page 83:

Answers will vary. Here are some possible ones.

2. Michael loaded the motorboat onto the trailer <u>that was sitting near the boat ramp.</u> (Adj)

3. The people sat down and the meeting started <u>after everyone stopped talking.</u> (Adv)

4. <u>When he returned from Mt. Olympus,</u> Prometheus warmed his hands by the fire. (Adv)

5. Bill Gates, <u>who owns Microsoft,</u> and Steve Jobs began to argue. (Adj)

Pages 90-91:

Answers will vary. Here are some possible ones.

2. At the front door a man holding a briefcase talked to Herman.

3. Here are the nifty new bowling shirts for the team.

4. Leave the door open.

5. Ted and Sandy drove to the beach and went for a swim.

Pages 92–93:

Answers will vary. Here are some possible ones.

2. The confused polar bear paced in its cage; it did not look at all happy.
3. The orangutan had escaped from its cage five times; as a result, the zookeeper decided to consult an expert locksmith.
4. Jenna will visit China this fall, **or** she will take a trip to Fresno.
5. It rained for three hours yesterday; nevertheless, we had a picnic.

Page 93:

2. compound:	S:	mouse	V:	had become	
	S:	he	V:	had made	
3. simple:	S:	two	V:	found	
4. compound:	S:	They	V:	had	
	S:	they	V:	chased	
5. simple:	S:	Gomer	V:	wondered	
6. simple:	S:	They	V:	had found, had formed	
7. compound:	S:	He	V:	admired	
	S:	they	V:	should have run	
8. simple:	S:	It	V:	was	
9. compound:	S:	they	V:	did want	
	S:	they	V:	wanted	
10. compound:	S:	They	V:	enjoyed	
	S:	they	V:	lost	

Pages 94–95:

Answers will vary. Here are some possible ones.

2. While Nero fiddled, Rome burned.
3. Sylvester looked at the car that had just crashed into a brick wall.
4. Because he was late for the movie, Cyrus did not stop to buy popcorn.
5. The man who had a large bulldog looked at the man who had a wolf.

Page 96:

Answers will vary. Here are some possible ones.

2. Barbara liked the fish although it was burned; however, she avoided the okra.
3. The jockey who had won the Kentucky Derby died two days later; however, no one suspected foul play.
4. Because I had lost my job, I didn't have any money, so I could not afford to take my mother out to dinner when she came to visit.
5. I like to drink coffee with my friends when I am not in class; on the other hand, I like to study in the library too.

Page 97:

2. compound:	S: versions	V: are	
	S: stories	V: do give	
3. complex:	S: slippers	V: appeared	
	S: version	V: was translated	
4. simple:	S: shoes	V: were made	
5. compound-complex:	S: story	V: used	
	S: word	V: was	
	S: that	V: meant	
	S: that	V: meant	
6. complex:	S: Charles Perrault	V: was	
	S: who	V: translated	

7. simple:	S: versions	V: depict
8. compound:	S: Cinderella	V: is helped
	S: versions	V: use
9. compound-complex:	S: mother	V: is
	S: she	V: appears
	S: she	V: takes
10. compound:	S: cows, goats	V: assist
	S: mice	V: come

Pages 106–107:

Answers will vary. Here are some possible ones.

2. *fragment:* The koala that came out during the day because it was hungry.

   possible correction: The koala that came out during the day because it was hungry thrilled the zoo visitors.

3. *fragments:* Using a lead pipe. While he was in the library.

   possible correction: Using a lead pipe, Mr. Green committed the crime while he was in the library.

4. *fragment:* To do well on the next test.

   possible correction: Study this chapter carefully to do well on the next test.

5. *fragment:* When the boy had used all of the excuses that he could think of.

   possible correction: When the boy had used all of the excuses that he could think of, he mowed the lawn.

6. *fragment:* Probably because I had forgotten to set it.

   possible correction: The timer on the oven failed to go off probably because I had forgotten to set it.

7. *fragments:* Even as Rupert was dashing across the street. Begging for her to let him in.

   possible correction: The Chocolate Shoppe owner was locking the door even as Rupert was dashing across the street begging for her to let him in.

8. *fragment:* Although he knew he might cause a shipwreck.

   possible correction: Ulysses wanted to hear the Sirens' song, although he knew he might cause a shipwreck.

9. *fragment:* To remind her of her senior year in high school.

   possible correction: Her daughter's behavior always seemed to remind her of her senior year in high school.

10. *fragment:* Stooping to pick up fallen rocks. That separates his property from mine.

    possible correction: Stooping to pick up fallen rocks, my neighbor and I repaired the stone wall that separates his property from mine.

Pages 110–111:

Answers may vary. Here are some possible ones.

2. F   When Gomer looked into the cabinet, all he could see was Spam.
3. C
4. CS   Chuck Berry was playing "Hail, Hail, Rock and Roll" on the radio; meanwhile, Gomer and Homer finished the catfish and hushpuppies.
5. F   Every day Gilligan searches the horizon, and he even climbs a tree for a better look.
6. CS   Dido begged and begged Aeneas; finally, she gave up and jumped off the cliff.
7. F   Pluto kept feeding Cerberus chocolate turtles; even though Cerberus knew they were not good for him, he ate them anyway.
8. C
9. F   Hortense watched *The Fellowship of the Ring* ten times, so soon the ushers knew her by name.
10. CS   When Mr. Nosferatu came over for dinner last night, he kept staring at my fiancee's neck.

Chapter Three

Pages 147–148:

2. The server apologized to the (customers) sitting by the front door.

3. Swimming silently under the ship, (Nessie) avoided the monster hunters.

4. Standing alone on the beach, (Robinson) stared at the footprint in the sand.

5. Henrietta will not watch any (movies) produced by that studio.

6. The (Spam) hidden under Homer's bed had started to mold.

7. The old grouch yelled at the (children) selling Girl Scout cookies in his neighborhood.

8. Angered by his rude response, (Barb) headed for his front door.

9. Walking past the lingerie counter (Byron) brooded about his sore foot.

10. The (coach), confused by the umpire's call, asked for a time out.

Page 149:

2. Sailing across the Pacific, (Cameron) and (Peter) wondered if their supplies would last.

3. Luckily, William Tell knew the correct (way) to aim a crossbow.

4. Bitten by a radioactive spider, (Peter Parker) dreamed about houseflies.

5. Ellen's obsessive (desire) to make money drove away many of her friends.

6. Jack traded his cow for some magic (beans) to plant in his garden.

7. Yelling loudly, the (Rebels) charged up the hill toward the Yankees.

8. Frustrated by the rainy weather, (Sarah) stayed home and watched television.

9. Ruben could not decide which (flower) to give to his wife.

10. Once the basketball game started, Brent completely forgot about his (promise) to arrive home early.

Page 157:

2. (*The Tunnel*) which was written by William Gass, was a labor of thirty years.

3. (Everybody) who attended last night's baseball game received a free yo-yo.

4. (Zen Buddhism), which is an ancient religion, is practiced by many (people) who live in the United States.

5. (Maurice Ravel) who was a famous French composer, wrote (*Bolero*) which became one of the most popular concert

pieces of the twentieth century.

6. The frustrated contestant could not name the (planet) that was third from the sun.

7. Toots was looking for a (place) where he could play his tuba in peace.

8. The (women) who were arguing about the baby decided to ask Solomon for advice.

9. The (train) that left the station at noon had to stop for a (cow) that was standing on the railroad tracks.

10. (Wolf Moonglow) who was an exceptionally hirsute man, was telling us about the (time) when he first began to study

lycanthropy.

Pages 158–159:

2. Gothic cathedrals are often ornamented with (gargoyles), grotesque sculptures of evil spirits.

3. Homer and Hortense were asked to endorse (Spam Lite), a new product.

4. (Harry Houdini), a famous American escape artist and magician, spent many years exposing fraudulent mediums

and mind readers.

5. The one-armed (man), Richard Kimble's elusive enemy, was recently seen playing the slot machines in Las Vegas.

6. (Patrick Stewart), the former Captain Picard of the *U.S.S. Enterprise*, has also starred as Captain Ahab of the

Pequod.

7. Christopher picked up his favorite (instrument), a handcrafted classical guitar, and began to play.

8. Thomas had always wanted to visit (Utopia), a city not found on most maps.

9. (Diamonda), a jeweler from Switzerland, collects antique clocks.

10. Bill Liscomb was a pioneer in (hang gliding), a popular sport among the Peter Pan crowd.

Pages 159–160:

Answers will vary. Here are some possible ones.

2. Amelia Earhart, <u>a famous aviator</u>, vanished while flying over the Pacific Ocean.
3. Professor Emerson asked me to write a report on Edgar Allan Poe, <u>who wrote "The Tell-Tale Heart."</u>
4. Wile E. Coyote, <u>my favorite cartoon character</u>, carefully constructed the trap.
5. An angry old man <u>who had lost his two front teeth</u> barged into the office and headed toward the dentist.
6. The pilot flew fearlessly into the Bermuda Triangle, <u>where many strange accidents have occurred</u>.
7. Buffy, <u>the famous vampire slayer</u>, was honored when Count Dracula invited her to dinner.
8. The librarian hopped into his car, <u>a 1985 Ford Mustang in mint condition</u>, and drove to his favorite fishing spot.
9. Homer smiled in delight as Hortense brought out his favorite dessert, <u>Spam in prune sauce</u>.
10. Mount Vesuvius, <u>which killed thousands of people when it erupted</u>, still smolders over the ruins of Pompeii.

Page 168:

2. Mr. Martinez asked me <u>often</u> to eat dinner with him.
   Mr. Martinez often asked me to eat dinner with him. (Other answers are possible.)
3. Correct
4. The commando who had been approaching <u>silently</u> signaled to me.
   The commando who had been approaching signaled to me silently. (Other answers are possible.)

5. By the time he had <u>almost</u> eaten the entire case of Spam, Homer was feeling a litte woozy.
By the time he had eaten almost the entire case of Spam, Homer was feeling a litte woozy.

6. Peyton Farquhar <u>nearly</u> crept to the edge of the trees before he saw the Union soldiers.
Peyton Farquhar crept nearly to the edge of the trees before he saw the Union soldiers.

7. Although Charlene had many relatives in the area, she decided <u>just</u> to visit her aunt Mary.
Although Charlene had many relatives in the area, she decided to visit just her aunt Mary.

8. The counselor advised Fred <u>frequently</u> to attend the meetings.
The counselor advised Fred to attend the meetings frequently. (Other answers are possible.)

9. Vernon was disappointed to see that the menu <u>only</u> offered two side dishes.
Vernon was disappointed to see that the menu offered only two side dishes.

10. Frodo <u>almost</u> slept twenty hours once he got rid of that stupid ring.
Frodo slept almost twenty hours once he got rid of that stupid ring.

Pages 170–171:

2. Vera gave a cake to her boyfriend <u>soaked in rum.</u>
Vera gave a cake soaked in rum to her boyfriend.

3. Scratchy Wilson yelled at the stray dog <u>dressed in his colorful Sunday shirt.</u>
Scratchy Wilson, dressed in his colorful Sunday shirt, yelled at the stray dog.
(Other answers are possible.)

4. Consuelo introduced her daughter to the surgeon <u>who had just entered second grade.</u>
Consuelo introduced her daughter who had just entered second grade to the surgeon.

5. Sabrina gave the fruit to her mother-in-law <u>full of worm holes.</u>
Sabrina gave the fruit <u>full of worm holes</u> to her mother-in-law.

6. Claude took his rifle to the gun shop <u>that had a broken trigger.</u>
Claude took his rifle that had a broken trigger to the gun shop.

7. Homer daydreamed about Hortense <u>chewing on his plug of tobacco.</u>
Homer, chewing on his plug of tobacco, daydreamed about Hortense.
(Other answers are possible.)

8. The two border collies growled at the teenagers <u>with their tails wagging.</u>
The two border collies with their tails wagging growled at the teenagers. (Other answers are possible.)

9. Anse Bundren drove the cart carrying the coffin of his dead wife <u>complaining the entire way about his bad luck.</u>
Complaining the entire way about his bad luck, Anse Bundren drove the cart carrying the coffin of his dead wife.
(Other answers are possible.)

10. Amber showed her pond full of koi to her class, <u>which had bright orange and black markings.</u>
Amber showed her pond full of koi, which had bright orange and black markings, to her class.

Page 172:

2. D
3. C
4. D
5. D

Pages 173–175:

2. <u>Waiting for the game to begin</u>, Michael's stomach was upset.
While Michael was waiting for the game to begin, his stomach was upset.
(Other correct answers are possible.)

3. <u>After telling the lie</u>, Pinocchio's nose began to grow.
After Pinocchio told the lie, his nose began to grow.
(Other correct answers are possible.)

4. Correct

5. <u>Running swiftly up the hill</u>, the flag was raised by the warrior.
   Running swiftly up the hill, the warrior raised the flag.
   (Other correct answers are possible.)

6. <u>Attempting a comeback in the Daytona 500</u>, Darryl's driver's license was revoked.
   While Darryl was attempting a comeback in the Daytona 500, his driver's license was revoked.
   (Other correct answers are possible.)

7. <u>To join the choir</u>, a signup sheet is on the wall.
   To join the choir, you should put your name on the signup sheet on the wall.
   (Other correct answers are possible.)

8. <u>Huffing and puffing as hard as he could</u>, the house of bricks would not blow down.
   Huffing and puffing as hard as he could, the Big Bad Wolf could not blow down the house of bricks.
   (Other correct answers are possible.)

9. <u>Burned in the explosion,</u> a bandage was placed on Curt's right hand by the paramedic.
   Because Curt's right hand had been burned in the explosion, a paramedic placed a bandage on it.
   (Other correct answers are possible.)

10. <u>To show remorse</u>, Mary received flowers and an apology.
    To show remorse, Ramon sent Mary flowers and apologized.
    (Other correct answers are possible.)

Chapter Four

Pages 210–211:

2. The **dogs** next door **have** barked all day.

3. My **friend** often **visits** me at school.

4. **A soldier** sometimes **writes** several letters each day.

5. Low **grades** always **make** me feel unhappy.

Pages 212–213:

        S
2. An old bicycle with two flat tires (<u>does</u> do) seem to be a strange gift.

       S   S
3. Every surfer and skateboarder in Pacific Beach (<u>thinks</u> think) that the new law is unfair.

      S   S
4. A Spam omelette and a glass of buttermilk always (starts <u>start</u>) Homer's day well.

     S
5. Some of the corn (<u>was</u> were) harvested too early.

       S   S   S
6. Since he had started to speak, every soldier and archer (<u>was</u> were) listening to Agamemnon.

     S
7. Somebody from one of our local schools (<u>has</u> have) won the prestigious Peacock scholarship.

        S   S
8. The car's upholstery and paint job (<u>make</u> makes) it look almost new.

     S
9. Some of the fans in the audience (was <u>were</u>) standing and cheering.

     S
10. A squirrel with two cats chasing it (<u>is</u> are) running down the street.

Page 214:

2. A flock of geese (<u>has</u> have) just landed in my backyard.
   (S over "flock")

3. Rory is one of the dogs that (plays <u>play</u>) Frisbee so well.
   (S over "Rory", S over "dogs")

4. Neither the first officer nor the seamen (wants <u>want</u>) Captain Vere to hang Billy.
   (S over "officer", S over "seamen")

5. Her trip to Disneyland or her two vacations to Nepal (seems <u>seem</u>) to be all that Amanda thinks about.
   (S over "trip", S over "vacations", S over "Amanda")

6. The mob in Paris (<u>loves</u> love) to watch the executioner at work.
   (S over "mob")

7. Henry is the only citizen in Concord who (<u>refuses</u> refuse) to pay taxes.
   (S over "Henry", S over "citizen")

8. (<u>Has</u> Have) your mother or your brother arrived yet?
   (S over "mother", S over "brother")

9. The debate team that Ray coaches (<u>wins</u> win) every year.
   (S over "team", S over "Ray")

10. Henrietta is one of the women who (has <u>have</u>) recently joined our lawn bowling club.
    (S over "Henrietta", S over "women")

Pages 215–216:

2. Fifteen inches of rain (fall <u>falls</u>) in Murrieta every winter.
   (S over "inches")

3. One of Charlie's favorite British dishes (<u>is</u> are) bangers.
   (S over "One")

4. According to Bruce, the news of his lottery winnings (<u>was</u> were) exaggerated.
   (S over "news")

5. (<u>Has</u> Have) the mumps ever seemed like a serious disease to you?
   (S over "mumps")

6. After deliberating for three days, the jury in the Mallory trial (<u>has</u> have) not yet reached a verdict.
   (S over "jury")

7. Barbara says that two hundred pounds of tuna (<u>is</u> are) too much for her freezer.
   (S over "Barbara", S over "pounds")

8. There still (<u>are</u> is) people who believe that the earth is flat.
   (S over "people")

9. Randall's only source of income (<u>is</u> are) his stocks and bonds.
   (S over "source")

10. Ten miles of unpaved road (<u>lies</u> lie) between my house and the beach.
    (S over "miles")

Page 222:

2. Most people are very nervous even if **they** have studied for the test.
3. An applicant should get a good night's sleep if **he or she** wants to do well on the test.
4. When I drove my daughter to her first test, **I** could see that she was worried.
5. During my driving test, **I** needed to drive on the freeway for three miles.

Page 224:

2. Everybody who wanted to attend the meeting had to say the secret password before **he or she was** let in the door.
3. When visitors tour the local dairy, **they** should watch where **they** step.
4. correct

5. Neither Galileo nor Copernicus could keep **his** eyes focused on the ground.
6. Someone from the Halloween party left **his** (or **her** or **his or her**) giraffe costume on the couch.
7. correct
8. Once a skier tries snowboarding, **he** or **she** will never go back to skiing.
9. correct
10. A camper in these woods will often see a bear wander though **his or her** campsite.

Pages 226–227:

Answers will vary. Here are some possible ones.

2. When Tom told Huck about finding the lost treasure, Huck became very excited.
3. I tried to help in the dispute between my mother and my sister, but my mother would not give in.
4. When Gary introduced his in-laws to his parents, he hoped his parents would not reveal his secret.
5. Seymour refused to eat his soup when he found a cockroach in it.

Page 228:

Answers will vary. Here are some possible ones.

2. Zeda had always wanted to visit the San Diego Zoo, but she wasn't able to do so on her last trip to San Diego.
3. There were empty M & M wrappers all over the couch, but Randy said that he had not eaten the M & Ms.
4. Dan is a sailor, and every weekend he takes his boat out on the bay.
5. Because Daniel loved the snow and was an avid skier, he decided to buy a house in Colorado.

Page 230:

2. Alberto and I knew that we were the best snowboarders on the mountain.
3. Homer and Hortense sent a dehydrated Spam omelet to **us** for Christmas.
4. Even though Jerry and **she** were tired, they stayed up for *The Late Late Show.*
5. Cecilia and Ebony were sure that they could drive to Yellowstone by **themselves.**

Page 230:

2. The Gallo family and **I** will visit the winery next week.
3. My accountant **made the government suspicious when** he filled in my tax return in pencil and took a large deduction for jelly doughnuts. (Other correct answers are possible.)
4. Sherri asked **if her mother's clock** was right. (Other correct answers are possible.)
5. The faculty voted to give a $25,000 bonus to Bill and **her.**
6. I would like to listen to a CD on the stereo, but I don't have **a stereo.** (Other correct answers are possible.)
7. I have always enjoyed the genius of Picasso, **whose paintings** I saw two of at the museum. (Other correct answers are possible.)
8. They decided to treat **themselves** to a weekend by the seashore.
9. Bean **broke his nose when he** stuck a peppermint stick in it. (Other correct answers are possible.)
10. Madame Bovary told Edna Pontellier that **Edna's** husband was a bore. (Other correct answers are possible.)

Page 237:

2. obj
3. sub
4. obj
5. obj
6. sub
7. obj
8. obj
9. sub
10. obj

Page 239:

2. me

3. her

4. he

5. me

6. me

7. him

8. she

9. she

10. they

Page 240:

2. who

3. who

4. whoever

5. whomever

Page 240:

2. her

3. he

4. he

5. me

Page 241:

2. me

3. he

4. her

5. I

Pages 241–242:

2. I

3. I

4. she

5. whomever

6. him

7. her

8. me

9. whom

10. she

Chapter Five

Page 271:

2. Hortense served the Spam over vermicelli, but Homer refused to eat it.

3. correct

4. Hortense refused to speak to Homer, for she loved hushpuppies.

5. Homer decided to eat the hominy, so Hortense ate the Spam and rice.

Page 272:

2. Quentin looked at the sky and dreamed about applesauce, sweet potato pie, and creamed corn.

3. Martin finished the ninety-five items, grabbed a hammer, and nailed them to the church door.

4. We spotted trout in the clear, cold river.

5. Elmer was exhausted, for the neighbor's dog had barked all night long.

6. The dirty, unkempt man stumbled into camp, and the first thing he wanted was a Popsicle.

7. correct

8. Ms. Caudillo could have gone to the play, or she could have gone to the concert.

9. LaVere bought some flowers, visited her sick friend, caught the trolley, and went to work.

10. Daniel looked at the soft, inviting pile of pine needles and decided he would take a long, refreshing nap.

Page 274:

2. In a cave high on a mountain in Tennessee, Homer was setting up his still.

3. Scanning the world, Keats knew he had never seen anything like Chapman's Homer.

4. When we got to the top, we wrote a message to those who would follow us.

5. Yes, I have always wanted to have a wisdom tooth pulled without any anesthetic.

6. Approaching the crash site, Matt Scudder slowed to a stop.

7. As the artist looked up at the ceiling, he hoped the Pope would like it.

8. After spending a sleepless night, Dr. Scarpetta knew who the main suspect was.

9. In a final ironic twist, Abner's job in prison was making matches.

10. To find the Holy Grail, Perceval spent years wandering throughout Europe and Great Britain.

Page 275:

2. Charlie Moon, on the other hand, knew exactly where the old woman was going.

3. Homer wanted to impress Hortense; therefore, he saved enough flour sacks to make her a dress.

4. Peter Decker, however, was late getting to the synagogue.

5. Ms. Mendoza disliked flying on airplanes; in fact, she even turned down a free flight to Hawaii.

Pages 276–277:

2. *The Simpsons,* which was created by Matt Groening, presents a cynical view of the American family.

3. My best friend, who served with me in Vietnam, has been visiting me in San Diego.

4. correct

5. The *Titanic,* which was supposed to be one of the safest ships ever built, sank on its maiden voyage.

Page 277:

2. correct

3. Inspector Morse, embarrassed by his first name, refused to reveal it.

4. Polonius, trying to look important, told the director that he was an actor.

5. Masayo, determined not to insult her hosts, told them that the food tasted wonderful.

Page 278:

2. Persephone stared at the pomegranate, the only fruit in sight.

3. Gary, an avid hiker, did not mind being called a tree hugger.

4. *The Sopranos,* a series about Italian families, is my favorite television program.

5. The Australian shepherd, an intelligent dog, was introduced into Australia to herd sheep.

Pages 279:

2. The package that was mailed on Friday, September 13, 1875, from Transylvania, Ohio, never made it to Carlsbad, California.

3. Homer asked, "Which pasture contains the best cow pies?"

4. The multi-colored togas arrived at The Debauchery, 415 Cicero Street, Rome, Arkansas, on the day before Saturnalia began.

5. Please close the door to the basement, Chelsea.

Page 280:

2. A misanthrope, who is a person who dislikes other people, is usually not well liked.

3. *The Tell-Tale Tart,* a novel by Dulcinea Baker, will soon be a movie.

4. Ahab, how do you like my wide-wale corduroy pants?

5. Paul Revere's famous ride took place on April 18, 1775, although he did not really ride alone and never made it to his intended destination.

6. The missing coprolite was found on August 10, 1954, in Rome, Georgia.

7. Dave Robicheaux sadly considered his po'boy sandwich, dropped during the vicious gunfight.

8. "The spiders have arrived," said Harker, "and I'm ready."

9. Sherrie, in fact, sent me a postcard from the St. John Coltrane African Orthodox Church in San Francisco.

10. Francis, please tell Mr. Ed, who will not stop talking, that we are tired of his silly horse jokes.

Pages 287–288:

2. Who is on first?

3. Stop, I can't breathe!

4. Homer wondered if he would have enough Spam for Christmas.

5. Does Roscoe want to visit the Liberace museum?

6. What is the weather like outside?

7. Never again!

8. Rosemary studied for her Ph.D. at Yale.

9. Are his anapests as clever as usual?

10. Jack asked Carlton if it was time to leave.

Page 289:

2. Homer bought the following items: bag balm, cow chip hardener, and an okra peeler.

3. Billy thought he had hidden all of the rope; however, Claggart found a piece long enough.

4. correct

5. Dee wanted some keepsakes for her house; therefore, she asked her mother to give her a quilt.

Pages 290–291:

2. In spring the rains come; then the small animals emerge.

3. Whose last words were "My kingdom for a horse"?

4. My favorite Mae West quotation is "When I'm good, I'm very good, but when I'm bad, I'm better."

5. Miles picked up his horn and said, "Let's begin this gig."

6. "Where is the ring?" asked Gandalf.

7. Was it Mark Twain who said, "I believe that our Heavenly Father invented man because he was disappointed in the monkey"?

8. When he got to the top of the hill and watched the stone roll back to the bottom, Sisyphus shouted, "Not again!"

9. Queequeg never hesitated; he just picked up the harpoon and threw it.

10. Oscar Wilde once said, "Consistency is the last refuge of the unimaginative."

Page 292:

2. Mr. Jones's friends placed an inappropriate sticker on his car's bumper.
3. Did you enjoy Emma Thompson's part in that movie?
4. When I quit, I was given a month's salary.
5. Maria's brother wouldn't admit that he had read his sister's diary.
6. It's a shame that the meteor shower won't be visible from here.
7. As he looked at his car's fender, he knew that it could've been worse.
8. His brother-in-law's judge gave him two weeks' reprieve.
9. Staring over the rim of Sylvia's soup bowl was a cockroach.
10. The children's pet Gila monster ran away to the desert.

Page 293:

Answers will vary. Here are some possible ones.

2. Louis's new car certainly looks expensive.
3. My father-in-law's house was robbed last night.
4. Do you think the mice's cage should be cleaned?
5. Ms. Lewis's new house didn't withstand the earthquake.

Page 299:

2. In Nathaniel Hawthorne's short story "Young Goodman Brown," the main character loses his faith in the goodness of people.
3. On the table in the coroner's office was a stack of <u>Time</u> and <u>Wonderful Endings</u> magazines.
4. Brent has memorized W. S. Merwin's poem "The Last One."
5. The movie <u>The Wizard of Oz</u> mixes both black-and-white and color photography.

Page 301:

2. <u>A Morning for Flamingos</u>, a novel by James Lee Burke, takes place primarily in the South.
3. <u>Newsweek</u> magazine had a picture of New York on the cover this week.
4. Uncle Javier was humming the song "My Way" when he heard that Frank Sinatra had died.
5. Several prominent citizens of Sioux Falls, South Dakota, are veterans of Operation Desert Storm.
6. During the Christmas holidays, one can see beautiful decorations in Santa Fe and Albuquerque.
7. In California, the Native American tribes are having a legal battle with the state government over gambling.
8. Every actor wants a chance to play the leading role in William Shakespeare's play <u>Hamlet.</u>
9. Charlie showed Marisa his collection of <u>T.V. Guide</u> magazines.
10. The thrift store run by the Episcopal church on State Street has decided to move three blocks north this summer.

Page 303:

2. Jessica fed her goldfish at 6:00 and then again at 8:55.
3. For the retirement party, Charlie brought 15 pastries, Woz brought 1 Clark Bar, Barbara brought 115 pounds of fresh tuna, and Carlton brought 3 chocolate cheese cakes.

or

For the retirement party, Charlie brought fifteen pastries, Woz brought one Clark Bar, Barbara brought one hundred fifteen pounds of fresh tuna, and Carlton brought three chocolate cheese cakes.

4. After August 6, 1945, the world seemed a more dangerous place.
5. correct

Chapter Six

Pages 340–341:

2. drunk
3. swum
4. laid
5. sat
6. lying

7. shrunk
8. drunk, sitting
9. sung, raise
10. lain

Pages 350–351:

2. an, conscience
3. accept, effect
4. among, break
5. An, disinterested
6. advice, affected
7. already, uninterested

8. anxious, all right
9. number
10. complements
11. our, break
12. choose, break

Pages 355–356:

2. fewer, than
3. Your, principal
4. past, through
5. led, lose, their
6. their, personal
7. led, principles

8. Two, too, to
9. number, fewer, than
10. lose, proceeded
11. quite, quiet
12. were, where, an

Page 363:

2. received, friend
3. ceiling, sufficient
4. sleigh, quiet, relief
5. Neither, achieve, their

Page 364:

2. angriest, angrier, angrily
3. portrayed, portrays, portraying, portrayal
4. business, busier, busiest
5. employer, employed, employable

Page 365:

2. requring
3. inspiring
4. lovable
5. lovely
6. managing

7. management
8. completely
9. judgment
10. noticeable

Page 366:

2. wildest
3. referred
4. proceeding
5. dimmer
6. cleaner

7. committed
8. forgettable
9. happening
10. compelled

Pages 367:

2. unnatural
3. dissatisfied
4. illegible
5. mistrial
6. immoral

7. misspell
8. irreversible
9. illicit
10. unethical

Pages 369:

2. monkeys
3. echoes
4. knives
5. matches
6. forgettable

7. kisses
8. stereos
9. candies
10. phenomena

Pages 369–370:

2. a lot
3. athlete
4. behavior
5. brilliant
6. business
7. carefully
8. career
9. competition
10. definite
11. desperate
12. develop
13. different
14. dining
15. describe
16. doesn't
17. embarrass
18. environment
19. exaggerate
20. February
21. fascinate
22. government
23. grammar
24. height
25. immediate

26. interest
27. knowledge
28. mathematics
29. necessary
30. occasion
31. opinion
32. opportunity
33. original
34. particular
35. potato
36. perform
37. perhaps
38. probably
39. ridiculous
40. separate
41. similar
42. sincerely
43. studying
44. surprise
45. temperature
46. Thursday
47. unusual
48. writing

Index